More than any car builder of the time the rise of E. L. Cord followed with practically absurd fidelity the formula of the old American success legend—the poor boy from the country, with practically no education, who fights his way to wealth at an age when most men are just fitting their necks to the drag of effort, who in early middle age is able to enjoy palaces and yachts and leisure, a movie script existence, who goes into the wicked purlieus of Wall Street and battles triumphantly with the giants of finance.

—ARTHUR D. H. SMITH
in *Men Who Run America*

CORD
GRAND
PRIX
WINNER
MODEL
ON
DISPLAY
HERE
AUBURN
CORD
WHICH WAS
GIVEN
HIGHEST
AWARD
EVER ACCORDED
AN
AMERICAN
AUTOMOBILE

CORD
Without Tribute to Tradition

THE L-29 FRONT-DRIVE LEGEND

Dan Post

POST-ERA BOOKS
Arcadia CA 91006

Library of Congress Catalog Card Number 72-96734
ISBN-0-911160-50-7

Foreword

When the motor books *Duesenberg, the Mightiest American Motor Car* and *The Classic Cord* were published a generation ago they brought to Special Interest car enthusiasts a focus on these makes never before seen.

In the ensuing years, as more early car collectors broadened their perspective to respect generally automobiles built after the earliest models, these readily available references for the Duesie and the Cord helped lay enthusiasts to become "experts." Scattered interest spread until a new generation of motor hobbiests was carefully coaching itself in the proper spelling of *Duesenberg* as a mark of classic car authority.

Discriminating collectors sought out the scarce surviving examples of these automobiles and they began to climb in value as demand mounted among the many. Formal recognition of the thoroughbred status of Duesenberg and Cord cars followed shortly after with the formation of a special national club to promote their worthy preservation.

The Duesenberg book, a study which J. L. Elbert had developed with great depth, has persevered to this day as the standard reference on this exciting marque.

The Cord book, while certainly a volume to instill interest in this undoubted classic, had been published, on the other hand, following only limited story research. Not long after publication the author became aware that it required revision and enlargement to relate the Cord story in a form permanently worthy of the subject.

What occurred next was certainly neither planned nor intended. As a number of veteran Cord enthusiasts know, the revised edition was not immediately forthcoming after the original edition had been permitted to lapse out-of-print. Months became years. Among the heartiest core of collectors existing copies of *The Classic Cord,* themselves, became collectors' items.

What really happened? The author, with the best of intentions, had become increasingly involved with the subject. A mountain of additional material was at hand. The revision task which originally had been viewed as a light tune-up had taken on the proportions of a major overhaul.

Finally, as work progressed the revision approach was completely abandoned. Clearly, proper documentation of the Cord saga required a fresh start — from the beginning. The "wheelbase" of the assembled material, meanwhile, had grown to such length it would not "garage" in a single volume of popular size.

To permit broad use of key reproductions to supplement the story lines the subject was then expanded comfortably into a two volume work. *Cord, the Front-Drive Legend* is the result.

You are reading *Volume I: Without Tribute to Tradition,* the story of the model L-29.

If the subject *CORD* is your cake you will also enjoy *Volume II: The Timeless Classic,* the story of the model 810.

Acknowledgements

While *CORD/THE FRONT-DRIVE LEGEND, Volume I: Without Tribute to Tradition* stands by itself as a finished work it necessarily reflects a pooling of the efforts of a considerable body.

A book of this scope cannot be produced authoritatively without access to many records, public and private, and without special assistance from expert sources. The author was fortunate in obtaining the substantial support of a number of individuals who, by experience or developed inclination, were possessed of key information.

The author is particularly grateful to seasoned Cord enthusiast Ron Irwin, whose research pursuits, and studious review of the developing work through many painstaking sessions, helped measurably in bringing this project to fruition.

Lasting thanks are expressed to the Duesenberg historian J. L. Elbert for his suggestion in 1951 to do a Cord book, and for much company literature used in the resulting original *The Classic Cord* — material, in turn, reissued in this new revised and expanded volume.

Important contributions were prepared specially by Bob Fabris, the country's leading authority (as the Auburn-Cord-Duesenberg Club's official historian for this particular make and model automobile), and by Henry Blommel, the prominent Connersville, Indiana, automotive historian whose latter-day "finds" have sparked new interest in an established subject.

A special note of gratitude is due professional illustrators Strother MacMinn and Willis B. Dobson for their fresh and original L-29 artwork which was specially commissioned to enrich this book.

A debt of acknowledgement is due Arthur D. H. Smith for his profile of E. L. Cord in the book *Men Who Run America,* from which the author has drawn freely, and to various American periodicals from which contemporary details were confirmed, and to staff members from the Arcadia, Pasadena and Los Angeles Public Libraries.

Additional details were also developed through the much appreciated individual interest of Richard Beagle, Gordon Buehrig, Charles Cord, Randy Ema, the late Warren Fitzgerald, Bob Foldenauer, Bob Gegen, Franklin Hershey, Bill Kinsman, Dr. Alfred S. Lewerenz, W. Everett Miller, Charles Mooney, Roy Schneider, C. R. Van Ranst and others.

The cover illustration is reproduced from an original oil painting by the celebrated transportation artist Harlan Hiney.

The anonymity of some photographs does not permit a credit for every illustration used, but acknowledgement of individual sources where established — though some are secondary — appears below:

Richard Beagle: 14 above, 61, 123, 124, 154-155. Roy Beagle: 86. Henry Blommel: 13. Gordon Buehrig: 173. Peter dePaolo: 92. Denny Duesenberg: 10. Bill Dobson: Pre-title drawing, 69, 98, 120. J. L. Elbert: 17-33, 35, 38, 44-46, 48-49, 52, 62-63, 71 above, 72 below, 82 below, 83, 100-105, 111, 113-114, 169, 171-172, 174. Randy Ema: 36, 40-41, 125, 129-153, 164-165. Bob Fabris: 37, 43, 47, 53-60, 72 above, 73-74 above, 75 above, 84 above, 89, 93, 95, 106, 158-159. Murray Fahnestock: 121. Warren Fitzgerald: 74 below, 84 below. Bob Gegen: 85. P. E. Guerrero: 39. Frank Hershey: 64 below, 65-68. Ron Irwin: 12, 15-16, 42, 50, 51 above, 115, 117-119, 126-127, 161-163, 167, 170 above. Bill Kinsman: 70 below, 75 below, 88 below, 89 above. Strother MacMinn: 14-15 above, 82 above, 87-88 above, 90-91, 99, 107-109. Harry Morrow: 70 above, 71 below. Free Library of Philadelphia Automobile Reference Collection: 2, 4, 6, 112, 122. Roy Richter: 94. Arthur D. H. Smith: 11. Ray Wolff: 64 above.

Contents

1. The Limitless Horizon

The only limitation of a business in America is the limitation of the men running it.

Each chapter opens with a lead paragraph in bold type. These observations have been selected from various pieces of automobile advertising copy composed by E. L. Cord.

In that galaxy of American automobile builders—past and present—one smaller star in particular sparkles more brilliantly than all the others of its comparatively minor magnitude.

This car maker secured for his time a public prominence for his product far greater than its nebulous production figures in usual circumstance would have earned.

No one in the whole American motor car saga made so much, from so little, for so long, with such spectacular splash, as the innovative, brash E. L. Cord, whose youthful energies first attracted attention in the automobile world by reviving the moribund *Auburn Automobile Company* from virtual collapse before he turned thirty.

When he secured control of this company a little later the exercise would prove only a warm-up for bigger acts to follow. Soon Cord would add *Duesenberg, Lycoming* and others in steps towards the construction of an empire almost fictional in its fascination.

Young Cord didn't become as rich as some, though he seemed to enjoy every moment of his ascendency more than most men. In the decade between 1924 and 1935 he accomplished things faster than any other man who strove for material success. It is safe to say that E. L. Cord had a lot of fun.

Unhampered by tradition, and with unfaltering courage in the commercial possibilities of his private convictions, E. L. Cord demonstrated a fan-

Fred Duesenberg had achieved an invincible position in the motoring world as the builder of racing cars and engines that made their mark at the Indianapolis 500. By the fall of 1920, when he began to make a passenger car of custom production it secured immediate public stature.

tastic capacity for bringing through to indelible fruition automotive concepts *apart from convention* in features, styling and pricing.

Errett Lobban Cord

By brilliant planning none of his car designs would remain obscure after hitting the market. Each one made major news in motordom and caught the public eye because it was possessed with the kind of *"IT"* that contemporary actress Clara Bow was reputed to impart on the silver screen.

Today these automobiles live on in the eyes of men as the most conspicuous enterprise of a career that attained epic scale.

To the substantial number of investors who helped finance what later was to become a hurricane of promotions, Cord was one of the most characteristic entrepreneurs produced by the 'twenties boom years and the depression. What distinguished him from others was the flexibility he demonstrated in riding right on through the depression.

2. *Without Tribute to Tradition*

I believe the passport to public patronage is the value of the car itself. That is why Auburn says: drive the Auburn and if the car does not sell itself, you will not be asked to buy.

Auburn's sterling record even in barren years was the result of several factors. Among them were good management, which was quick to recognize a trend and capitalize on it; a tradition of production economy; and a flexibility which enabled their happy combination.

Cord had never had surplus money to play with. He had never wanted much except as it was earned. Every year had been a lean year for him. It was possible, therefore, for Auburn to show a profit when fatter companies would fail to break even.

In an era when styling was disciplined by reality quality materials were everywhere at hand, and labor took pride in its crafts. Cord managed to come up with products of instant character.

Cord knew the public cherished an unconscious desire for longer, lower, faster cars—cars that *looked* fast too. So Auburn was quick to offer streamlined bodies and liberal wheelbase for the price. Yearly models retained a family resemblance comforting to the owner who kept a car more than a season.

"It is not necessary to change a car radically if it is built right," wrote Cord. "The car builder is the custodian of the car owner's investment, and he should do nothing to jeopardize or depreciate that investment."

An early advocate of common sense traffic laws, E. L. Cord was among the vanguard to suggest adoption of uniform regulations among the states and speed limit increases commensurate with technical progress in the industry.

LONG BEACH PRESS-TELEGRAM — SUNDAY, FEBRUARY 20, 1927

SPEEDING LAWS ARE DECLARED OLD-FASHIONED

Simultaneously with the action of the House of Representatives of Indiana to amend the LaFuze bill calling for an increase in the speed laws of that State from thirty-five to forty miles an hour, E. L. Cord, President of the Auburn Automobile Company, indorsed a nation-wide movement for more liberal speed restrictions.

Mr. Cord, in a radio address during the Chicago automobile show startled his listeners when he termed the present day speed laws as "old-fashioned and inadequate," claiming they are seriously retarding record as in sympathy in faster and safer driving.

The automobile manufacturer's action in this matter is entirely reverse from the campaigns recently launched by various State and community organizations. It is the popular opinion that speed should be retarded. The State of Indiana, however, is one of the first to take steps toward solving the traffic problem which is becoming acute.

Cord set forth a fixed group of laws which he believes should be rigidly enforced and which would be uniform laws in every section of the country. They are as follows: Drivers entering highways from side streets must stop. Slower traffic must stay closer to the roadside. Any motorist found incapable of driving under these regulations should be stopped and examined, if found inexperienced or otherwise incapable, he should be prohibited from driving. Cars in unsafe condition should be barred from the streets.

"I recommend that instead of trying to retard progress, instead of hampering the full use of motor cars and getting the utmost value from their time-saving facilities, that we release motor car owners from these old-fashioned, inadequate restrictions.

"As people grow, expand and change, their laws must be kept up to date. Main arteries, such as Michigan Avenue in Chicago, should be free streets for fast driving. Drivers should be educated to respect these right of ways just the same as we have grown to respect the right of ways of the railroads," Mr. Cord told his listeners.

THE SATURDAY EVENING POST

It Will Pay You to Wait

We greatly regret that thousands, whose first choice was for an Auburn car, have had to have their deposits returned because they could not wait for delivery. We anticipated and prepared for a vastly increased consumer demand when we announced these new Auburn models. It was the fact that Auburn was oversold in 1928 that justified us in anticipating a greatly increased sales volume for 1929 and increasing our production 100% for this year by the transfer of the production of the Auburn cars to our new Connersville plants. We want to ask all whose first choice is for Auburn cars to be a little patient. We believe Auburn cars are worth waiting for. Production is steadily increasing consistent with good business tactics and without impairing quality. It is significant that each month from January to May this year our production has exceeded the output of the entire year of 1924. And in May alone, production was 50% greater than for the twelve months of 1924. This is our pledge, that the character of Auburn cars will continue to excel in both kind and degree.

E. L. CORD

AUBURN

POWERED BY LYCOMING

6-80 Sedan $1095; 6-80 Sport Sedan $995; 6-80 Cabriolet $1095; 6-80 Victoria $1095; 8-90 Sedan $1495; 8-90 Sport Sedan $1395; 8-90 Speedster $1495; 8-90 Phaeton Sedan $1695; 8-90 Cabriolet $1495; 8-90 Victoria $1495; 8-90 7-Passenger Sedan $1595; 120 Sedan $1895; 120 Sport Sedan $1795; 120 Speedster $1895; 120 Phaeton Sedan $2095; 120 Cabriolet $1895; 120 Victoria $1895; Prices f. o. b. Auburn or Connersville, Indiana. *Equipment other than standard extra.*

AUBURN AUTOMOBILE COMPANY, AUBURN, INDIANA

Airmail postage has been reduced to 5 cents for the first ounce and 10 cents for each additional ounce. Use Airmail daily for quicker communication. The development of Aviation is vital to American progress.

Cord's pioneer interest in air progress was evident in the institutional plug for AIR MAIL that appeared as a bottom line in Cord Corporation trade and consumer magazine advertising.

The depression Auburn had been shrewdly built to appeal to buyers without benefit of four-color double spreads or high-pressure salesmen. It was made longer, heavier, and higher-powered than competing cars. Forethought was evident in wider doors, easy steering, oversize instruments and other conveniences unexpected for the money.

3. *The Ultimate Prerogative*

There are plenty of ways of winning attention. I am speaking only of favorable attention. One of my first principles is to be different—not spectacular or contrary, but different.

AUBURN
POWERED BY LYCOMING
Straight Eights and Sixes
and
CORD
FRONT-DRIVE
AUBURN AUTOMOBILE COMPANY, AUBURN, INDIANA

A simple orthographic frontal line sketch of the L-29 by Albert H. Leamy represented an initial step towards body development after the design had been set.

After his marathon strides had lifted Auburn from the shadow of death, and his re-energizing of a faltering Duesenberg had created a new monarch, it came as a practically natural event that Cord would keep business humming—on the verge of the stock market collapse as it chanced—by bringing yet another new and different car to market in 1929. The project had been known at the plant as the front-drive or FWD car.

With the interest generated by the front-wheel drive successes in speedway driving it was natural for Cord to consider capitalizing on such prominence by applying the principle to a passenger automobile. He talked with Harry A. Miller, the leading advocate, whose patents appeared basic to the idea.

Auburn's best engineering talent was assigned the task of converting the Miller system from track to street. Working closely with Cord, whose own sense of line was well-seasoned, a lithe body configuration was developed by Auburn design head Al Leamy who shaped a frontal mood that was to precurse the whole industry in design. John Oswald as the body engineer would translate Leamy's sketches into three dimensions.

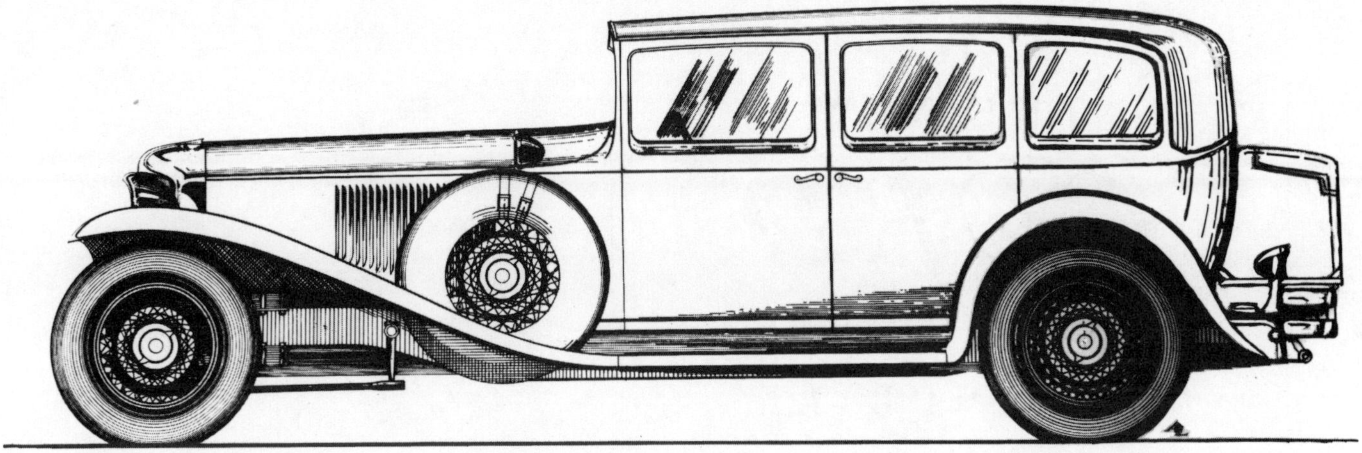

Motor legend has it that at the big banquet before the annual New York Automobile Show, when nearly every important automobile manufacturer was present, according to a report in *Business Week,* someone asked:

" 'Where's Cord?'

"The young man who had won first rank leadership in the industry in record time was the only notable absentee. It transpired that he had run off for a cross-country ride in a new, unnamed front-wheel drive car—he and one mechanic.

"That was just like the 35-year-old president of the Cord Corporation. On the trip he told nobody who he was. But the car, novel in design, attracted universal comment. At the curbstone, at the roadside, Cord listened. He listened to gas station attendants, garage hands, casual strangers, men and women all along the way. They, he knew, were the final critics. When he came home he had improved the view of the car he proposed to make. His engineers had said their last word and were ready to go into production. Cord said:

" 'Wait!'

"Structural changes were not necessary, but modifications for looks, riding comfort and driving ease were swiftly imposed before the FWD car was set for production.

This side view by the designer was expanded to full size by John Oswald on a wall drawing board so actual production data could be established.

As an initial step in chassis design the clutch was related to the forward location of the transmission by turning the standard Lycoming engine fore to aft. A common housing could then be designed to enclose the transmission, differential and front axle.

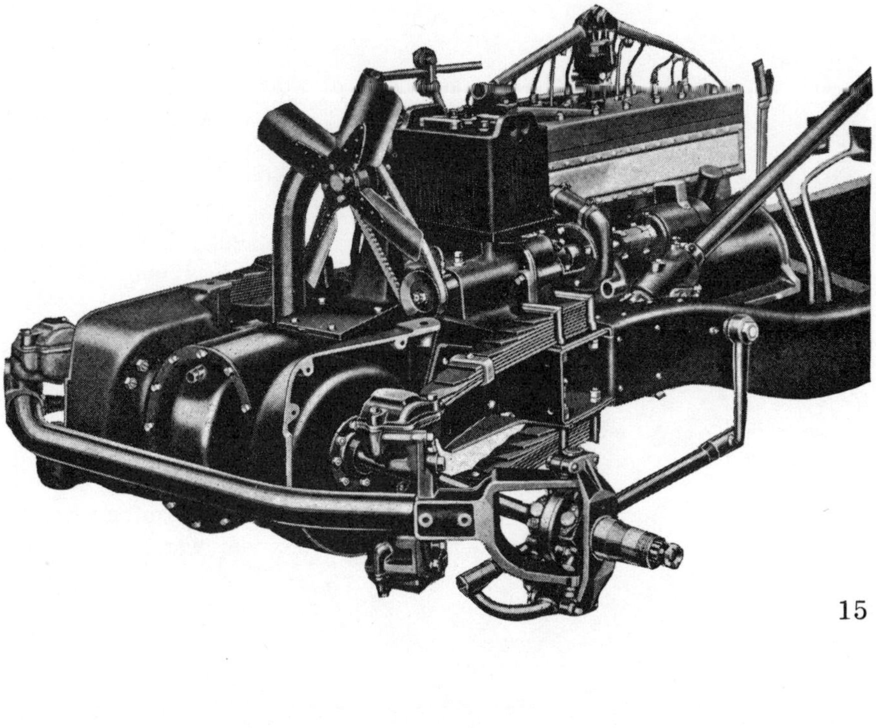

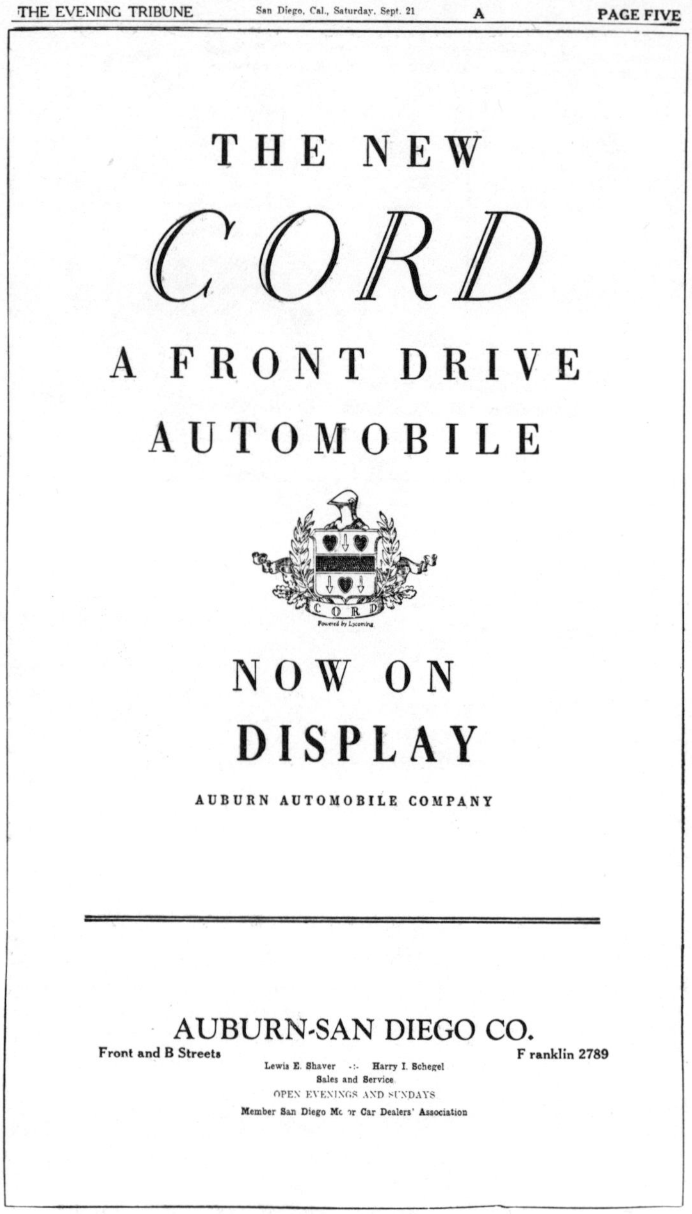

THE EVENING TRIBUNE San Diego, Cal., Saturday, Sept. 21 A PAGE FIVE

THE NEW

CORD

A FRONT DRIVE AUTOMOBILE

NOW ON DISPLAY

AUBURN AUTOMOBILE COMPANY

AUBURN-SAN DIEGO CO.

Front and B Streets F ranklin 2789

Lewis E. Shaver -:- Harry I. Schegel

Sales and Service

OPEN EVENINGS AND SUNDAYS

Member San Diego Motor Car Dealers' Association

Formal announcement in major newspapers judiciously omitted an illustration of the new car which might have saved a thousand words. Readers with qualified interest in front-drive were compelled to go to an Auburn showroom for a look at the new car. Dealers were swamped.

"Tall, slender, good looking with dark eyes and an intriguing cleft chin, Errett Lobban Cord has been described as the man who substituted 'pull' for push in the automobile. His outstanding faculty was an insatiable curiosity which led to dominant action. He was a great listener. Yet, oddly, he hated the limelight, and even more being the subject of an interview."

While others had talked of longer, lower cars, E. L. Cord, applying his natural sense for the unforgettable, had gone right ahead and made one—with a smartness all its own.

The FWD car, all but unique for its time, had no reputation to trade on; it had to be good.

It introduced the first X-frame design for torsional rigidity in American automotive history. Sleek styling was accentuated by elegant paint and trim. Open bodies were the product of Limousine Body Co. at Kalamazoo; closed bodies came from Central Manufacturing Co. in Connersville. Both were Cord subsidiaries. The car was a round one knockout with the public.

CORD

Powered by Lycoming

AUBURN has introduced America's first production front wheel drive automobile—the CORD. The Cord creates a place for itself no other car has ever occupied, fitting in between our complete line of Auburn and Duesenberg cars. Many drastic claims could truthfully be made for exclusive advantages in having a car pulled instead of pushed. The tremendous public acceptance has proved that its easier handling and safer control have a decisive appeal to even more people than we expected. But we do not choose to prejudice you. We prefer to let the car sell itself to those who can afford it. You are entitled, however, to know that many years have been devoted to it; that being first, Auburn was privileged to benefit from all previous experience, and able to obtain the services of as many expert engineers as we wanted. It is unusually substantial in construction, is of very highest quality in every respect, and offers a satisfactory and economical investment for many years.—E. L. CORD

AUBURN AUTOMOBILE COMPANY · AUBURN, INDIANA

***SEDAN* $3095 · *BROUGHAM* $3095 · *CABRIOLET* $3295 · *PHAETON* $3295**

Prices: f. o. b. Auburn, Indiana. Equipment other than standard extra.

Cord managed to exercise his ultimate prerogative in only six years of management. Earlier it had taken William C. Durant, founder of General Motors nearly a generation, and Walter P. Chrysler nearly as long to advance their ultimate prerogatives.

At the age of just thirty-five E. L. Cord had exercised every car maker's ultimate prerogative: *a new automobile distinctive enough, by his own private standard, to bear his own name.*

Even after the depression had made its effects fully manifest, and the industry was wallowing in red ink, Cord's companies, with the unique, front-wheel drive model as their latest baby, made a profit of more than three million dollars.

A full reproduction of the original 1929 grand catalog begins on the next page . . . Private residences in Beverly Hills, California — where Cord's own two-story stucco of fashionable early California Spanish architecture was at 616 N. Arden Drive — provided elegant backdrops in staging publicity shots for this catalog . . . The entrance to the wooded Harold Lloyd estate, for example, was reportedly used to pose the Cabriolet (pp. 21). (This location on Benedict Canyon Road has since undergone some change.) . . . The Phaeton (pp. 25-26), as another example, was posed in the forecourt of the Spanish-Moorish Tower Road estate of George O. Kolb, of the Philadelphia baking family. (This location was acquired in 1962 from the original family by the actor James Coburn. It reposes today almost exactly as it did in 1929. Only a plain iron gate replaces the colorful original of carved wood.) . . . Beyond this property, at the end of Tower Road, John Barrymore had purchased a five-room hacienda from the noted director King Vidor not long before the L-29 staging . . . Could it have been on the very day of this photography that the Great Profile, enroute to his lair, had first glimpsed the new CORD, and, turning to his companion, in characteristic prose, commanded "Buy a a CORD instantly!"?

Auburn Automobile Company
Auburn, Indiana, U. S. A.

Why We Introduce a Front Drive Automobile

By E. L. Cord

AUBURN'S policy for five years has been to strenuously seek new ways to improve, develop and originate better automobiles. In the course of this earnest search it was inevitable that we should investigate the possibilities of the established principle of front-wheel drive. We had as a precedent the progress of aviation where puller planes were adopted instead of the original pusher types. Our long experimental work has conclusively demonstrated that automobiles that are pulled, instead of pushed, have pronounced exclusive advantages. Therefore in order to continue to grow and maintain our own leadership we are introducing America's first production front-drive automobile. The Cord car is a specialty car, different from others. Its purpose is not to obsolete rear-drive cars. Being the very latest automotive development however, it creates an entirely new place never before occupied by any other car. We offer it as an addition to our other products, being priced between our complete line of Auburn and Duesenberg cars. No automobile built can have all the advantages nor appeal to all people, no more than one house can embrace every residential advantage and meet the needs of every family. We found in our thorough sales tests that the front-drive car has inherent features that attract more people even than we anticipated. Its favorable reception has been universal and decisive. Its exclusive advantages in safety, easy handling, comfort and durability have already won a host of

Cord Cabriolet—Open

converts! In order that the attributes peculiar to the front-drive may be fully enjoyed by those who desire them, we are determined to build the Cord car so substantially and of such unquestioned quality in every respect, that owners will have an extremely satisfactory and economical investment for many years. The basic difference of the Cord makes possible many drastic claims, but we prefer that the public learn of these exclusive advantages from the car itself. No technical explanation nor description could convey the difference in roadability, sense of safety and sure control of this new kind of automobile. These things are revealed and appreciated only through driving. Therefore this brochure is confined to reproductions of actual photographs of the four Cord models, a few of its structural features and its specifications. It seems fitting however to refer to the significance of the leadership of the Cord in this inevitable progress. Years have been devoted to its development. Being the leader, we were unhurried. Being first we have had many advantages no longer available to others. We could deliberate and exhaust all of the possibilities. Nothing has been spared; time, money nor effort to make this a strictly quality car in every respect. We have had a free hand to benefit from the best that the whole world offered. We have been privileged to pick and choose from all designs and patents. We have been able to procure the exclusive services not of one, but of as many of the most experienced and leading front-drive engineers as we wanted. We have had ample time to design, test and experiment. We have the rights, for as long as we care to use them, to the patents of the famous Harry Miller, internationally famed for his front-drive racing cars. We submit it as a simple statement of fact that this car requires no selling to those who can afford it.

Cord Sedan for five

Comfortable rumble seat in Cabriolet

Exceptional ease of steering and control

Distinctive and pleasing front end appearance

Custom type Convertible Phaeton Sedan body

Smart cadet type visor

Doors of unusual width for convenience

Cord Phaeton Sedan—Enclosed

Low body design but no sacrifice of head room

Fenders of long, sweeping lines

Headlights and cowl lights of special design

Long, low, racy lines

Complete comfort for five

Narrow corner posts for clear vision

Cord Cabriolet—From the rear

Cord Four Door Brougham

Cord Phaeton Sedan—Open

The Cord is the first production car with a unit power plant, engine, transmission, differential and front brakes being in one assembly. Thus the power is applied near its source, greatly increasing efficiency. A long drive shaft with its tendency to vibrate at high speeds is eliminated.

The universal joints operate at wheel speed and not at motor speed as in rear-drive, or approximately five times slower, thus insuring longer life. The double universal joint gives constant velocity and permits the steering of the front wheels up to an angle of 42 degrees while power is being applied. This angle is sharper than the average rear-drive car can turn. Joints are provided with an oil reservoir making oiling necessary only about once every 8,000 to 10,000 miles.

Heavy double quarter elliptic springs prevent undue oscillation of the front axle and provide the utmost ease and comfort in riding. This double type elliptic springing is a departure in passenger car design and provides a total of 91 inches in spring length for the front end of the chassis. Ends of the springs are mounted in rubber shackles. Hydraulic shock absorbers are mounted between the springs and control both up and down action.

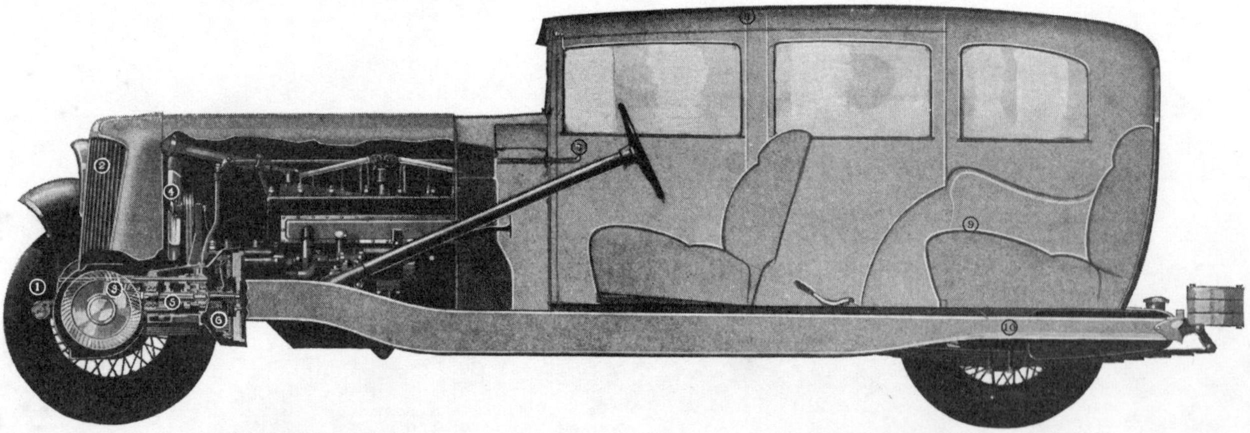

1 Tubular Front Axle.
2 Automatic Radiator Shutters.
3 Differential.
4 **Six-Blade Fan.**
5 Transmission.
6 Single Plate Clutch.
7 **Gear-shift lever.**
8 Greater head-room.
9 Both seats on same level.
10 **Straight frame—no kick-up.**

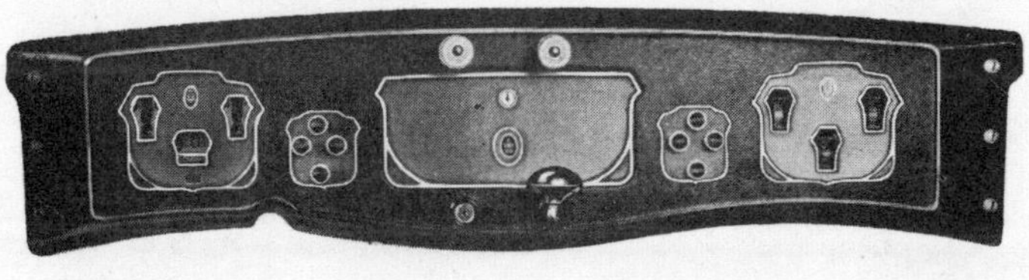

The metal instrument panel is in three divisions. The left group contains the speedometer, motor temperature indicator, oil pressure gauge, spark control, throttle, instrument lamp and left windshield wiper. In the center is a glove compartment and just below this is the ignition lock and the gear shift lever. Instrument Panel lamp and cigar lighter are mounted above glove compartment. The group on the right contains the starter, choke, manifold heat control, right windshield wiper, gasoline gauge, engine oil level gauge and ammeter. Background of the panel is in a rich crackle finish and instruments are of the approved aviation type, white figures on black background. Special attention has been given to arrangement of instruments for ease in operation.

Three quarter view of the chassis of the Cord front-drive showing how direct power is applied to the wheels, the constant velocity universal joint in the spindle, double quarter elliptic springs, front axle, front wheel brake drums, steering arrangement and bumper mountings.

Ring and pinion gears are hypoid, designed 30 percent stronger than for cars of similar weight. This assures an unusual margin of safety.

Bridge like construction of the chassis frame (right) giving the Cord front-drive the strongest frame under any passenger car built. The X-cross member is an innovation in chassis frame bracing and is possible through the absence of a drive shaft. Illustration below shows the straight side rails with front and rear cross-members. Side rail stock is 7/32 inches thick. No tramp, shimmy, nor wobble with a frame like this. Absence of frame "kick-up" at rear makes lower body possible and enables Cord designers to place rear seat on same level as front.

SPECIFICATIONS

AXLE—Front

Type	¾ floating—Tubular
Axle End Type	Reverse Elliot
Trans. Inclination of King Pin	None
Trans. Inclination of Spindle	1½ deg.
Castor Angle	2 deg.
Toe-in	Nothing
Inside Universal Joints	Universal Products
Outside Universal Joints	Mechanics—special constant velocity
Final Drive	Inverted Hypoid
Gear Ratio	4.076-1, 4.416-1, 4.818-1

AXLE—Rear

Type	I Section

BRAKES—Foot

Type	Internal Hydraulic
Operate on	4 wheels
Front Drum Diam.	12″
Rear Drum Diam.	15″
Division of Braking Effort	60% front, 40% rear

BRAKES—Hand

Type	Internal Mechanical
Operate on	Rear Wheels

This system operates the serv. brake shoes in rear drums.

CLUTCH

Type	Dry Disc
Driven Discs	1
Facings	2

COOLING

Type	Centrifugal Pump
Pump Drive	Chain
Radiator Type	Tube
Thermostat	Dole
Radiator Shutter	Automatic

ENGINE

Make	Lycoming
Cylinders	8 in line en bloc
Valve Arrangement	L
Crankcase	Separate
Bore and Stroke	3¼ x 4½
Piston Displacement	298.6 cu. in
Tax HP	33.8
Maximum Developed HP	125
Compression Ratio	5.25-1
Rotation of Engine	Counter-clockwise
Points of suspension	4
Mixture Heated by	Exhaust around riser
Heat Control	Manual
Vibration Dampener	Tortional—Lanchester
Crankshaft	Counterbalanced
No. Main Bearings	5
Main Bearing Diam.	2⅜″
Camshaft Drive	Chain
No. Camshaft Bearings	6
Camshaft Bearing Diam.	2″
Timing Chain Adjustment	Automatic
Connecting Rod Material	Steel
Connecting Rod Length	9″ center to center
Connecting Rod Bearing Diam.	2⅛″
Piston Material	Bohnalite
Piston Type	Invar Strut
Piston Rings	3 compression, 1 oil
Piston Rings Location	All Above Pin
Valve Port. Diam.	1-5/16 Exhaust, 1-7/16 Intake
Valve Lift	11/32″
Exhaust Valve Material	Silicrome

FUEL SYSTEM

Tank Capacity	20 gallons
Fuel Feed	Pump
Carburetor	Schebler 1¼″ Dual

FRAME

Channel Depth	7″
Flange Width	3″
Thickness	7/32″
Cross Members	3 Straight, 2 Diagonals

IGNITION & ELECTRICAL

Make	Delco Remy
Generator Drive	Chain
Starter Drive	Bendix
Battery Make	U. S. L.
Battery Capacity	104 a. h. at 5 amp. dis.
Battery Location	Under Hood
Spark Control	Semi-automatic
Automatic Advance	15 deg. engine
Manual Advance	15 deg. Engine
Firing Order	1-6-2-5-8-3-7-4
Ignition Switch	Delco Remy

LUBRICATION

Chassis	Bijur

Points Reached—

Rear Springs	6 points
Fan	2 points
Water Pump	1 point
Clutch	1 point
Clutch and Brake Pedals	2 points

Engine	Gear Pump
Capacity	8 quarts

Pressure to—

- Main Bearings
- Camshaft Front Bearing
- Rod Bearings
- Timing Case

SPRINGS—Front

Type	Double ¼ elliptic
Shackle Type	Rubber
Leaf Material	Silico-Manganese

SPRINGS—Rear

Type	Semi-elliptic
Length	62″
Shackles	Metallic
Leaf Material	Silico-Manganese

STEERING GEAR

Type	Worm and Roller
Gear Ratio	20-1
Turning Radius	23 ft.

TRANSMISSION

Location	Unit—in front

Gear Shift

Std. in Transmission, 1 3
reversed in lever * *
****
* *
R 2

Transmission Ratios—

Low	3.11-1
Second	1.69-1
High	Direct
Reverse	3.78-1

Note: All driving and front braking torque taken directly on the frame. Rear braking torque taken by the springs.

GENERAL FEATURES

Height of Sedan	61″
Height of Phaeton-Sedan	58″
Head Room—Rear of Sedan	36″ - 37″
Wheelbase	137½″
Tread	58″ front, 60″ rear
Wheels	Wire

Horns, 1 on each side, tuned to give beat note

Instrument Board—

Left Inst. Group	Water Temp. Gauge; Oil Pressure Gauge; Speedometer
Left Con. Group	Left Windshield Wiper; Spark Control; Throttle; Inst. Light Switch
Center Group	Gear Shift Lever; Ignition Switch; Glove Compartment
Rt. Con. Group	Rt. Windshield Wiper; Starter; Choke; Carb. Heat Control
Rt. Inst. Group	Gasoline Gauge; Oil Level Gauge; Ammeter

All instruments are of the rotating dial type.

Two Cowl Ventilators.

Two Windshield Wipers.

Emergency Brake Lever placed well forward in center.

Gear Shift Lever—sliding rod type through instr. board.

Hand crank in conventional position.

CORD crest on starting crank hole cover, glove compartment lid, and gasoline tank cover.

Front Seat adjustable fore and aft.

Steering column adjustable vertically.

Four Houdaille shock absorbers.

Torchieres in rear corners and dome light in all closed cars.

Courtesy light on running board of all models.

Tail light on left rear, stop and back up light on right rear.

Lights controlled by knurled knob in center of steering wheel.

Speedometer drive off differential shaft giving proper recording with all gear ratios.

Front fenders approximately 80″ in length.

Hood 46″ in length.

Tires 18 x 7.00 standard.

Unique and original theft-proof spare tire lock.

Cord Cabriolet—Enclosed

4. *The Talk of the Town*

Car owners are too experienced and too critical to be satisfied with superficial changes. Improvements must be real and fundamental.

No fewer than a dozen other makes put in a first appearance at the automobile show along with the new Cord. Marmon introduced a junior nameplate, the *Roosevelt*—honoring Teddy. Stutz brought out a lower priced companion in the *Blackhawk*. Moon christened the *Windsor White Prince*. The up-and-coming Chevrolet upset Ford's recent Model A by standardizing on a six. Publicity appeared for a car called the *Ruxton*.

General Motors provided a big new car for Oldsmobile dealers named the *Viking*. It came up with a smaller model for Buick dealers dubbed the *Marquette,* and with this courted disaster. Buick people had been extolling the superiority of "valve-in-head" power for many years. Suddenly they were loaded with a junior edition which, as a flat head, refuted traditional values. The Marquette engineering—which had simply borrowed from existing Oldsmobile engine patterns—proved to be the kind of top level mistake that smaller companies couldn't afford to make and still survive as corporate entities. The Viking, which had been shown as a LaSalle-looking V-8, never reached standard volume. General Motors was big enough to quietly bury them both shortly after.

Within the Auburn Automobile Company there existed no margin for product error. E. L. Cord had groomed the car to bear his name for an indelible reception when it was slipped into automobile exhibitions along with the Auburn in the summer of 1929. He was not to be disappointed.

In the eyes of car men the unforgettable Cord was to have a devastating effect on the shape of other makes of conventional proportion.

To many show attendants of rural ken the sudden appearance of the new Cord before them as they sauntered along the aisle, came as a complete surprise. Some gaped in shock. Thousands knotted around the car wherever it was shown.

The appeal of front-wheel drive was as compelling as a magnet. Everyone wanted a demonstration and the "feel" of the car was sensationally different to many, from an operator's standpoint. Auto enthusiasts of every age fought for trials in the only car in the country with this new approach to roadability, cornering and control. Outside in the street the Cord literally stopped traffic where demonstration units, engulfed with onlookers six-deep, found it impossible to swing away from the curb for that all-important pull around the block.

The fluid, classic lines of the new car were those schoolboys had been drawing in their daydreams on the margins of their foolscap. The Cord was so advanced in appearance, yet so earthly, it looked like it would last and last for years—like a piece of hand-tooled machinery that never needs oiling, where you lock up the parts when you make it and send it out with a lifetime guarantee. Among arbiters of good taste the Cord seemed the tacit archtype of the future in that great unwritten textbook of motor car design.

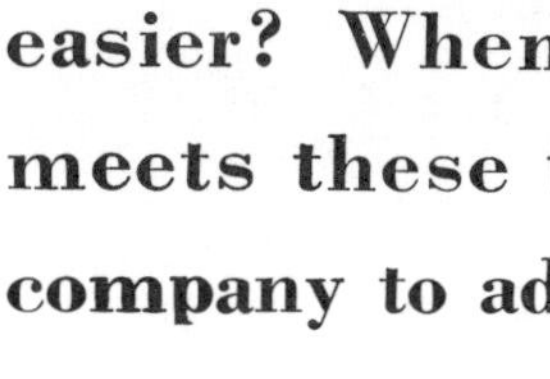
CORD

CORD

PLUS DE SÉCURITÉ

Puissance contrôlée
Pas de dérapage
Facilité de conduite

PLUS DE CONFORT

Aménagement plus normal des sièges
Augmentation du poids suspendu

BEAUTÉ

Crée le style

La Cord à traction avant est exposée actuellement. Demandez à en faire l'essai.

Une avance définitive en technique automobile

CORD

À TRACTION AVANT

Dès sa présentation, il y a plus d'un an, la Cord à traction avant a recueilli les suffrages des connaisseurs par sa valeur technique et son élégance. Aujourd'hui, tous ceux qui l'ont adoptée sont unanimes à témoigner de ses merveilleuses qualités de performance et de confort, qui lui assurent la première place des voitures de luxe. Le choix d'une Cord s'impose nécessairement à tous ceux qui veulent obtenir maximum de sécurité, absolue facilité de conduite car, seule, la traction avant est à même de garantir ces avantages.

Distributeur Général pour la France :

OMNIUM AUTOMOBILE

SERVICE STATION : 98, RUE DE COURCELLES PARIS MAGASIN D'EXPOSITION : 114, CHAMPS ÉLYSÉES

3 A-30

AUBURN AUTOMOBILE COMPANY

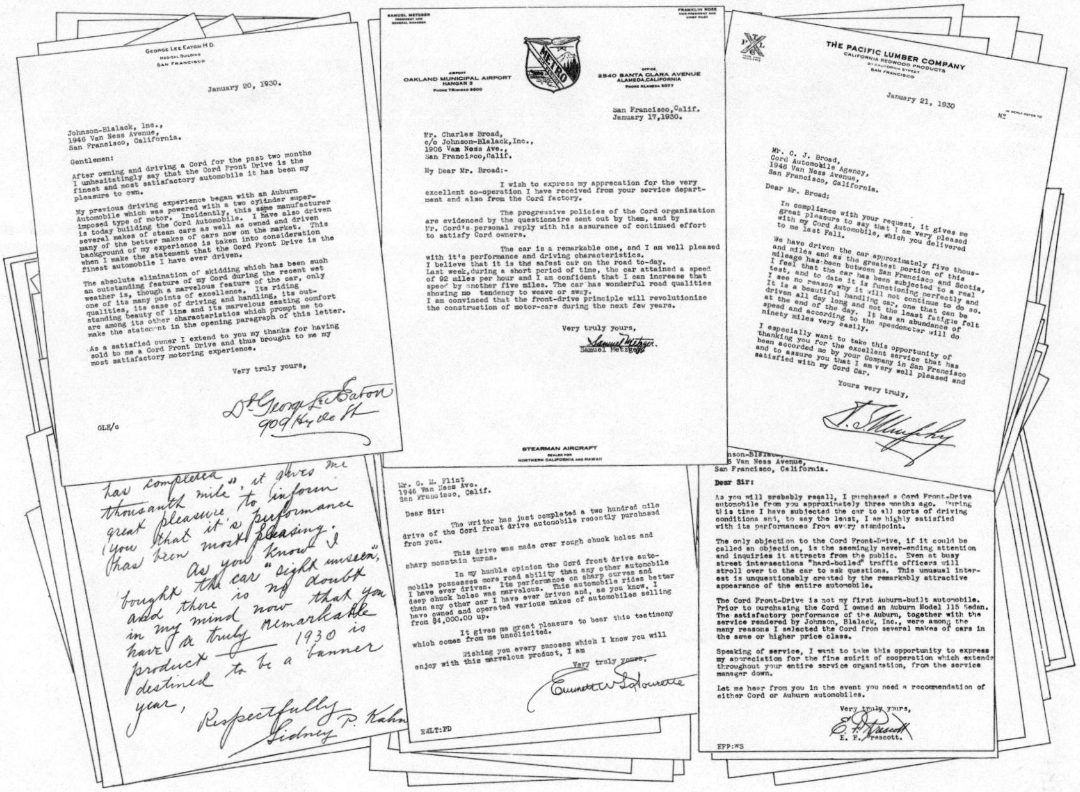
GEORGE LEE EATON M.D.
MEDICAL BUILDING
SAN FRANCISCO

January 20, 1930.

Johnson-Blalack, Inc.,
1946 Van Ness Avenue,
San Francisco, California.

Gentlemen:

After owning and driving a Cord for the past two months I unhesitatingly say that the Cord Front Drive is the finest and most satisfactory automobile it has been my pleasure to own.

My previous driving experience began with an Auburn Automobile which was powered with a two cylinder super-imposed type of motor. Incidently, this same manufacturer is today building the Cord Automobile. I have also driven several makes of steam cars as well as owned and driven many of the better makes of cars now on the market. This background of my experience is taken into consideration when I make the statement that the Cord Front Drive is the finest automobile I have ever driven.

The absolute elimination of skidding which has been such an outstanding feature of my Cord during the recent wet weather is, though a marvelous feature of the car, only one of its many points of excellence. Its riding qualities, its ease of driving and handling, its out-standing beauty of line and its marvelous seating comfort are among its other characteristics which prompt me to make the statement in the opening paragraph of this letter.

As a satisfied owner I extend to you my thanks for having sold to me a Cord Front Drive and thus brought to me my most satisfactory motoring experience.

Very truly yours,

Dr George Lee Eaton
909 Hyde St

GLE/c

SAMUEL METZGER
OAKLAND MUNICIPAL AIRPORT
HANGAR 3
OFFICE
2540 SANTA CLARA AVENUE
ALAMEDA, CALIFORNIA
PHONE ALAMEDA 5077
FRANKLIN ROSE

San Francisco, Calif.
January 17, 1930.

Mr. Charles Broad,
c/o Johnson-Blalack, Inc.,
1906 Vam Ness Ave.,
San Francisco, Calif.

My Dear Mr. Broad:-

I wish to express my appreciation for the very excellent co-operation I have received from your service department and also from the Cord factory.

The progressive policies of the Cord organization are evidenced by the questionaire sent out by them, and by Mr. Cord's personal reply with his assurance of contimued effort to satisfy Cord owners.

The car is a remarkable one, and I am well pleased with it's performance and driving characteristics.
I believe that it is the safest car on the road to-day.
Last week, during a short period of time, the car attained a speed of 92 miles per hour and I am confident that I can increase that speed by another five miles. The car has wonderful road qualities showing no tendency to weave or sway.
I am convinced that the front-drive principle will revolutionize the construction of motor-cars during the next few years.

Very truly yours,

Samuel Metzger
Samuel Metzger

STEARMAN AIRCRAFT
DEALER FOR
NORTHERN CALIFORNIA AND HAWAII

THE PACIFIC LUMBER COMPANY
CALIFORNIA REDWOOD PRODUCTS
SAN FRANCISCO

January 21, 1930

Mr. C. J. Broad,
Cord Automobile Agency,
1946 Van Ness Avenue,
San Francisco, California.

Dear Mr. Broad:

In compliance with your request, it gives me great pleasure to say that I am very pleased with my Cord Automobile, which you delivered to me last Fall.

We have driven the car approximately five thousand miles and as the greatest portion of this mileage has been between San Francisco and Scotia, I feel that the car has been subjected to a real test, and to date it is functioning perfectly and I see no reason why it will not continue to do so. It is a beautiful handling car, one that can be driven all day long and not the least fatigue felt at the end of the day. It has an abundance of speed and according to the speedometer will do ninety miles very easily.

I especially want to take this opportunity of thanking you for the excellent service that has been accorded me by your Company in San Francisco and to assure you that I am very well pleased and satisfied with my Cord Car.

Yours very truly,

has completed "thousandth mile", it gives me great pleasure to inform you that it's performance has been most pleasing.
As you know I bought the car "sight unseen", and there is no doubt in my mind now that you have a truly remarkable product — 1930 is destined to be a banner year,

Respectfully
Sidney P. Kahn

Mr. G. M. Flint
1946 Van Ness Ave.
San Francisco, Calif.

Dear Sir:

The writer has just completed a two hundred mile drive of the Cord front drive automobile recently purchased from you.

This drive was made over rough chuck holes and sharp mountain turns.

In my humble opinion the Cord front drive automobile possesses more road ability than any other automobile I have ever driven. Its performance on sharp curves and deep chuck holes was marvelous. This automobile rides better than any other car I have ever driven and, as you know, I have owned and operated various makes of automobiles selling from $4,000.00 up.

It gives me great pleasure to bear this testimony which comes from me unsolicited.

Wishing you every success which I know you will enjoy with this marvelous product, I am

Very truly yours,

Emmett W LaTourette

EWLT:PD

...nson-Blalack,
...6 Van Ness Avenue,
San Francisco, California.

Dear Sir:

As you will probably recall, I purchased a Cord Front-Drive automobile from you approximately three months ago. During this time I have subjected the car to all sorts of driving conditions and, to say the least, I am highly satisfied with its performances from every standpoint.

The only objection to the Cord Front-Drive, if it could be called an objection, is the seemingly never-ending attention and inquiries it attracts from the public. Even at busy street intersections "hard-boiled" traffic officers will stroll over to the car to ask questions. This unusual interest is unquestionably created by the remarkably attractive appearance of the entire automobile.

The Cord Front-Drive is not my first Auburn-built automobile. Prior to purchasing the Cord I owned an Auburn Model 115 Sedan. The satisfactory performance of the Auburn, together with the service rendered by Johnson, Blalack, Inc., were among the many reasons I selected the Cord from several makes of cars in the same or higher price class.

Speaking of service, I want to take this opportunity to express my appreciation for the fine spirit of cooperation which extends throughout your entire service organization, from the service manager down.

Let me hear from you in the event you need a recommendation of either Cord or Auburn automobiles.

Very truly yours,

E. P. Prescott
E. P. Prescott.

EPP:WS

Representative initial reaction to the front-drive as prepared to illustrate a brochure distributed by Johnson-Blalack, Inc., San Francisco.

The Cord was first exhibited abroad at the Paris Salon and the next week at the Olympia, in London, in October 1929. More than a score of Auburn distributors from all over Europe and North Africa went wild.

Fall shows were also held in Brussels, in Amsterdam, in Berlin, in Prague and in Lisbon. In the Spring of 1930 Cords were shown at the Geneva Motor Show and later in Milan. Precursors of Fashion became anxious for delivery in every market where the car appeared. One of the first cabriolets to go out of the office on the *Champs Eysées* was ordered by Dieundone Costes, an aviator then in the news for his speed attempts in the name of France.

In Cairo the distributor put five members of the Royal family, as well as numerous bankers, sportsmen and other notables, into the Cord. Everywhere the front-drive seemed to attract leaders of the land. In Mexico City early owners numbered among them three governors. Chile's Ambassador to Peru chose a phaeton sedan and took time to write to Auburn, "The Cord has everything that can be asked for in the best of cars; a powerful engine, great speed, solid construction and to this splendid mechanical ensemblage is added a unique smartness of lines . . . a revolution and an advancement in the automotive industry."

Among international figures to recognize the superiority of front-drive (on land or ice) was Sonja Henie, the Norwegian ice skating queen, age nineteen, whose *first car* was a cabriolet.

Distribution points were also established in Athens, Tokyo, Durban, Syria, Palestine, Johannesburg, and even in Manchuria, China. Markets such as Australia, South Africa, Brazil and Colombia, while passing through severe economic conditions still supported the Cord with more than the average percentage for the industry. Exclusive of the U. S. and Canada, it was distributed in twenty-two foreign countries through a network of thirty-five distributors.

FOREIGN TO EUROPE

So foreign is the originality of the Cord design, that it stands out with sharp contrast against the background of the finest motor equipage that Europe has to offer. As a result, in competition in the important Continental Rallyes, the Cord has emerged victorious in thirty-nine events.* No other American automobile has ever gained such overseas renown. In Europe, as elsewhere, the influence of the Cord is felt as the model for others to pattern after. Cord dealers are now showing models of the winning Cord cars chosen by various members of Royalty for their personal use.

*Included are such outstanding awards as: Grand Prix, plus Cup of Honor, at Monte Carlo; Grand Concours d'Elegance Prize at Jaun Les Pins; First Grand Prize, Concours d'Elegance, Cannes, France; First Prize, Concours d'Elegance, Berlin, Germany; Gold Band, Concours d'Elegance, Prague

CORD
FRONT DRIVE

Sedan · Brougham · Cabriolet · Phaeton Sedan · Auburn Automobile Company, Auburn, Indiana

Frank Lloyd Wright (1869-1959) may go down as the original owner of longest record. FLW was still in possession of the Cord he called "heroic" at the time of his passing nearly thirty years after he had originally fallen for its precursory form — at the age of sixty, in 1929.

In the free-wheeling days just before that Black Friday in October, 1929, when history records the beginning of the Great Depression, brand new, along with the *automobile radio* and the *Aerocar*—which provided a new mode of transportation as a house trailer—the front-wheel drive Cord was the stuff of standup comedians, the focus of cab drivers' discussions and the talk at dinner parties. The Cord brought interest to the scene.

"The Cord had taken several foreign prizes for body design and it was the nearest thing to a well-designed car I had ever seen outside Europe," observed the world's foremost architect in his monumental autobiography. ". . . when several large commissions loomed in the foreground, I [bought] the Cord, taking it on an installment-plan contract that ran us ragged for years. . . ."

From all over the world men came to see and to marvel at the fresh, free spirit of Frank Lloyd Wright. European architecture was probably more profoundly influenced by the work of this vigorous American than by any other force that had struck it in a century. His selection of the L-29 for personal use *in effect* bestowed yet another silver medal on the automobile—for Wright's judgment at once underscored the validity of the Cord as the design of substance for the *avant-garde.*

". . . right here the feeling comes to me that the Cord should be heroic in this autobiography somewhere," Frank Lloyd Wright recalled with compassion. ". . . The Cord seemed to have the right principle—front-wheel drive pulling instead of pushing along . . . [It] certainly looked becoming to my houses—the best design from my 'streamline' stand point ever put on the market . . . The Cord was an innovator along right lines that changed the whole field of body design for the better."

WHAT A FEW OF THE

WESTERN UNION

91C A 50 DL

HOLLAND MICH 220 P SEPT 7 1929

AUBURN AUTO CO ATTN MR ROY FAULKNER

AUBURN IND

AM VERY MUCH PLEASED WITH MY NEW CORD IT IS THE LAST WORD IN ROAD ABILITY AND EASE OF HANDLING ITS SMALL TURNING RADIUS IS A GREAT SURPRISE THE MOTOR SEEMS TO HAVE UNLIMITED POWER AND SPEED YOU HAVE ACHIEVED A NEW LEVEL IN MOTOR CAR BUILDING YOURS FOR SUCCESS

CHAS R SLIGH JR

314P

WESTERN UNION

96C 40 5 EXTRA

MINNEAPOLIS MINN 1238P SEPT 7 1929

R H FAULKNER

ESQ AUBURN AUTO CO AUBURN IND

SO FAR CORD AUTOMOBILES PERFORM BEAUTIFULLY AS A STOCKH
AUBURN BELIEVE EXECUTIVE MANAGEMENT OF COMPANY LACKING
IS NOT COMMENSURATE WITH MERCHANDISE VALUE PRICE SHOULD
SIX THOUSAND AND EIGHT THOUSAND DOLLARS

HAROLD L WARNER PRESIDENT HAROLD L WAR

1258P

WES UN

4C A 101 NL

TOLEDO OHIO SEPT 7 1

ROY FAULKNER

VICE PRESIDENT AUBUR

LIKE MOST LAWYERS BANKERS I LACK E
MOTOR VEHICLE STOP HOWEVER I HAVE
TEN AND AFTER PUTTING TWO THOUSAND
FRONT WHEEL CORD OVER ALL SORTS OF
I FEEL I AM QUALIFIED WHEN I UNHES
SAFETY AND COMFORT WILL AMAZE THE
CROWDS THAT FLOCK AROUND IT EVERY
ALLY TO ITS ORIGINAL BEAUTY STOP I
MAKING AUTOMOBILE HISTORY AND WILL

WESTERN UNION

83C A 46 D L

PITTSBURGH PENN 238P SEPT 7 1929

R H FAULKNER VICE PRESIDENT

AUBURN AUTO CO AUBURN IND

VERY MUCH PLEASED WITH MY SEDAN STOP EASIEST CAR I HAVE EVER OP
STOP IT HAS BEEN EXAMINED AND ADMIRED BY OVER ONE THOUSAND PEOPLE
IN LAST TEN DAYS COMMA AND KNOW OF NOTHING YOU COULD ADD TO INCREA
THE EFFICIENCY OF THE CAR STOP CONGRATULATIONS

DR H E MCGUIRE

210P

VE TAKEN DELIVERY OF CORD
I PREDICT IT WILL MAKE

WESTERN UNION

125C A 75 NL

LOSANGELES CALIF SEPT 9 1929

ROY FAULKNER

AUBURN AUTO CO AUBURN IND

I HAVE DRIVEN AUTOMOBILE FOR MORE THAN TWENTY YEARS AND HAVE NEVER HAD A CAR THAT HAS GIVEN ME THE SATISFACTION MY CORD HAS STOP ITS POWER SPEED EASE OF RIDING AND HANDLING AND ITS ROADABILITY UNDER ALL CONDITIONS IS A REVELATION OF WHAT AN AUTOMOBILE SHOULD BE STOP THERE IS NOTHING IN MY OPINION THAT COULD BE ADDED TO THE CAR TO ENHANCE ITS ALL AROUND DESIRABILITY STOP WHEN WILL MY CABRIOLET BE SHIPPED

WM B JOYCE JR 707P

1C A 13

GLEN

ROY FAULKNER AUBUR
DRIVING FACILITIES AN
KEENEST EXPECTATIONS

WESTERN UNION

109C A 46

GI CHICAGO ILL SEPT 8 1929

ROY FAULKNER VICE PRESIDENT

AUBURN AUTO CO AUBURN IND

NEW CORD CAR PERFECT MY ONLY CRITICISM BEING THAT WHEN I PARK
TOWN IT TAKES THREE POLICEMEN TO CLEAR A PATH THROUGH THE CROW
FOR ME TO GET IN AND OUT SO FAR THE CROWDS FORTUNATELY HAVE NOT
STARTED TAKING SOUVENIRS MY PERSONAL REGARDS

HOMER HARGRAVE

613P

WESTERN UNION

87C A 103

PITTSBURGH PENN 314P SEPT 7 1929

R H FAULKNER VICE PRESIDENT

AUBURN AUTO CO AUBURN IND

AFTER DRIVE OF TWO THOUSAND MILES IN THE CORD WITH MY KIDDIES I HAD BECOME A PEST I FEAR TO MY FRIENDS IN PRAISE OF ITS PERFORMANCE WE WERE ALWAYS ON THE RIGHT SIDE NEVER CROSSING CENTER LINE EXCEPT IN PASSING CAR A POINT OF SAFETY TO BE STRESSED STOP OUR KIDDIES ALWAYS SUFFER FROM CAR SICKNESS UNTIL THIS TRIP PROVING THE EASY RIDING QUALITIES I TOLD THIS TO MY PHYSICIAN AND HE SAID THAT IS THE BEST PROOF YOU CAN GIVE ME THE ELIMINATION OF SWAYING ESPECIALLY ON CURVES IS MARVELOUS EVERY CLAIM HAS BEEN EXCEEDED IN MY EXPERIENCE I CONGRATULATE YOU

E MCLAIN

W U

C G 20

TWO CHICAGO

FAULKNER

VICE PRESIDE

ORD CAR RUNNING BEAUTIFU
STERPIECE AND PREDICT FO

ST OWNERS THOUGHT

WESTERN UNION

49C G 78 DL

TDB MILTON MASS 1122A SEP 9 1929

R FAULKNER

V P AUBURN MOTORS AUBURN IND

CAN SUGGEST NOTHING LEFT UNDONE IN NEW CORD TO GIVE OWNER SATISFA[CTION] IN FREEDOM FROM ALL ROAD FATIGUE COMPLETE SENSE OF SECURITY AT HI[GH] SPEEDS AND RESERVE PERFORMANCE BEYOND ALL USUAL DEMANDS IN ADDITI[ON] SMARTNESS OF LINE AND APPOINTMENTS THOROUGHBRED IN EVERY PARTICUL[AR] STOP CAR HAS PROVED WHOLLY SATISFACTORY HAVE OWNED TWENTY SEVEN [...] OF EUROPEAN AND AMERICAN CARS AND BELIEVE CORD TO BE REGARDLESS [...] PRICE AS VALUABLE AN AUTOMOBILE AS HAS YET BEEN BUILT CONGRATULA[...]

ALEX W MOFFAT

1112A

WESTERN UNION

110C A 87 NL

HR CHICAGO ILLS SEPT 6 1929

ROY FAULKNER VICE PRESIDENT

AUBURN AUTO CO AUBURN IND

AT DIFFERENT TIMES HAVE OWNED A FORD DODGE HUDSON TWO JORDANS TWO LINCOLNS CADILLAC TWO AUBURNS AND MY NEW CORD CAR IS THE GREATEST AUTOMOBILE I HAVE EVER DRIVEN STOP OVER THE SAME ROADS TRAVELED BY THE LINCOLN HAS IT SKINNED TO DEATH DRIVING THE CAR HAS CAUSED SO MUCH COMMENT AND CURIOSITY IT IS EMBARRASSING TO GO DOWN THE STREET STOP ON THE STRENGTH OF SEEING MY CAR TWO OF MY FRIENDS PLACED ORDERS AND CONGRATULATE YOU ON YOUR SUCCESS THINK YOU WILL REVOLUTIONIZE THE AUTOMOBILE BUSINESS

WESTERN UNION

92C A 43 DL

DALLAS TEX 238P SEPT 7 1929

R H FAULKNER VICE PRESIDENT

AUBURN AUTO CO AUBURN IND

AM EXTREMELY WELL PLEASED WITH MY NEW CORD PERFORMANCE FAR EXCEEDS MORE COSTLY CARS I HAVE OWNED STOP MY PURCHASE OF CORD LARGELY BASED ON AUBURN FACTORY INTEGRITY WHICH I FIND WELL FOUNDED STOP YOUR POSITION UNIQUE PRODUCTION NOT SALES YOUR PROBLEM

J V LINCOLN

316P

WESTERN UNION

72C A 64 DL

BARNESVILLE OHIO 100P SEPT 7 1929

R H FAULKNER

V P AUBURN AUTOMOBILE CO AUBURN IND

HAVE DRIVEN NEW CORD CAR OVER THOUSAND MILES OVER EAST AND BACK STOP CAR HANDLES AND STEERS WONDERFULLY STOP BELIEVE IT IS THE FINEST RIDING CAR IN THE WORLD AND I HAVE DRIVEN LOTS OF CARS STOP ONLY TROUBLE IS KEEPING CROWD OFF OF CAR WHEN YOU STOP AND THINK YOUR ONLY TROUBLE WILL BE IN SUPPLYING DEMAND STOP WILL WANT ANOTHER MYSELF

GIBSON BRADFIELD

106P

WESTERN UNION

103C G 111 D L

MV CHICAGO ILL 305P SEP 9 1929

ROY FAULKNER

AUBURN AUTO CO AUBURN IND

I HAVE HAD INTIMATE CONNECTION WITH THE VARIOUS CARS AND COMPANIES SINCE THE INDUSTRY STARTED BUT MY NEW CORD CAR HAS REVIVED IN ME THE MOTORING SPIRIT AND HAPPINESS THAT HAS BEEN DEAD FOR YEARS STOP THE INDUSTRY GETS ITS SECOND WIND IN THIS NEW CAR STOP THE NEW CORD CAR HAS THE APPEAL OF VENUS DEMILO DISTINCTION OF THE STATUE OF LIBERTY PERFORMANCE OF JOAN OF ARC ENDURANCE OF HELEN OF TROY STRENGTH OF ATLAS GUTS OF JACK DEMSEY SPEED OF MAN-O-WAR LEADERSHIP OF LINDY COMFORT OF OLD BURGUNDY THRILL OF SUCCESS AND COURAGE OF MY WIFE STOP YOU HAVE MY ORDER FOR ANOTHER CORD CAR

FRED J ROBINSON

351P

A 169 NL

LOSANGELES CALIF SEPT 6 1929

FAULKNER VICE PRESIDENT

AUBURN AUTO CO AUBURN IND

NEW CORD CAR HAS BEEN THE SENSATION OF LOSANGELES DURING THE TWO EEKS I HAVE BEEN ITS PROUD OWNER WHICH IS A BIG STATEMENT BECAUSE OBBY JONES AND THE ROUND THE WORLD GRAFZEPPELIN HAVE BOTH BEEN HERE URING SAID PERIOD STOP THOUSANDS OF PEOPLE HERE HAVE ADMIRED THIS CAR WHEREEVER I DRIVE CROWDS CONGREGATE AND THE UNFAILING EXAMINATION IS QUOTE WE HAVE NEVER SEEN SUCH A BEAUTIFUL CAR IT MUST BE A CORD FRONT DRIVE UNQUOTE THE MECHANICAL PERFORMANCE OF THE CAR AS WELL AS THE DESIGN AND DETAIL IS MARVELOUS I EXPECTED SOMETHING WONDERFUL BUT THE CORD IS A MASTERPIECE HUNDREDS OF PEOPLE HERE ARE ANXIOUS TO OWN AND DRIVE THIS CAR STOP MY ESTIMATE FOR YOUR PRODUCTION NEXT YEAR IS MINIMUM TWENTY THOUSAND FRONT DRIVE STOP THE WHOLE AUBURN STAFF FROM E L CORD DOWN THE LIST INCLUDING ROY FAULKNER AND NEAL MCDARBY IS TO BE CONGRATULATED FOR BUILDING THE AUTOMOBILE THE AMERICAN PUBLIC HAS BEEN WAITING FOR STOP REGARDS AND BEST WISHES FOR INEVITABLE SUCCESS

LYNDOL L YOUNG

630A

Touring Is Turning

Front-Drive Makes It Easier, Safer, and Requires Less Effort

WHETHER motoring in the country or in the city, you seldom drive in a straight line. Every time you turn your car you have to change the direction of the momentum of its weight. You have to do this on curves, around corners, when passing cars, in traffic, when parking, etc., innumerable times!

Here are some of the principal reasons why front-drive construction enables you to steer easier, with safer control, and with less effort:

The Cord turns shorter than any other car of comparable wheelbase. No other car as long as the Cord turns as short nor with as few revolutions of the steering wheel. The Cord requires less motion of the driver's hands and arms.

Because the power is applied to the front wheels, the Cord always wants to go in the direction the front wheels are pointed. The power helps to steer.

Due to the high ratio of sprung to unsprung weight, possible only with front-drive construction, the Cord holds the road much better and affords greater riding comfort, especially under adverse road conditions.

The absence of any tendency of the Cord to tip or lean on turns means better control and greater safety. The rear wheels do not bounce around, but follow in a true manner. There is no inclination to sidesway over cobblestones and chuck holes.

Because the king pins in the Cord are practically perpendicular, you do not have to jack up the weight of the car in order to steer it. The only steering effort required is simply the turning of the wheels.

Owners tell us that in driving the Cord there is a very noticeable difference; less mental and physical effort; and a sense of comfort, ease and security that is exclusive with the Cord.

You are invited to drive the Cord and judge for yourself the advantages of this new kind of motoring.

Cord Sedan

SEDAN $3095 . . BROUGHAM $3095 . . CABRIOLET $3295 . . PHAETON $3295 Prices F. O. B. Auburn, Indiana. *Equipment other than standard, extra*

AUBURN AUTOMOBILE COMPANY · AUBURN, INDIANA

CORD FRONT DRIVE

Not all of those taken with the Cord proved to be immediate prospects for sales. "I was about ten when I saw the L-29 for the first time," recalls a veteran airline pilot. "It was at a dirt airstrip in the country just outside our town in the midwest where I had biked out to look at a big Stinson plane that had come in for an emergency landing.

"The crippled aircraft was regarded by everyone as the most newsworthy event in our town since the town hall had burned to the ground the week Lindbergh was greeted in Paris. But when I saw the new Cord out near that aircraft—a long, long, low, low sedan—my interest in the plane wilted away. That sleek automobile reflected such a welcome and 'right' design departure that I remember feeling like I had been born again as I pedaled back home. The experience of seeing that first Cord became one of the pleasant memories I cherish from childhood."

The silhouette of the Cord contrasted unmistakably with the commonplace. Motor-conscious people everywhere held the commanding appearance of the new front-wheel drive car in special esteem. Not only had the Cord more than enough beauty but it gave unique performance and a speed made even more dazzling by the rider's closer proximity to the ground.

But the L-29 sold for a lot of money at a time when that commodity was scarce and getting scarcer. Initially it was offered at about the price of six Model A Fords and invited comparison with the highly regarded Packard 7-40 and the Cadillac and Lincoln V-8's. The amenities Cord offered were unique. Excitement among dealers reached a new high. One cabled the factory: ". . . expected something wonderful but the Cord is a masterpiece!" It looked like just about everyone wanted one.

While thousands everywhere did *wish* for the Cord, actual sales were consumated only among the daring. Cord remained for the IN group which it endowed with a *touch of tomorrow*. Cord parked next to Cord at the country club and vied with the niblick and the eagle as a topic at the nineteenth hole.

While presence of the Cord merely added dimension to a bright life among the Four Hundred it *made the scene* for others with the foresight to buy one. One band leader of later renown recalls a time when he was a struggling youth with the baton: ". . . even though we were living very close to the bone, we looked as if we were rolling in wealth because we were traveling in a beautiful white Cord [cabriolet] . . . Years before, when we first came to Yankton and were making . . . good money, I had bought my first 'big' car. I remember walking by a showroom late one night while we were playing a date at the Rigadon Ballroom in Sioux City and seeing that car. It was an Auburn, gleaming and sleek under the lights in the window. I wanted that car almost as much as I had wanted the accordion back on the farm, and I spent most of the night trying to decide whether to buy it or not . . . I've always had a weakness for sporty cars—and I've always been able to figure out some reason why I should have one.

"That night I finally remembered George T. Kelly's advice about always looking as prosperous as possible. 'Put up a good front, Lawrence,' he told me. 'If you look as though you're doing well and you're happy, other people will be happier, too.' I decided he was absolutely right, and the next morning I was waiting at the door . . . when the dealer arrived . . . Later on," remembers Lawrence Welk in his autobiography *Wunnerful, Wunnerful!* "I traded the Auburn in on that Cord."

Exclusive Advantages of the CORD Front D

WITH a rear drive car the motor is in front but propelling power is transmitted to the rear axle where it is applied. This means that the horsepower PUSHES your car from the rear. With Cord front drive the horsepower PULLS your automobile because the power is applied to the front wheels.

At left: Rear Drive "Skeleton" frame, impossible to adequately reinforce due to presence of transmission, propeller shaft, rear axle drive, etc. At right: CORD FRONT DRIVE reinforced frame. No moving parts; cross-braced to insure proper reinforcement against weave from every possible oblique angle.

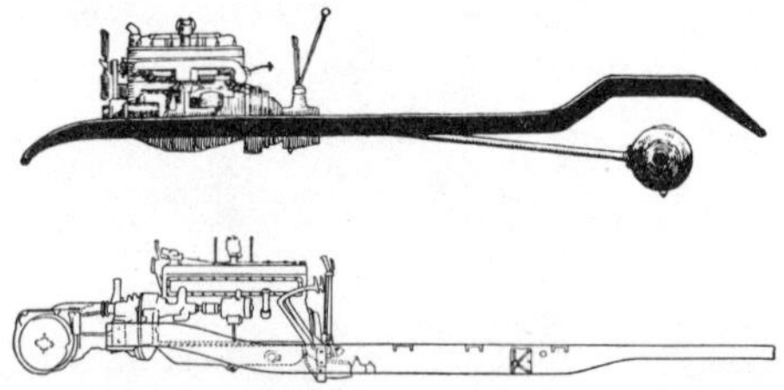

Upper illustration: Frame in rear drive car must have elbow at end to go up and over differential and rear axle. Lower illustration: With Cord Front Drive car frame can be perfectly straight, therefore much stronger.

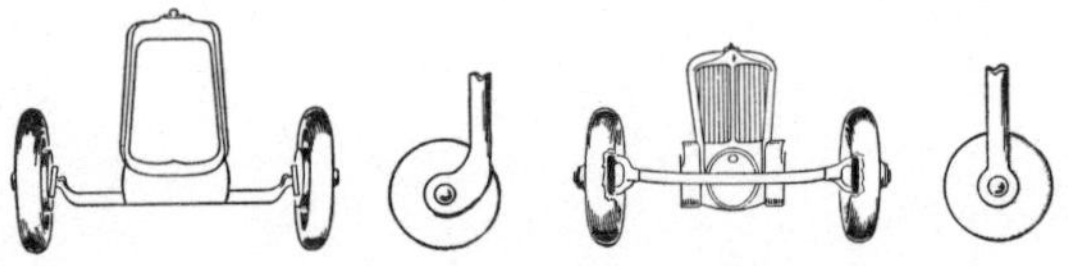

In rear drive cars, king pin is away from center of wheel and at an angle. Compare this with caster in illustration on left. Center of caster is not in center of chair leg. Push chair, and casters turn in different directions. The Cord Front Drive is comparable to casters, whose center would be same as center of chair's legs making front wheels travel in a straight line where pointed.

The Cord Front Drive is easier to steer. The brake is not mounted on the wheel, making it possible to put king pin practically perpendicular. Line from center of king pin is practically in direct line with center of wheel.

With rear drive car considerable operating mechanism is under passengers; clutch, transmission, battery, propeller shaft, differential and rear axle. With Front Drive, none of this is under passengers. They are not disturbed by noise, rumble or vibration of these operating parts.

Left picture shows a rear drive car. The center of gravity is higher, because of frame kickup to clear rear driving axle, causing top heaviness. Right picture shows a front drive car. Due to very light rear axle and straight frame, body is lower, therefore lower center of gravity.

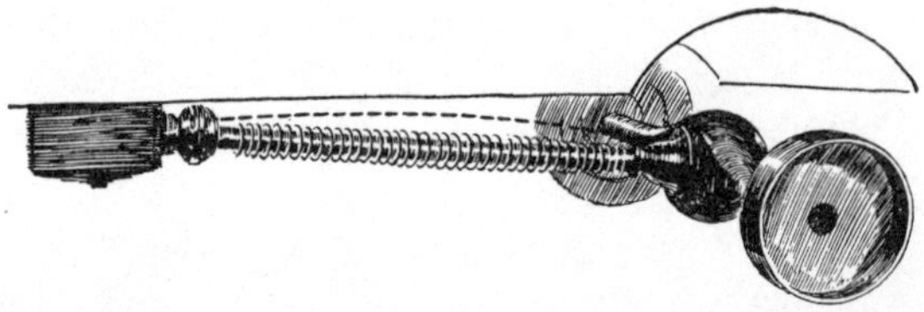

Propeller shaft of rear drive car, revolving at speed of motor. Every bump in the road throws rear axle in the air. The tendency is for this rotating shaft to bend enough to throw it out of balance and set up vibration. With front drive, none of this mechanism is under car, therefore none of the noise of the transmission, propeller shaft or rear axle and none of their vibration.

Left: Rear drive car with all four wheels in ruts. Power on rear wheels is aimed and pushing straight ahead, but driver has his front wheels turned to the right, trying to get out. Front wheels are being shoved ahead, in the ruts. This continues until with a lurch, the car leaps out. Right: With the Cord Front Drive car, when driver turns his front wheel, car climbs up and out, because power is applied to front wheels in the direction they are aimed. The power lifts or rolls front wheels out of rut, while rear wheels simply trail behind.

rive car that make it Easier and Safer to Drive

At left: Rear Drive automobiles: No easy accessibility except to motor. Rear axle, differential, drive shafts, propeller shafts, universals, transmission, muffler, clutch, gearset and battery all under floor. At right: CORD FRONT DRIVE 100% accessibility: All moving parts, clutch, transmission, muffler, gearset and battery located ahead of instrument board and UNDER THE HOOD.

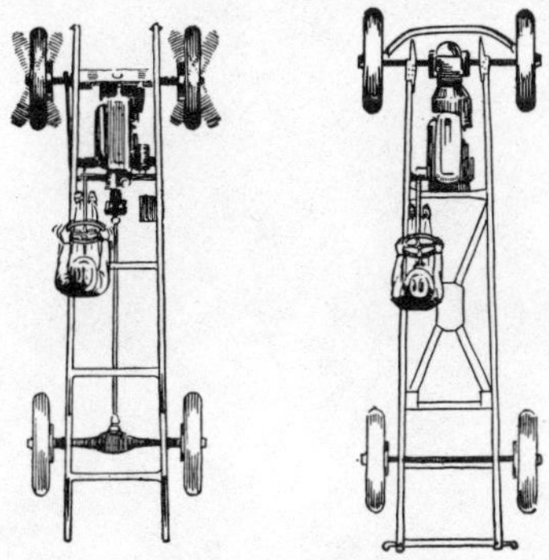

Left picture: A plan view looking down upon driver steering a rear drive car. Due to play and deflection in tie rods, tendency is for wheels to turn this way and that. Front wheels "fight" each other. The result is "shimmying." Right picture: Shimmying eliminated with Front Wheel Drive. Front wheels pull in straight line because they are not being pushed, but are pulling the mass behind them.

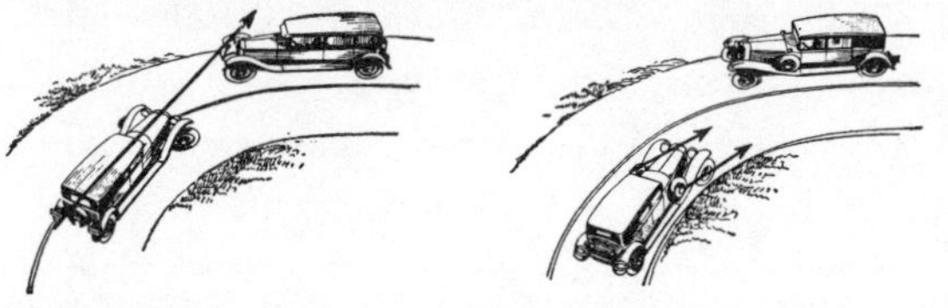

Left: Shows rear drive car going around turn. Power is going the way rear wheels point, the direction of arrow but driver is steering front wheels to the right. The tendency is for car to go the way arrow points, that is to the left, or wrong side of road. Right picture: With Front Drive car it is easy to stay on your side of road. The power is pulling in the direction you steer front wheels. Your Front Drive car goes exactly in direction front wheels go.

Two cars stop on crown of a slippery road. At the signal "Go", this happens: On rear drive cars, with power applied at rear wheels, the rear wheels spin and slide or skid to side because it is easier for them to go to the side than to push mass of car forward. With Front Drive car, even if wheels do spin, you can steer them and go forward. The power is applied the way wheels point. It is pulling the mass instead of pushing it.

The rear drive as a result of kick-up in its frame, compels passengers to ride *on* the car rather than *in* it. In addition, its springs are designed to take driving torque and for propulsion efficiency—NOT passenger comfort.

CORD FRONT DRIVE automobiles (below), have all driving mechanism in front, under the hood; consequently body, frame and springs are engineered for RIDING EASE. With the Cord Front Drive car the frame is perfectly straight. Rear seats are on same level as front seats. Rear passengers have same line of vision as front seat passengers. Top of car comes much lower down and at same time gives rear seat passengers more head room.

Rear drive cars have but ONE purchase for traction in mud or sand or on ice—immediately in front of rear power wheels. CORD FRONT DRIVE power wheels may be swung in an 80 degree turn. Purchase for traction possibility is increased over 1000 per cent.

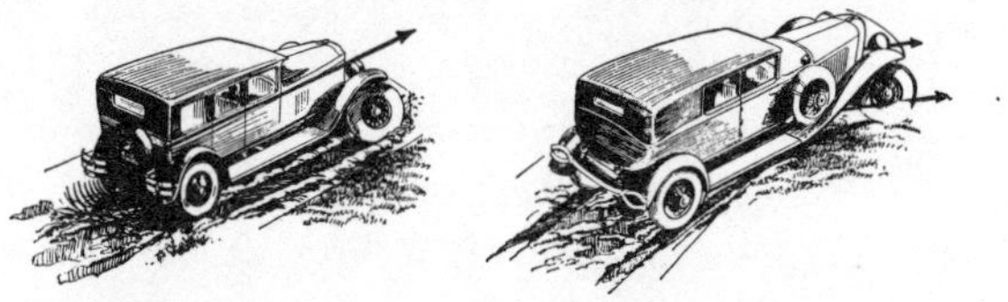

Left picture: One of the first types of airplanes, the "pusher" type with propeller in rear. All of the first planes were of the "pusher" type. But imperative need in aeronautics for utmost efficiency soon forced aeronautical engineers to adopt the tractor type of plane with propeller in front, (as in the right picture below), to pull the plane through the air.

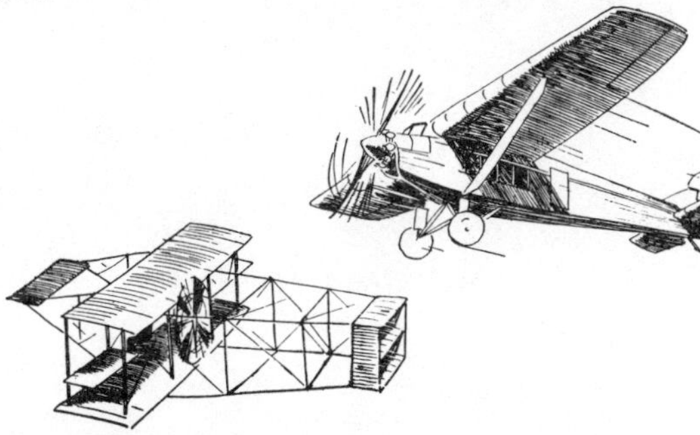

FRONT DRIVE IS SAFER

Now comes the season for rain, sleet, ice, snow; slippery streets and frozen ruts. The handling of a motor car under these adverse conditions is safer, steering is easier, and control is surer, when you are at the wheel of a Cord front-drive.

A year ago this claim was challenged by some who wanted to wait for proof of front-drive's superiority. Today this proof is abundant and conclusive. The exclusive advantages of the Cord are being enjoyed in every part of the nation. Front-drive success is so complete and unqualified that the Cord has immediately become the standard of value among fine cars.

The advantages found only in the Cord can be summed up in one statement—a Cord does all the things any other fine car can do, with less driver effort, with greater riding comfort, with better roadability, and with greater safety.

There are three ways you can verify this claim: Ask Cord owners who have had six to twelve months' experience; drive the Cord yourself and compare it with any other fine car; study its structural difference and mechanical excellence. You will learn that the Cord has a lower center of gravity; that there is less tendency to tip or lean on turns; that the rear wheels do not bounce around but follow in a true manner; that there is no inclination to side-sway over cobble stones and chuck holes; that the car always wants to go the way you aim it; that the front wheels lift up, tractor-like, out of ruts; that it holds the road much better, due to a minimum of unsprung weight in the rear; and that you enjoy a new kind of comfort possible only when you ride *in* a car and not *on* it.

AUBURN AUTOMOBILE COMPANY · AUBURN, INDIANA

Prices F. O. B. Auburn, Indiana. *Equipment other than standard, extra*

SEDAN $3095 CABRIOLET $3295
BROUGHAM $3095 PHAETON $3295

CORD

CORD FRONT DRIVE

Formerly known as the Four Nightingales, Arthur "Harpo" and Julius "Groucho" in the tonneau, Leonard "Chico" and Herbert "Zeppo" at the wheel were all musicians of note. As the Marx Brothers they had just completed their second feature film "Animal Crackers" for Paramount Pictures.

Film folk moved to front-wheel drive with a flourish. Among celebrities who became Cord owners at the Hollywood Branch were "America's Sweetheart" Mary Pickford, Ronald Colman, Edward "Hoot" Gibson, the western star who had been driving an Auburn speedster, Charles Mack, Ann Harding, Harry Bannister, Jeanette MacDonald, Bert Wheeler, Jack Smith, Wynne Gibson, John Miljan, Merwyn LeRoy, Monte Blue and the Four Marx Brothers, each of whom, reputedly, had his own Cord.

The simple straight lines that made the Cord immediately known and admired at every turn on the roads of America and the boulevards of Europe were retained in their maiden form, providing the car's owners with a long style life and dealers with a stable product in the showroom.

An important "seller's market" was sometimes maintained by Cord dealers so that short supply could act as a bargaining virtue. Demand for the heart-pounding front-wheel drive marque was permitted deliberately to outstrip supply, while the production of the L-29 was actually geared to dealers' firm orders.

The uniqueness of the car's appeal would generally have permitted a bargaining advantage for the buyer of a particular unit on the dealer floor. The prospective owner might say, in effect.

"I wanted a tan car; the one you have in stock is green. Drop the price and I'll accept this 'damned' green one." Short supply properly prevented such encounters as this.

ANNOUNCING THE NEW 1931 PROGRAM FOR THE CORD FRONT DRIVE

In keeping with our long standing policy, we are again able to make the public the beneficiary of the savings obtainable through better manufacturing methods and greater buying power. For the first time, a Cord Front-Drive car is now offered to a larger market. Owners of the Cord Front-Drive will tell you it is the finest automobile in the world. Nothing less than a totally new *kind* of motoring could make possible the successful invasion of the Cord into the fine car field. Its sales in its first year represent nearly twenty per cent of all cars sold above $3000. The Cord became the model for the entire automobile industry to pattern after. It is this car, which is the standard of fine car values, with its exclusive front-drive advantages, which we are now able to offer for the first time at the extremely low price of— $2395

BROUGHAM $2395 · SEDAN $2395 · CONVERTIBLE CABRIOLET $2495 · CONVERTIBLE PHAETON SEDAN $2595

Prices f. o. b. Auburn, Ind. · Equipment other than standard, extra · AUBURN AUTOMOBILE COMPANY, AUBURN, IND.

CORD

FRONT DRIVE

FOREMOST AUTOMOBILE

Out of approximately 44 different makes of American automobiles, the Cord offers the exclusive advantages of front-drive. . . . When introduced about a year and a half ago, the Cord was an original, distinct advancement against the background of all other cars. Since then, its margin of fine-car leadership has widened daily due to the experience of the increasing number of Cord owners. . . . That it is foremost in design, is evidenced by the great number of 1931 models patterned after it, both here and abroad. . . . Now for the first time a Cord is available at the extremely low price of $2395.

BROUGHAM $2395 · SEDAN $2395 · CONVERTIBLE CABRIOLET $2495 · CONVERTIBLE PHAETON SEDAN $2595. Prices f. o. b. Auburn, Indiana. *Equipment other than standard, extra*

AUBURN AUTOMOBILE COMPANY AUBURN, INDIANA

CORD

FRONT DRIVE

Captures Speed Officer's Fancy

CAPT. LE ROY F. GALYEN, veteran California State Highway patrol officer, admiring the lines of the Cord convertible phaeton-sedan, driven by Miss Polly Watters and Ruth Hall, First National Studio players. Captain Galyen caught them with his White Auburn 8-90 state patrol coupe after a thrilling chase, only to ask them about the performance of the Cord. The two officers are "Brad" Coombs and Pat McCune.

At Half-Way Mark

NASH 970 SEDAN from Thompson-De Jarnette Company, distributors, being checked in at Zion Canyon Lodge. Left to right are F. C. Keyto, H. Roberts, driver, and O. G. Reinhardt.

OIL 'SURVIVES' ECONOMY TEST

With 74,000 miles recorded on his 1929 Chevrolet sedan, R. A. Marshall finds that by using Gilmore Lion Head motor oil he can travel more than 3500 on six quarts, and on draining the crankcase, the oil that came out was still light in color and oily.

R. A. MARSHALL

"A service station man advised me to use it for 2000 miles," said Marshall, "but I was a confirmed believer of the 1000-mile oil change theory, so drained it out at the end of the 1000 miles. The oil looked so good that I decided to try it for 2000 miles.

"At 1600 I lost my nerve and had the Lion Head oil drained out. Again it looked so good I persuaded myself to go to the limit.

"I just finished a drive of 3554 miles and the oil still looks good. However, I am draining and refilling with Lion Head, because I feel I got three times my money's worth."

The car's appeal was universalized the second selling season by the expedient of price reductions of about one-fourth. While still equivalent to the price of a number of Fords, the car then attracted the next lower price group of buyers, competing with La Salle, Marmon, Franklin, Stutz and the smaller Packard. Production for the year averaged slightly fewer than 150 cars per month. Clearly, many of those who were most in love with the Cord did not seal their affection with a purchase.

By 1932, the whole world was inundated in depression. To counter a second annual reintroduction of the same automobile, however advanced its lines and appeal remained, horsepower was boosted from 115 to 125 by the expedient of increasing the cylinder bore ⅛ inch.

More than two years after its debut the Cord lines proved as excitingly ahead of their time *in proportion* as they had been originally—with one flattering difference. By this date the precursor was meeting second and third rate copies of itself over every mile of the road, for its design had inspired the whole industry with a new design tack. Imitations, within the awkward frame of rear drive limitations, were generally superficial and confined to the radiator area. Baldface copies appeared at the bow of the Nash, Willys and De Vaux. Chrysler not only transgressed in grille design to adopt the motif practically in toto, but lowered and shaped its bodies in slavish imitation.

"Somewhere, sometime, someone, said that 'If a man builds a better mouse trap the world will beat a path to his door.' and we have certainly found out the truth of this statement," wrote Roy Faulkner, then president of Auburn.

"They not only beat a path to your door but they steal your design!

"There has been some resentment about this influence of CORD design on new models among our friends and we have been criticized somewhat for not taking cognizance of it in our advertising, but we at Auburn feel it is the greatest compliment that could be paid us, and that we have been placed in the position of style leaders and given a standing in the industry that cannot help but reach to our benefit.

"Imitations always fall short of the original . . . every kid along the highway says as they pass, 'That's not a CORD! That's a copy . . .'

"There is a certain fundamental sportsmanship in the heart of every American, and the fact that we have chosen to ignore this tendency to imitate has created a great fund of good will for us. It must warm the cockles of the heart of CORD owners to see great manufacturers put the stamp of approval on their judgment."

A full reproduction of a representative issue of the Auburn Automobile Company's monthly house organ The Accelerator begins overleaf . . . A clinical road test from the authoritative British weekly The Autocar follows.

For the most part, the unforgettable body lines of the Cord had been roughly translated into quite forgettable forms among the competition. Walter P. Chrysler's studied emulation of the L-29 in his top-of-the-line Imperial may have been an exception.

LOS ANGELES EXAMINER

SUNDAY, OCTOBER 18, 1931

EXTRAORDINARY OWNER ALLEGIANCE

No car ever built has a greater hold upon its owners than the Cord Front-Drive. The man or woman who has never driven a Cord, regardless of how much other fine car experience they have had, cannot appreciate the difference. The ease of handling, comfort, sense of safety, and the difference in maneuverability of the Cord are a revelation. We invite you to find out, by actually driving a Cord, why owners say "It spoils us for any other type of car."

BROUGHAM $2395 - SEDAN $2395 - CONVERTIBLE CABRIOLET $2495 - CONVERTIBLE PHAETON SEDAN $2595. Prices f. o. b. Auburn, Indiana. *Equipment other than standard, extra. Prices subject to change without notice*

AUBURN AUTOMOBILE COMPANY, AUBURN, INDIANA

CORD

FRONT DRIVE

March, 1930

The Accelerator

PUBLISHED MONTHLY BY THE
AUBURN AUTOMOBILE COMPANY
AUBURN - INDIANA

Cord Front Drive with capacity load negotiating slippery grade on North side of Big Bear Lake, California, without the aid of chains.

In This Issue

VOLUME V

NUMBER III

The Cord Front Drive was the only automobile to arrive at Fawnskin, California, Sunday, January 19, without the aid of chains.

The Cord Front Drive - Southern California and Snow

By EVERETT C. HOWARD
Adv. Mgr. Auburn-Fuller Company, Auburn and Cord Distributor for Southern California.

Snow and plenty of it! That is a condition not at all uncommon, at this season of the year, to most Americans, but to the people of California, and particularly Southern California, it is a great novelty. And to those in Southern California who own Cord front-drive automobiles it meant the first opportunity to find out what this new car would do under real winter conditions.

Being somewhat of an innovation in the passenger car field, it was of interest to see what the car would do on mountain roads after the heaviest snow that has visited Big Bear Valley since 1920. Most of the roads were closed with snow anywhere from five to twenty feet deep. But one, by way of the Mojave desert over Cushionbury and Johnson grades had been opened with snow plows to Big Bear Lake.

The run was made from Los Angeles by way of Victorville to Big Bear, a distance of 143 miles, in three and one-half hours. The road through the desert was perfect but as we approached the snow we found a long line of cars, all with chains, slowly making their way up the grade. The snow had packed and was slick, but we, in the front-drive Cord found no need of chains and the car walked over the snow as though on snowshoes.

As the road was opened to a width of only one car, every car met from the opposite direction meant all hands out to dig a pocket in order to negotiate a passage for the two car. Such a task would probably seem a hardship to those dwelling in a snowclad country, but to the Californian with orange trees in blossom at his doorstep, getting on the business end of a shovel in this deep snow meant great sport.

The San Bernardino Sierras is the range crossed by most visitors who come to Southern California. It lies within the eastern section of the Angeles National Forest and is famous for its Big Bear Lake and Arrowhead, for its summits of San Bernardino and San Gorgonio and is cherished as one of the prize playgrounds of the Southland. On the one side lies the desert, on the other a land of fruit and flowers and between these a range rising from six to eleven thousand feet covered with a forest of giant pines with here and there a meadow which changes with the seasons from a riotous coloring of wild flowers to the pure white of Snow King's Carnival.

The scenes about Big Bear Lake are of surpassing loveliness. The ice-covered lake with its background of pines and giant crags; the quaint cottages of rustic bark with snowshoes, skiis, toboggans and gaily clad people scattered about everywhere.

The performance of the Cord was of interest to everyone up there and the Village Sheriff and the chap who had run the snowplow for sixteen hours to open the road, climbed aboard and we made a trip around the Lake to make contact with people who had been snowed in at their cabins for almost a week. The Cord was the only car to reach the Valley without chains and these men were curious to see what it would do. They saw plenty—for when the power is applied to the front wheels of a car it literally walks away over the snow and ice.

The Cord owners in our party who were so tremendously interested to discover what their Cord car would do under trying winter conditions returned home just 100% satisfied. As the old saying has it: "They marched up the hill and turned around and marched right down again". They made it almost too easy—those triumphant engineers of the Auburn Automobile Company.

AUBURN VALUE BRINGS MANY NEW DEALERS AND DISTRIBUTORS

Since January 1, 1930, nearly one hundred and fifty new dealers and distributors have been added to the Auburn dealer organization.

Distributing points closed include Buffalo, N. Y., Jacksonville, Florida; Oklahome City, Oklahoma; Roswell, N. Mexico; El Paso, Texas; Minneapolis, Minn., and Hastings, Nebr.

The dealer points closed represent important "key cities" in the various distributors territories giving Auburn a more thorough covering of the domestic market.

During the month of December new distributors were added for Fresno, California St. Joseph, Missouri; Pensacola, Florida; and Kalamazoo, Michigan.

The interesting feature of these additions is that in practically every case the distributor has given up a well known, firmly established make of car, and reports that his January and February volume of this year with Auburn and Cord exceeded his January and February volume of 1929.

This is additional and conclusive proof that Auburn's policy is right and Auburn cars represent the greatest "Value" on the market.

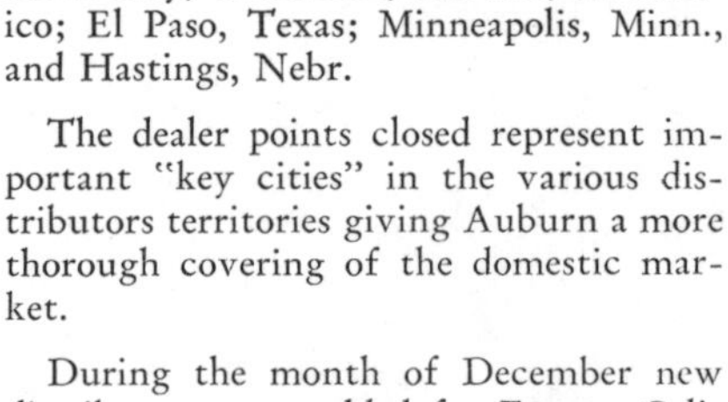

Buck Lucas finds a new use for the Auburn Phaeton Sedan.

WHAT OWNERS SAY

HATS OFF TO THE CORD!

UNITED PLUMBERS SUPPLY CO. *Inc.*
New York City
March 15, 1930.
Executive Dept.

Mr. N. N. Mason,
Auburn Automobile Sales Co.,
1848 Broadway, New York City.

Dear Mr. Mason:—

I have just completed a round trip drive from New York to Miami and return in a new CORD front drive. After twenty-five years of driving all makes, I didn't suppose I had a thrill coming to me—but——I was wrong. I was thrilled to my finger tips.

Driving in speeds up to ninety miles per hour without vibration or fatigue to either passengers or car was nothing short of a revelation. In going through towns the password was "SLOW DOWN TO 60"

GOOD LUCK to the new CORD!

Cordially yours,
(Signed) E. A. LONDON.

EAL:LL

"IT COULD BE SOLD FOR A $2,000 JOB"

Tomahawk, Wisc.

Auburn Automobile Co.,
Auburn, Indiana.

Gentlemen:—

On March 15, 1928, I purchased an Auburn 76 Sedan from Badger Garage, Wausau, Wisconsin, which has been driven ever since in all kinds of weather. Sometimes 40 below zero and in a cold garage.

Starting means nothing to Auburn in cold weather. This Auburn could be sold for a $2,000.00 job I honestly believe as you have a large roomy and powerful and trouble free automobile when you buy an Auburn. I bought my first Auburn in 1921 and drove that till March 15, 1928.

Yours forever,
(Signed) ARTHUR CROSS.

HAS DRIVEN 35 DIFFERENT MAKES IN PAST 19 YEARS

519 No. Washington Ave.,
Lansing, Michigan.

Auburn Automobile Co.,
Auburn, Indiana.

Gentlemen:—

I wish to thank you for the interest you have taken in my car so far and also for the fine job done in getting it in the condition as it is now. The changes made were simply the best thing I have ever seen and the car surely runs much better and steers easier than ever, so I am really in love with this car.

I have owned in the past 19 years 35 different cars and some of them I paid as high as $5400.00 which was some price for the class I got at that time. I will say this car has everything beat I have ever driven in every way. You may publish this letter if you desire to do so.

Again thanking you for the way this car has been taken care of and wishing you every success in the future in selling them to folks who really will appreciate a MIGHTY FINE CAR, I am

Sincerely,
(Signed) DR. EDWIN E. SALISBURY.

L. E. Searles, Sales Manager of Habig Motors Co., Miami, Florida, congratulating W. L. "Young" Stribling on his purchase of a Cord Brougham.

REALLY, I CAN'T TELL YOU HOW PLEASED I AM WITH THE LITTLE WAGON

Mr. W. W. Rice,
Rice Motors, Inc.,
2410 Gilbert Ave., Cincinnati, Ohio.

Dear Mr. Rice:—

I must take my pen in hand to tell you that the Auburn 8-90 was the biggest surprise I have ever experienced. The darned thing apparently will hold seventy-five miles an hour forever. It will go considerably over eighty, checked by Sam's speedometer, without any fuss. We made wonderful time all the way down and I didn't have a bit of trouble all the way. The motor sounds just as quiet as when I started. I think our driving time for the full distance, about 1,300 miles, would be about fifty-five miles an hour and any car that can stand up under that racket has to be good. Really, I can't tell you how pleased I am with the little wagon. I stopped in the Auburn place the other day and discovered that they have sold five Duesenbergs this season.

Best regards,
(Signed) FRANK CROSS.

15 YEARS OLD AND STILL GOING

Mr. R. C. Sackhoff of the Auburn Sales Company, Inc., of Birmingham has just advised us they had the privilege of seeing a 1915 model Auburn touring car owned by a party in the suburbs of Birmingham and that in spite of its 15 years is still running good and has been serving the owner very faithfully.

AND THAT'S THAT

By Phil M. Daly

John Eberson, leader among theatre architects, also takes his place as a leader among automobile owners when his new specially Eberson-designed Duesenberg rides the ways and purrs out into 5th Ave.

The car has the grace of a swan, the dignity of a carriage, the comfort of a home, the power of a battleship, plus the speed of an airplane. When we were told that it could develop a speed of 80 miles an hour in second within half a city block, and could do 116 an hour in comfort, we had to be shown. So, we were, and how!

Next time John Eberson intends to make a flying trip to Chicago all he needs is this car and a passenger to keep his radio programs diversified. Oh, yes, it has a radio, too.

—From "The Film Daily", March 3rd, 1930.

The ACCELERATOR

Published monthly by the Auburn Automobile Co., Auburn, Indiana, in the interest of its Distributors, Dealers, Salesmen and everyone connected in any way with the Auburn organization.

VOL. V Auburn, Ind. March 1930 No. III

Faulkner Speaking

If You Care to Listen

Dr. Gardner of the Mayo Clinic told me the best story on salesmanship I've heard in years.

"Doc" said he was waiting between trains in a little town in Minnesota so he dropped in at a barber shop for a hair cut. The barber, noticing the hair was a little thin on the top, asked the Doctor if he didn't want to try some of his hair restorer which he put up himself. The Doctor said "Yes." The barber opened a drawer, took out a pair of rubber gloves similar to those used by housewives who are proud of their hands, and proceeded to pull them on. "What are the gloves for?" guilelessly asked Dr. Gardner, the leading dental authority of the United States and Europe. "What do you think I want to do—grow hair all over my hands", answered the barber.

Boy, that's salesmanship, faith, knowledge of your product and everything else all in one lump.

But, seriously, I am of the opinion that the little old salesman is coming into his own—

I don't think times are hard but I would be crazy if I didn't know that we are no longer in a seller's market. People are analyzing their purchases; salesmen are under the microscope. It takes better men to do a good job, and somehow I think that in this organization of ours we have the better man.

Ours has never been an easy task. We have never been able to "high hat" the customers. Fighting our way upward over the last five years; overcoming the resistance of small production; wrestling the business away from strongly entrenched competitors who thought they had it on ice, have given us a training and a courage that will make us meet the new conditions with a high heart and a conception of the situation that may be granted to but few. Our business during January and February demonstrated this.

But we must not let down. We must know our product as we never knew it before. We must have faith and put on rubber gloves. We must analyze our customers. We must remember that a man who comes into our store to buy a car is entitled to attention and courtesy.

We should be able to tell him why we built Front Drive automobiles. The Front Drive is not an experiment. For years it has been tested and proven on the race tracks of the world. For over two years Auburn engineers worked in California in the plant of Harry Miller developing parts that would make the Front Drive commercially acceptable. New universal joints had to be developed as the universals used in race cars were not practical for commercial purposes. They were built up and torn down, tried out and discarded until finally the first car came to Auburn. It was a sorry sight compared to the Front Drive as you know it today. At Auburn a special crew of engineers went to work upon it. Radiator after radiator was designed and redesigned. Wooden models and clay models of the entire car were built only to be thrown in the discard by Mr. Cord. Sample cars were built—some of them costing upward of ten thousand dollars, only to be dismantled because something was lacking. Over three quarters of a million dollars were spent in getting ready to build this automobile. Cars were tested at Indianapolis by day and night shifts. Four cars in the hands of competent engineers were sent across country, through sand, mud, over mountains, beaten and pounded in every way, to find out any weakness they might have. Then Mr. Cord alone took a car and drove it many miles down through Texas, Oklahoma, Arizona, trying to break it before he would put his stamp of approval on it.

That is the story of the inception of the Cord Front Drive. Cost meant nothing. New methods of manufacture had to be devised; new machines installed.

So when somebody asks you why other manufacturers haven't Front Drive automobiles, don't tell them you don't know but tell them the truth. Tell them cost is the greatest deterrent.

This Front Drive car was not an accident. It was the result of time, money and effort well spent and as surely as electric light pushed out the lamps, so will the Front Drive obsolete rear drive cars in the high priced field.

In a certain city a customer asked a salesman why the Cord was high priced and the answer was, "A lot of people made money in Auburn stock and we have a good market among them." That's terrible. It's so dumb it isn't even funny.

Front Drive has an appeal that no other car has.

Let us look at this thing for a minute. Before the coming of the Cord Front Drive what reason was there for a man to buy a car in the field above three thousand dollars

Some great automobiles were built in the field around two thousand and, building the Auburn line, we know some great automobiles were built in the field below two thousand.

People could buy speed, beauty, power, riding qualities, durability, almost anything their hearts could desire, for anything from $1500 up to $2500.

Sales above three thousand depended upon prestige, nameplates on bodies, broadcloths, broadlace, trick cigar lighters, clocks and what nots. Now for a sum a little over three thousand what do we offer—

Prestige? At Miami and Palm Beach Cord Front Drives were more a mark of distinction than the most foreign foreign car and American makes were not even in the running.

Bodies? In our own plants under the supervision of men who have set a pace for the entire industry to follow, who have designed bodies so beautiful that they are the center of crowds wherever the car is parked, we are building bodies as fine as those built by custom body builders of note—because a nameplate cannot be a substitute for ash lumber, angle irons, glue, long screws, padding, etc., nor do nameplates give anyone a corner on all the brains and craftsmanship in the body building industry.

Broadcloths and broadlace, cigar lighters? We have them.

But we also have—

Greater steering ease than any car at home or abroad, because our car goes where it is pointed. A woman can park it without feeling that she's been working over a washtub all day.

It is safer than any automobile on the market due to its low center of gravity and the manner in which it negotiates turns without sidesway or skidding.

It is rigid and solid and already we have cars that have negotiated from thirty to forty thousand miles of the most gruelling work imaginable—over any and all kinds of roads between Auburn and Connersville, Chicago, Detroit, day in and day out, with a minimum of repairs and no breakdowns. These are our courtesy cars.

It has an abundance of speed but it is loafing at a speed of sixty miles per hour which can be maintained for hours at a time with no danger, no fuss, no effort and absolutely no fatigue to the driver.

It has a seating arrangement scientific in design and absolutely alone in comfort and restfulness. There isn't any car that can compare with it in riding qualities, and youngsters or elderly folk can ride days in it without car sickness.

It brings a new thrill and a new joy to motoring. People drive their Cord cars for the thrill they get out of driving them.

We offer something definitely new—something typically American.

Competition has as little chance of stopping people, who have enjoyed the privilege of a long ride in a Cord car, from buying one as a person would have of making my wife give up her vacuum cleaner and get a broom.

But do not let us underestimate competition.

No car ever introduced has had as many knockers. There are people in your city who cross the street when they pass your store because somebody has told them Cord Front Drives do somersaults on unwary bystanders.

There is only one way to sell Cord cars—that is by letting people ride in them and drive them.

The salesman does not live who can describe the thrill of a Cord Front Drive car. After the first nervousness has passed away and one gets the feel of it, there are no words to describe the joy one gets in steering it with a slight twist of the wrist, learning the little pause that makes the gears change without clashing, feeling the power impulse as you press the accelerator and feel it go on up—forty, fifty, sixty, seventy, eighty miles an hour, with no roaring in your ears, no vibration, no sense of speed—but, here I'm trying to describe it and it can't be done, so let us ride people in this Cord car. Let them drive it themselves. Let them find out that here at last is something that is low priced in comparison with the advantages, safety and pride of ownership it brings.

The Cord car stands alone today but the Cord car represents what people who can afford it will demand in all high priced cars in the future.

* * * * *

PANIC——

There is a great article in the March issue of the "American Magazine" on *Panic*. It is by Clarence Budington Kelland. A great traveler and correspondent, it has been his lot to go through train wrecks, motor accidents, bombings, tornados, battles, fires—a long list of experiences that do not happen in the lives of ten ordinary men. He has seen men and women under the stress of a great terror and his findings are interesting. For instance, he tells of an experience in an old-fashioned theater in a foreign country as follows:

"I sat one evening in a huge theater, an old-fashioned theater in a foreign city. There was but one exit down a long, narrow passageway. Suddenly smoke rolled over the audience; there was a shout of "Fire!" and then the thunder of feet in the galleries above—and the sound of those thundering feet I shall not soon forget! Somehow, it was more terrible than the screams and cries which came in its wake. It was as if something had erupted in the middle of that auditorium. The audience split into four parts, one rushing the stage, one rushing the rear and the exit, one blindly charging each side wall. Men and women fell and no one heeded them. Faces were dreadful and inhuman. I think in that brief interval I completed and passed the examinations in a full course in *Terror*. With me was my young son. If he had not been there, I think I should have been one of those scrambling, screaming madmen. It was curious; perhaps it was absurd. But the thought held my mind that I could not bear to have my son see me as those others were; that if he did see me so, I never should be able to face him again. Also, there was the responsibility—the *Discipline*. I had taught myself, or some gracious power had instructed me since his birth, that I was responsible for him, that he came before myself, that I must *always* answer his need. It was Discipline of a sort. I remember I said to him, 'Fellow, sit tight. For God's sake, let's be dignified'."

And in a short time they walked out unharmed.

Then again he covers this country's situation:

"But Panic is Panic. Human beings cease to function as normal human beings. And Bankers as well as Brokers are human just as the rest of us, subject to the same laws which govern all men, weak with the same weakness and strong with the same strength. They were the standing army of Finance, but in them was not Discipline. Many of them had never before encountered such conditions as existed in late October and in November, and had not been trained to stand firm and calm in the midst of a financial storm.

"So we observe the phenomenon of Panic. We find that its root is in man's consciousness of his powerlessness, of his futility to stem the inevitable. We find that this consciousness, suddenly reached, drives some men to madness and despair, to hysteria and insanity, for the moment. We find, I believe, that every human being may be attacked by Panic, and that nothing but Discipline of the body and the soul can make him immune. Bravery will not do it. Resolution will not do it. Nothing will accomplish it but Discipline.

"The discipline of an army is splendid; the discipline of a ship's crew is splendid; the discipline of a police force, of an engineer and his fireman, are admirable. But there is another Discipline which is not imposed from without, and that is the Discipline which can avert panics, whether in face of fire, flood, poison gas, or loss of fortune. It is the Discipline which may be had by scrutinizing the great known facts of human life, by accepting them as facts, by bowing to them, and by inuring himself to live his life in submission to them, and with fortitude in spite of them.

This is a great sermon. It seems to me it should be in the hands of every good business man—every executive who holds the future of his employees and their families in his hands.

It is a time for balance. It is no time for hysteria. Great businesses can be ruined by fright. Control can be lost and great enterprises wrecked because of fear.

Premiums offered, trick advertising, hysterical propositions cannot serve as a substitute for true value, proper business methods and salesmanship.

Don't be stampeded into wild trading or service agreements beyond all reason. Realize that the present situation is only temporary and for the man who holds his house in order and does business on a business basis, the future holds greater promises than the past.

THE FIGHT'S THE THING—

I was much impressed by the following introduction to an article by W. O. McGeehan in the same edition of the American Magazine:

THE FIGHT'S THE THING

"Made by adversity; broken by prosperity. Thus does Mr. McGeehan sum up the careers of some of our most famous athletes. It is a thought all of us may well heed.

"Adversity and prosperity are opposite phases of life, but either is apt to breed discontent. Adversity produces the kind of discontent that builds character and leads a man on toward his goal. But if mere wealth is the goal, he is likely to find that happiness, like the foot of the rainbow, vanishes as he approaches.

"After all, it's the fight, not the referee's decision, that shows the man."

This seems very apt to me right now.

We have been given a great opportunity. Men who were being created and carried on by the momentum of a great demand are finding out that the joy-ride is over.

People are getting smarter. Under the stimulus of a great need our country will progress more in new advertising ideas, new inventions, better business methods, better merchandising plans. I see its effect all around me. I seldom talk to men on trains, in clubs, in stores or offices but what they leave a new thought with me.

To my desk in one day came six different suggestions from employees outlining ways in which our company could save money. There is a new spirit in the air. Midnight oil is being burned. A great era lies just ahead of us in America. New names will be written on the honor rolls of success. Men will create business; business will not create men.

We of Auburn, at home and in the field, are fortunate. We know the joy of a *great* fight. We have not yet heard the referee's decision. Our goal is still ahead, and our last five years of fighting and plugging should stand us in good stead.

I was thinking the other night about a certain company that has fallen by the wayside. It was our ambition six years ago to catch up with them in registrations. Each month we kept climbing closer and closer to them until on one Grand Day the records came in and we had outsold them. I can remember how proudly I galloped in to Mr. Cord's office, laid down the registrations and said, "Well, there we are. At last we beat ———." He looked at the records a minute, then glanced up, smiled and said, "You're wrong there, kid, you didn't beat them—they simply fell down below us." My hat slipped down over my ears. In fifteen minutes he had me convinced we had done a terrible job and my mark was another company farther up the line.

That has been the secret of Auburn. The knowledge that "The Fight's the Thing" and the fact that each victory made us accept the challenge of a more worthy opponent.

(Continued to page 7)

EXPORT NEWS

Prince Leopold of Belgium visits the Cord and Auburn exhibit at recent Brussells, Belgium, Show.

Portion of Cord-Auburn exhibit at Buenos Aires, Argentina, Automobile Show.

Cord Front Drive on display in Amsterdam, Holland, exhibition.

AUBURN VERY POPULAR IN POLAND AMONG PROMINENT PEOPLE

Niktan Company, Nowy Swiat Nr. 7, Warsaw, Poland, have a very select clientele of Auburn owners as is evidenced by the following list of recent purchasers of Auburn cars:

Count Franciszek Puslowski.
Mr. Nuksa, Ambassador of Lotwa.
Count Wlodimierz Karski.
Count Constantine Przezeziecki.
Count Jaraslaw Potocki (Cord owner).
Minister of Public Works.
Minister of Labour.
Mr. Marjan Kiniorski, Senator.
Board of Directors of Stanislawow R.R.
District Council of Rowne.
Municipal Provision Establishment.
Doctor Lukwik Dydynski.
Doctor Edward Flatau.

CHILEAN AMBASSADOR TO PERU PURCHASES CORD PHAETON SEDAN

A Cord Front Drive Phaeton Sedan was delivered during the early part of March to Conrado Rios Gallardo, Chilean Ambassador to Peru. Delivery was effected at the Chilean Embassy in Washington.

Mr. Conrado Rios Gallardo is planning on returning to his headquarters in Lima, Peru, during the latter part of March.

Cord Convertible Models have proven especially popular throughout South America, and the ease in handling the Cord and its riding comfort has strong appeal for owners in those countries where discomforts in driving are greatly augmented by weather conditions.

CORD FRONT DRIVE PROVES ESPECIALLY ADAPTABLE FOR SEVERE DRIVING CONDITIONS IN THE INTERIOR OF ARGENTINA

During February Gomez Aguirre and Santiago Bengolea, Auburn-Cord Dealers in Beunos Aires, Argentina, desirous of ascertaining the adaptability of the Cord Front Drive for interior driving in the Argentine, took two Cords, a Phaeton Sedan and a Cabriolet and travelled more than 2000 miles over heretofore almost impassable interior territory.

The Phaeton Sedan was driven a distance of 650 kilometers (approximately 407 miles) to Carhue and was delivered to a wealthy rancher, and the Cabriolet a distance of 2500 kilometers (approximately 1600 miles) into the west towards Cordoba and southeast to Mar del Plata, the fashionable summer resort of the wealthy Argentinians.

Both trips were made without mishap. The Cords forced their way over hundreds of miles of the sun-beaten, terrifically hot Argentinian pampas, without faltering.

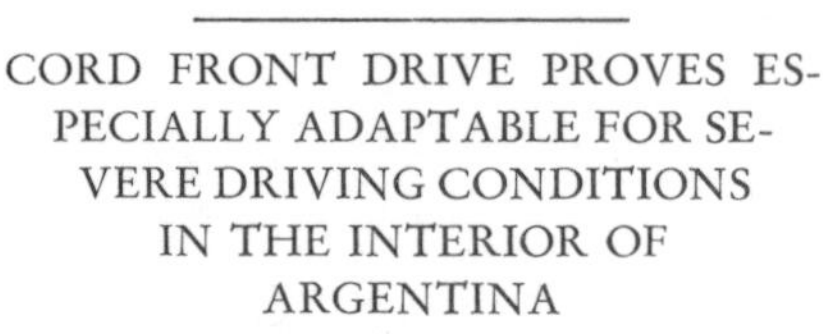

W. H. Golden, Auburn-Cord Distributor, Halifax, sends us the Cord's first photograph from Nova Scotia.

R. S. WILEY COMMENTS ON EXPORT BUSINESS

Shipments of Auburn and Cord Front Drive cars into Overseas markets have maintained more than the average percentage for the industry, with gains being shown in a large number of markets.

The total volume almost equals last year despite the fact that such important markets as Australia, South Africa, Brazil and Colombia have been passing thru severe economic conditions making it impossible for Auburn Distributors in these markets to purchase any considerable stock of cars during the past few months.

Substantial gains in shipments have been experienced in practically all European markets.

March shipments of Cords overseas were

40% more than any previous month since the car was introduced.

The Cord Front Drive is being distributed in twenty-two different countries of the world exclusive of the United States and Canada, by thirty-five Cord Distributors.

This remarkable showing has been made possible because of Auburn's outstanding values and the wide acceptance of the Cord Front Drive.

A. G. COLIN OF AUTOMOTOR COMPANY OF MEXICO CITY VISITS FACTORY

Mr. A. G. Colin, Auburn Cord Distributor in Mexico City visited the factory recently, making practically the entire trip to Auburn by airplane.

Auburn and Cord models are proving very popular in the Mexico City market, particularly the Phaeton Sedan Models and for 1929, which was Mr. Colin's second year as our distributor, Auburn ranked 11th in registrations.

The Cord Front Drive was introduced in Mexico City last October and already has established itself as a mark of social distinction and prestige. Numbered among the Cord owners of Mexico City are three Governors, several other important officials, and other prominent personages.

THE FIGHT'S THE THING—

(Continued from page 5)

Now we have come into our own. The present situation was made for us. We at the factory and our dealers in the field can go farther in the next five years than we could have gone had this incident not happened.

Our business is mounting steadily. At this writing it looks like March business would exceed last March and if it does, we will sell more automobiles in the first three months of this year than we sold in the first three months of last year.

We are spending more money to do the job, we are operating on a smaller margin of profit to put it over and we are spending more hours at our desks devising ways and means to make it possible to save money internally, but *we are doing it and that's the thing that counts.*

Greater than any monetary success this company has attained, greater than any glory that has come to us for our meteoric rise, are the faith, loyalty and application of our organization in the field and at the factory which have made this success possible and which are carrying us forward even in this trying time. *These are our greatest assets and they don't appear any place in our financial statement.*

So I say with the editor of the American Magazine, "The Fight's the Thing", and the world will reward the fighter.

—*Roy Faulkner.*

K. Ebb of Helsingfors, Finland, with fastest stock car in Finland.

A. D. O'DONNELL, PRESIDENT, O'DONNELL-MACKIE LIMITED, TORONTO

During the month of January, O'Donnell-Mackie, Limited, 577 Yonge Street, Toronto, were appointed Auburn-Cord Distributors for the Province of Ontario.

The firm of O'Donnell-Mackie Limited is operated by two young men, Mr. Arnold D. O'Donnell, President, and Mr. Dickson Mackie, Vice-President. Mr. S. J. O'Donnell is Wholesale Manager.

This young and aggressive distributing organization since its formation three years ago has created an enviable position as distributors of high quality automobiles and have grown from a small company to one of the largest and best known in Toronto with two show-rooms and a personnel of over fifty people.

A. D. O'Donnell, President of O'Donnell-Mackie, Ltd., Auburn-Cord Distributors located at Toronto, Ont., Canada.

The building is especially adaptable for their purpose. The ground floor, front-half is used as a sales and show-room. The rear half is taken up by the reception room of the Service Department where the shop foreman has his office. The building is fifty feet wide by about 150 feet deep.

The second floor is divided in half, the rear half being used for the Service Department repair shop and the front half for offices and the parts stockroom.

The third floor is used as an additional show-room and storage. In the full-sized basement are found the wash decks.

O'Donnell-Mackie Limited are very enthusiastic over the possibilities of Auburn and Cord Front Drive automobiles in the Ontario territory. They have recently established seven new dealer connections, all of very high calibre.

In commenting on their decision to take on the Auburn and Cord franchise, Mr. O'Donnell says:—"The Automobile business in our judgment is first a matter of management. If the management is sincere, far-sighted and progressive, the car itself and owners' satisfaction will follow with mathematical certainty. Therefore, we were unhurried in our study of the industry, paying particular attention to policies, personnel, history and programs of the various automobile manufacturers. Our admiration and confidence of long standing in Auburn was vindicated as a result of our investigation. During the past five years we have watched the amazing success and growth of Auburn. We have seen Auburn time and time again introduce improvements and advancements that invariably have been followed sooner or later by the industry.

"We have watched Auburn give consistently greater motor car value for the money than could be secured elsewhere and have seen Auburn lead in giving the public what it wants when it wants it—

"Primo" Carnera, Italian Heavy Weight Champion, visits the Auburn Graves Company of St. Louis and inspects the Cord Front Drive.

larger, better, more dependable merchandise at low costs which preclude comparison. Therefore it has been a real pleasure to announce to our clientele that we are fortunate in obtaining the distributorship for this line of automobiles."

KNOW YOUR JOB

During the past winter one of the outstanding Major League baseball pitchers has been appearing in vaudeville and at times suffered from "stage fright". He was asked by one of his friends, "Why he became frightened when on the stage in front of 3,000 friends, and yet, on the baseball diamond with the bases loaded and 80,000 frenzied rooters screaming at him he was the coolest man in the ball park?" He replied, "I guess when I'm in the pitcher's box I know my job".

There is nothing that gives a retail salesman more confidence in himself when talking with a retail prospect than an obsolute knowledge of his product and every Auburn salesman should know his car and be sure to bring out all the major advantages that makes Auburn the greatest value on the market today and is boosting Auburn sales to a new high level this year. Sell the prospect your new car—don't buy a used car.

Auburn salesmen have found that by analyzing and comparing it is easier to sell Auburn Cars and every interested prospect appreciates a clear and unbiased comparison. If a prospect can be definitely shown why the 8-95 is a better and greater value the sale is much easier and by following and comparing Auburn's features with whatever car the prospect might be interested in the greater value of Auburn is clearly evident.

There are many superior points of construction and features that are instantly visible to the prospects and the following is a list of features that should be incorporated into your sales talk with every prospect:—

100 Horsepower Straight Eight Motor.
4 door Closed Car.
125 Inch Wheelbase.
Bijur Chassis Lubrication.
Greater Frame Strength.
Metal Side Quarters—pioneered by Auburn.
Brewster Type Windshield.
4 Hydraulic Shock Absorbers.
Rubber Covered Steel Running Boards.
4 Wheel Internal Expanding Lockheed Hydraulic Brakes.
Starter Button located on Dash.
Light Control on Top of Steering Column.
Corona Proof Ignition Wires.
Large Headlamps.
Cam and Lever Steering.
Compensating Cylinder for Hydraulic Brakes.
Electro Lock.
Rubber Covered Foot Controls.
Treadle Type Foot Accelerator.
Pockets in Doors for Gloves and Small Parcels.
Wide, Deep Seat Cushions.
Ample Leg and Head Room.
Rubber covered felt carpet in front compartment.
Weather grooves in top of Doors.
Doors Close Flush Against Bottom Body Sill.
Lanchester Vibration Dampener.
Cowl Lamps.
Stop light Controlled by Rod from Brake Pedal.
Beautiful and Distinctive Lines.

These features are plainly visible to every buyer but it is necessary for the salesman to intelligently explain Auburn's inbuilt advantages and hidden features to every prospect.

In addition to these the prospect should be acquainted with Auburn's frame construction, an important feature that is hidden from view.

The Auburn 8-95 frame is the strongest frame under any stock car with the exception of the Auburn 125 model and the Cord Front Drive.

The front ends of the side-members are joined by a 2-inch tubular cross member; a U-shaped member joins the center point of the side rails, and an inverted pan crossbar out of 5/32-inch stock boiler plate nearly 16 inches wide is inserted at the rear of the frame which completely covers the top of the 18-gallon gas tank. One channel cross-bar is used and the rear motor mountings act as an additional safety factor and absolutely eliminate shimmy. A 5/32-inch reinforcement channel is placed inside of the side rails running from the front end of the frame horn to just behind the rear motor support.

In addition to the above described tubular and channel cross-members the 8-95 has a combination angular and step channel member joining the front of the side rails just back of the 2-inch tubular cross member. The front motor supports are strongly gusseted to this member as well as to the side members of the frame, which makes an unusually strong motor mounting. The radiator is also mounted on this box-like member which absolutely eliminates radiator shimmy.

A. R. Gribben, General Manager of Auburn Sales Co., Inc., New York City, held a special showing of Duesenberg, Cord and Auburn cars during the Brooklyn Automobile Show.

THE PACEMAKER AT INDIANAPOLIS WAS EQUIPPED WITH STEERING BY GEMMER

Wade Morton and "Pop" Meyers in the Cord Front-Drive that paced the cars starting at Indianapolis in the 500-mile Classic May 30th this year

"The most wonderful steering car I've ever driven" was the tribute Wade Morton paid to the Cord car in which he paced this year's Indianapolis race. This is a fine tribute to steering by Gemmer by the Sales Manager of the Cord Division of the Auburn Automobile Company. The only purely stock car to finish in the first ten, a Stutz, was Gemmer-steered.

Gemmer-steered cars have long been favorites of the men who contest with Time. Ralph De Palma, Major Segrave, Earl Cooper, Captain Campbell and Kaye Don are but a few of the scores of famous racing drivers who depend on Gemmer-type steering gears. And passenger car builders who recognize the importance of safe steering depend on steering by Gemmer to give their cars the finest, quickest and easiest control.

GEMMER MANUFACTURING COMPANY - - DETROIT

GEMMER

The Autocar Road Tests

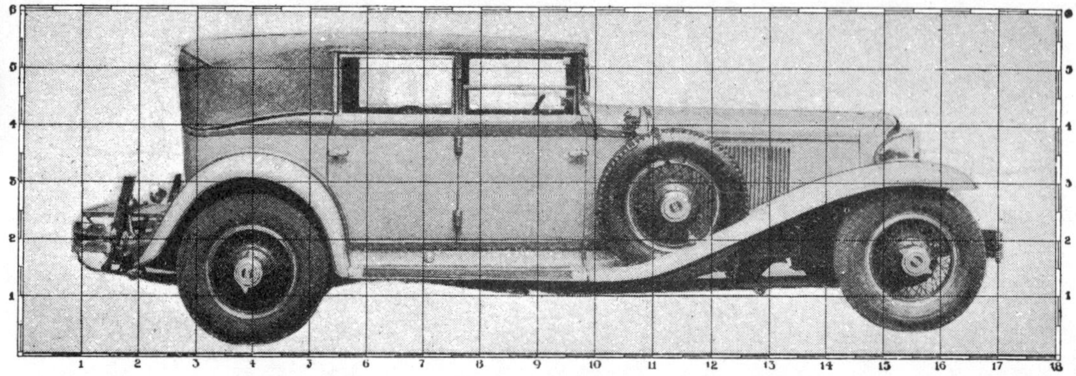

The illustration above indicates the size, in feet, of the Front Wheel Drive Cord

No. 642 (Post-War Series).—FRONT WHEEL DRIVE CORD

Sports Car Characteristics Allied with Great Comfort of Riding

OF the several cars which have appeared in recent years with front wheel drive, in many ways the most interesting of all is the Cord. For one thing it comes from America, where the majority of cars resemble one another closely in their conventional construction, and is developed, as regards the transmission, from the front wheel drive Millers which have raced so successfully at Indianapolis track. Yet in contrast to most other front driven cars the Cord is not produced as a sports car as the primary object, though the general feel of the car is very different, as would be expected, from that of the average transatlantic machine.

Yet the interesting thing about it is that under all ordinary conditions the driver and occupants are apt to forget that normal rear wheel drive is not employed, and the machine is handled like any other car, with the exception that it can be taken round curves and corners extremely fast for the size of car. What is more, it has a greater sense of stability than any front wheel driven machine previously tested, due probably to the weight, yet the suspension is soft in effect all through the range.

There is no denying that doubts exist in many motorists' minds as to the behaviour of a front driven car on a wet road; during the whole test, including a section of approximately 100 miles of rain-soaked surfaces, no skid or slide was experienced from this source, though on a wet good-paved surface, for instance, it was possible to make the front wheels spin by opening up the throttle more violently than usual, still, however, without deviation from the straight course. It is as well to deal with possible prejudices existing in connection with front drive before going on to the actual performance, and another point concerns the ability of such a car to restart on a loose-surfaced hill. It was not possible to find a really wet hill of this kind, but on a loose, dry gradient of approximately 1 in 6 several restarts were made with ease, the front wheels spinning only slightly.

There is no question that this is a fascinating car on the open road, yet it handles well also in traffic, despite its size, and is tractable on top gear. It is possible to maintain a high average on a long journey without necessarily using the maximum, since the cruising speed is anywhere up to 60 m.p.h., and the car climbs extremely fast on top gear, while second is a distinctly valuable ratio, since 52 m.p.h. is possible on it and 45 m.p.h. is normal, so that the ratio feels more like third in a fairly close-ratio four-speed box and can be used almost equivalently. In a little more than twelve hours, including all stops, a run of 340 miles was made. The engine is smooth to its limit, a certain roar which comes in high up being attributable chiefly to the air entering the carburetter.

An unconventional feature is the gear change, with the lever and its knob projecting horizontally and very conveniently from the instrument board. This is an arrangement to which the driver quickly becomes accustomed, and, the simple knack once mastered, gives a quick, light change that increases the sports machine idea. Second gear on this car produced a good deal of noise, which is partly because the occupants are travelling into the sound to a greater extent than is normal, the gear box being in front of the engine, of course; however, it is not at all an unpleasant sound, and somehow suggests power.

There is considerable interest in the fact that the car tested had covered a mileage equivalent easily to eighteen months' hard work in private hands, without, it is understood, the piston rings having been renewed. Thus the timed speed is all the better in the circumstances, especially considering that the comfort of the car for both back and front seats is better than that of most ordinary touring machines of similar size. Further, there was the most unusual point that the speedometer read slow, and during the timed test did not go above 74, while on the road the maximum reading obtained, slightly down grade, was 77, corresponding approximately to 80, which is excellent in view of the weight of the very stoutly built convertible body.

Because of the mileage and the exceptional conditions of use there was a certain slackness in the steering gear, and probably in the driving-shaft universal joints, which made itself apparent at high speed, though the car as a whole was essentially steady. It is interesting that the steering is very light and has full caster action, the wheel having a thin rim, while the car is easy to manœuvre and has an excellent steering lock.

The hydraulic brakes are light, progressive and entirely adequate to the speed of the car, while even when using the maximum effort on a normal road there is no deviation from the straight. The hand lever is convenient and the brake powerful, since it takes effect on all four wheels.

The phaeton, or all-weather body is a particularly good type, Continental rather than transatlantic in style, comfortable and smart, especially with the colour scheme of this car, which was silver grey and blue. For an all-weather that has had considerable use there were few rattles, and the hood is not too difficult to lower, while erecting it is simple enough. With the roof raised the car is equivalent in comfort and protection to a saloon, and with it down the full benefits of an open car are obtained. Also, the occupants sit well within the body, relatively very low, the whole car being low, too, and the leg room and space are exceptionally generous.

The single-piece front seat is not adjustable, though it is made to adjust in the normal saloon model, but the driving position is pleasant, the steering column being well raked. The upholstery is leather, and ease of entry and exit through each door is very great indeed. At the front, the instruments are grouped in two panels at each side of the board, and are remarkably complete, though there is not a clock. At the centre is a useful cupboard, which can be locked, while there are pockets in the scuttle sides. Ventilation is provided for by three big ventilators, and there are two separate suction screen wipers.

For its size the engine is neat; the plugs, with the exception of the rearmost ones, are accessible, and the distributor is convenient, which applies also to the oil filler and dipstick, as well as to the water pump and dynamo. Also under the bonnet are the reservoir for the hydraulic brake system and that for the one-shot chassis lubrication. The radiator shutters are opened and closed by a thermostat, and the engine starts easily.

The head lamps, as set, were not fully adequate to the speed of the car, but it is understood that special reflectors can be supplied to overcome this.

A car that attracts attention to a remarkable degree anywhere, and is exceptionally interesting and pleasing to drive. It was provided for test by Sinclair Motor Concessions, Ltd., 2, Mill Street, Conduit Street, W.1.

FRONT WHEEL DRIVE CORD

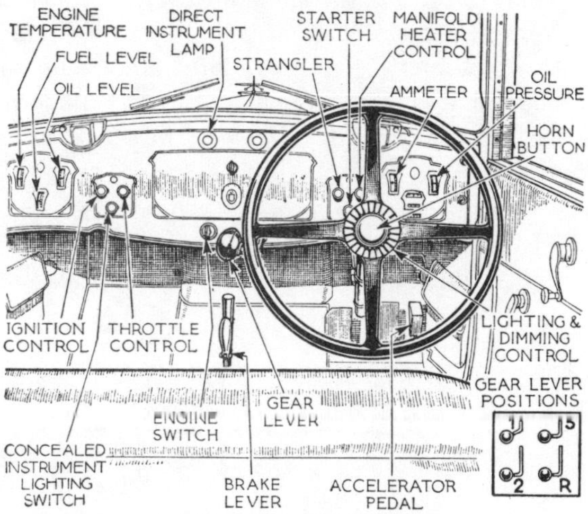

DATA FOR THE DRIVER

33.8 h.p., eight cylinders, 83 × 114 mm. (4,934 c.c.).
Tax £34.
Wheelbase 11ft. 5½in., track 5ft.
Overall length 17ft. 1½in., width 5ft. 11½in., height 5ft. 6½in.
Tyres: 32 × 7in. on detachable wire wheels.

Engine—rear axle gear ratios.	Acceleration from steady 10 to 30 m.p.h.	Timed speed over ¼ mile.
13.73 to 1	—	
7.45 to 1	6⅗ sec.	
4.41 to 1	9⅗ sec.	76.92 m.p.h.

Turning circle: 42ft.
Tank capacity 20 gallons, fuel consumption 12-14 m.p.g.
6-volt lighting set cuts in at 12 m.p.h., 10 amps. at 30 m.p.h.
Weight: 39 cwt. 3 qr. 4 lb.
Price, with phaeton body, £990.

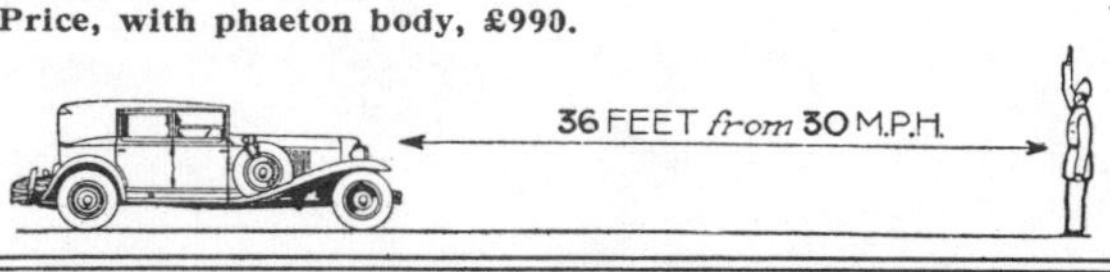

5. *Coachbuilders Strike a New Stature*

The Cord car creates a place for itself no other car has ever occupied.

With its bold traction parts exposed as prominently as the talons of an eagle, and the near-midpoint location of a squat windshield accenting the substantial stretch of its roadbound profile, the L-29 had spontaneously become a sensation wherever there were eyes to see.

Among those of the privileged life—in Westchester County, Newport, Palm Beach, Beverly Hills and other forefronts of fashion—this sleek, look-of-tomorrow automobile was to hit a new high in fashion, for E. L. Cord believed that Society should have the selection of special design and construction it enjoyed with Rolls-Royce and Duesenberg, even though the idea was all but unique for a chassis in the price class of the L-29.

Cord particularly wished to display custom line Cords at his fashionable new company showroom on Wilshire Boulevard in Los Angeles. Formal and sporting bodies were soon to be commissioned from the most able coachbuilders in the trade.

For Cord, who had just purchased a winter home high above the City of the Angels, it was a pleasant thirty-minute drive to skirt the foothills and slip across the landmark Colorado Street bridge over the arroyo into Pasadena, residential stronghold of the established rich. Behind the bricks at a Vernon street location just north of Colorado lay *Walter M. Murphy*, Coachbuilders, a firm youthful among its eastern peers but already hallmarked by contemporary, light-lined modern designs and superior custom body engineering for Lincoln, Minerva, Doble and other peerless chassis of the day.

Designs at Murphy's were produced by young men with an insatiable affection for cars. In this climate alive with youthful enthusiasm the resulting products were more *automotive* in appearance and less *carriage-like*

The streamer stripe which probably was first used as a style line to characterize the yacht-like Crane-Simplex, about 1915, came to production car prominence on Cord's Auburn. It was to become a recurring theme among custom body designers. Here it was neatly executed on a Cord coupe proposal by Franklin Hershey.

than styles then coming from most of the great, traditional coachmakers whose roots were down from the days of horsedrawn vehicles.

Murphy bodies were recognized for a common generally thin-pillared upperstructure, which in turn bestowed a lightweight feeling to the whole car's appearance. Even as a blind-quarter sedan with broadened B pillars this treatment was unmistakably Murphy and at once Frank Hershey.

Cord had first called upon Murphy a couple of seasons before to produce the prototype four-door convertible sedan for Auburn which then was translated at the factory into a production body type. The Murphy company was to prove most productive for the Duesenberg Model J chassis and would also account for a substantial share of the special bodies for the L-29.

Work began in Pasadena to supplement the standard Cord body styles following a visit from E. L. Cord with a request for design proposals for the new automobile.

The invitation generated excitement in the little design room upstairs at Murphy's. Under the administration of general manager Frank Spring, developing designers like Franklin Quick Hershey, and, for a time, Philip O. Wright—who was later to claim credit for the Pierce Silver Arrow—were anxious to impart their ideas to this chassis that clearly was a designer's dream come true.

Proportion was long, and low, and the limiting usual requirement of having to set the back seat higher than the front to clear a differential was not present. With its cowl established well aft on a frame perfectly flat in the rear, a designer was free to pick up the theme of length and lowness and apply lines he had only wildly wished for before.

These designers felt they were to be salaried for an effort their design dedication would have rendered freely. Unfortunately the general manager believed he knew exactly what E. L. Cord wanted. So proposed designs for this chassis were to be dictated by Frank Spring and simply executed by Hershey and Wright. Under this forced draft the young men were not encouraged to produce the Cord body styles that danced in their own heads.

Aflame with enthusiasm for the possibilities with the chassis Hershey resolved the matter by working nights, strictly on his own, to turn out designs for the Cord which did reflect the depth of his personal feelings. He developed a portfolio of exciting ideas which he showed to Phil Wright. But he was reluctant to show them to his boss. Wright responded by drawing several of his own at home.

As the day approached for presentation the products of young Hershey's moonlighting were still held in secret for he knew Frank Spring would summarily discredit the efforts as "too advanced." Days were spent in finalizing the house designs for Cord's study and approval. But it was not to be the last of this extracurricular work.

When the appointed hour arrived for the presentation the design room had been cleared and a large easel set up to dramatize individually the rather conservative, middle-of-the-road variety of designs Spring had directed his staff to turn out.

Fortunately for the *Walter M. Murphy* company, youth will out . . . Unnoticed by Frank Spring, the extra drawings reflecting the flare and verve of youth were slipped inconspicuously behind the establishment styling about to be shown by the general manager.

Cord, himself very much young in heart, arrived early for the appointment. He was unimpressed by a single design in Spring's presentation. The story is recalled by Hershey that Spring then casually became aware that someone had slipped extra work behind the group he was attempting to "sell" to Cord. Knowing nothing of the nature of these additional drawings that he had not authorized he avoided them by beginning a review of those already shown. Spring lost Cord's interest altogether.

"Come on, Frank," E. L. Cord had spotted the stack on the easel too. "You haven't shown me a thing that's worth a damn yet. Let's look at the rest of those drawings."

"Thank God he insisted on seeing them all!" recalled La Mar Bresee, Spring's assistant, and a man of advanced views.

With as much aplomb as he could muster Spring began to exhibit the unfamiliar balance of the work stacked on the easel. Hershey's spirited designs revived Cord's interest in a flash; he liked what he saw.

From the added designs, without further adoo, Cord commissioned construction of a complementary selection. Phil Wright's phaeton received the nod. Three of Frank Hershey's designs, a special thin-pillared "clear-vision" sedan, a cabriolet, and a special three-color phaeton were ordered.

Seven tri-color phaetons — one of the original designs to catch Cord's eye in the special showing — were eventually built, a record among L-29 customs of a single design. Hershey later joined the Art & Color section at General Motors where his Bentley-type front-end for the 1933 Pontiac, and his follow-up Silver Streak design for the 1935 model, proved early triumphs in American production car design.

Hershey's cabriolet and phaeton were so warmly received by Cord they were later to become custom catalog items. Three cabriolets and seven phaetons—many of them finished in the white[2] were eventually to be built.

A popular form of conspicuous consumption among the very rich was the purchase of custom cars in duplicate. Two tri-color phaetons went to the international sportsman W. A. Clark III, whose title as president of the Pilot Ray Corporation, a maker of popular night driving sportlights, brought him a special appreciation of advances in automotive design.

The Murphy body connection with Cord flourished. The chassis would lend itself invitingly to the most formal of body concepts—the town car. A first commission came soon after E. L. Cord's personal selection of the original group of designs. Phil Wright produced this on a 137½″ wheelbase for the petite screen idol Dolores del Rio.

[2]With color and trim held open for later completion to conform to a firm order.

When this ad appeared in the Sunday gravure section of the Los Angeles Times in 1937 skirted fenders and flaring rear quarters had become established style notes. To utilize a photograph of Dolores del Rio's home — in which her then vintage town car was prominently parked in the foreground — an artist was commissioned to retouch the car in the photo to contemporize it. The skirted fenders and ducktail rear depicted here were modifications never actually performed on this automobile.

The mini town car and its subsequent longer counterparts contributed a special sparkle to that great legend of a jewel case life in Hollywood of the 'thirties.

After its first film premiere the town car took Hollywood film folk by storm. The only car that could out charm that automobile in sheer hauteur would have to have been a stretched-out version of the same thing.

Since the original car offered scant seating comfort—through abbreviated foot room in both the cab and the chauffeur's compartment—and demand for more Cord town cars was immediate, the idea of an extended version was father to the deed. Two additional town cars, with wheelbase increased to 152½″ were redrafted from the original drawings, and built for display on Wilshire. The two were individualized by their spare tire mountings, one carrying sidemounts, the other rear tandem wheels fixed at a rakish tilt.

It was another latin actress, one Lola Montez, who reportedly soon became identified with the car with sidemounts. The other quickly became the trademark property of John Barrymore who used it, in effect, as an extension of his own "Great Profile."

Except for the Murphy designs by Frank Hershey which were to become custom catalog body types, specials for the L-29 generally proved to be one of a kind. A number, properly in keeping with the nature of the Cord chassis itself, were to be *avant-garde*.

Coachbuilders and designers all over the world were magnetically attracted to the suave specs of the new Cord chassis. They followed up their

With the most extended wheelbase of all L-29 customs built the 152½" town cars probably exaggerated the long, low look of the Cord to the ultimate degree.

The arrow-lined double-cowled phaeton commissioned by E. L. Cord from a Wright design featured lines of spartan simplicity and preceded Wright's town cars in production.

This Saoutchik proposal for a Parisian notable affixed wind-wings for the chauffeur and accented the tail with a low-line trunk.

Traditionally, many automobile stylists developed their talents independent of the classroom by emulating the drawing techniques of other established designers. The work of Roland P. Stickney first inspired Hershey.

interest by developing original proposals, some of substantial merit. Designs that would have translated into great automobiles, regrettably, were often doomed to designers' scrapbooks after the creations failed to connect with wealthy buyers to commission the work. In Paris the international coachmaker *Saoutchik* and the spirited *Franay* were active with the chassis—at least on paper—as was the house of *Castagna,* in Milan.

Concurrently with the Murphy activity, at the internationally recognized *Le Baron* in New York, one of the great perfectionists among professional automobile renderers of the period, Roland L. Stickney, was sketching a town car along formal coach lines, characterized by razor-edge corners and

CHASSIS CORD
MODELE DEPOSE

CASTAGNA
MILANO

LeBaron's construction of the razor-edge town car design had been achieved with absolute fidelity to the Stickney rendering.

A Cord chassis presented, internationally, the first genuine opportunity for town car formality in a step-in (vs. traditional step-up) package. Shown here is the continental Proux.

the accoutrements of carriage practice such as continuous loop door handles. Commissioned primarily for shows this town car debuted in New York, then in turn appeared in Chicago, Los Angeles and San Francisco, late in 1929. Except for a report that the car was personally used for a time by the man whose name appeared on its hubcaps little of its lifeline is known.

Abroad, yet another town car was being constructed by *Proux,* another of the more progressive coachbuilders in France. With softer radius details, in keeping with French style tones traditional with other custom chassis of the period, it proved a high point of interest when spotlighted at the Paris

Automobile Show late in 1930. It appeared in the Auburn-Cord stand in a Pearl Essence finish which was as new at the time as the body it graced.

Formed in the late 'twenties in Los Angeles the *Auburn-Fuller* Company was to expand with the Duesenberg and the Cord as these marques appeared to supplement the Auburn line. The Spanish-Moorish architecture of its showroom at 6145 Hollywood boulevard kept elegant company with the palacial movie houses along the same avenue in screenland's golden age. The sales floor was rarely without representative Murphy-bodied customs in the main ring. The agency became a mecca for celebrities of the day.

Fuller's involvement with customs was to expand. The organization came to feel it had enough talent within the company to build custom bodies on its own. Several employees with complementary skills had joined the firm as a team from the old *J. G. Kirchoff* coachbuilders. In this group were Frank Zerbo, an engineer and designer; Rudy Stoessel, a woodworker; Paul Eros, a sheet metal worker; and Harry Fells, an upholsterer. The men composed a formidable group.

In a backshop building the group was assigned the job of producing two special cars. The first completed, according to one source, emulated the lines of Murphy's long-wheelbase town cars.

The second custom unit proved an original coupe design with rumble seat from the pen of Frank Zerbo. A fixed top was covered in leatherette and the sides were accented by a prominent molding applique which increased in width as it drew back to prominent termination in a down taper just behind the door. The windshield was balanced with a forward-facing visor—an interesting option that might well have been considered for production.

While old world precision prevailed in its craftsmanship a brute top line brought heavy, uninspired upper proportions to the Fuller coupe.

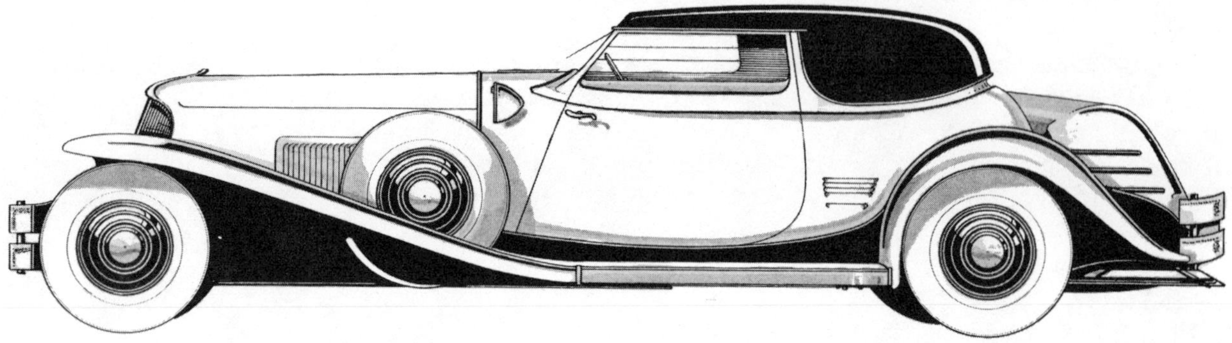

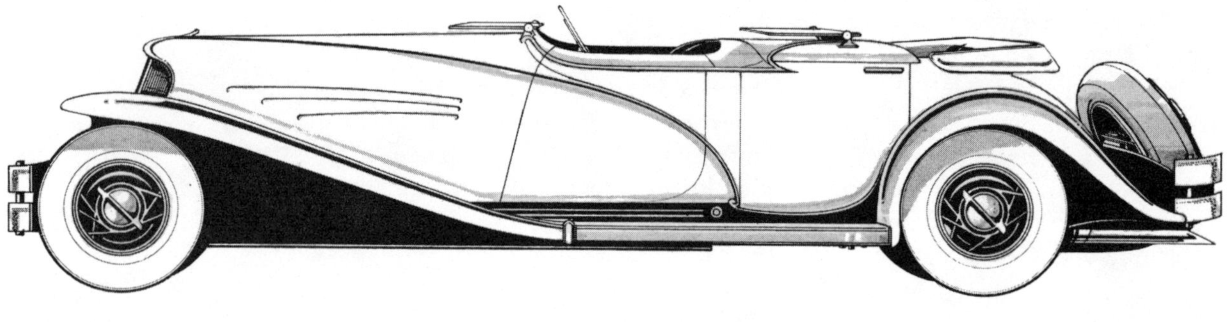

If Tony Gerrity incorporated more artist's fancy than fact in the slope of a grille or in the massive weight of a bumper the value of his creative contribution was still indeed quite real. To this lavish talent a precise observance of the minor contingencies of chassis reality was simply not of consequence. His spontaneous improvement of of the chassis to support his inspired body creations was consistent: presumably, it only remained for a wealthy client to order these chassis alterations included along with the body he was commissioning.

The late Anthony Gerrity, a wizard with the pen among wealthy clients in the early 'twenties, was one of the foremost "natural" stylists of the day. He was first recognized for work produced as a designer for the *John B. Brokaw* body works in Los Angeles. So great was the spontaneous latitude of his work that another automobile designer, the perfectionist W. Everett Miller—who himself had cut his teeth in the design department of *Walter M. Murphy* during the same period—has described Gerrity as a *"designer's* designer."

Lost to students of classic design for two generations, a portfolio of Tony Gerrity's inspired proposals to the golden proportion of the L-29 chassis was recently uncovered in a private collection. The lavish sketches from this sheaf are reproduced here for the first time in print.

Whether any of Gerrity's imaginative conceptions actually were built is not presently known, but the character of these body design proposals drawn for the *Auburn-Fuller Co.* in Los Angeles, on its own merit, establishes Anthony Gerrity as a creative artist of abundant talent.

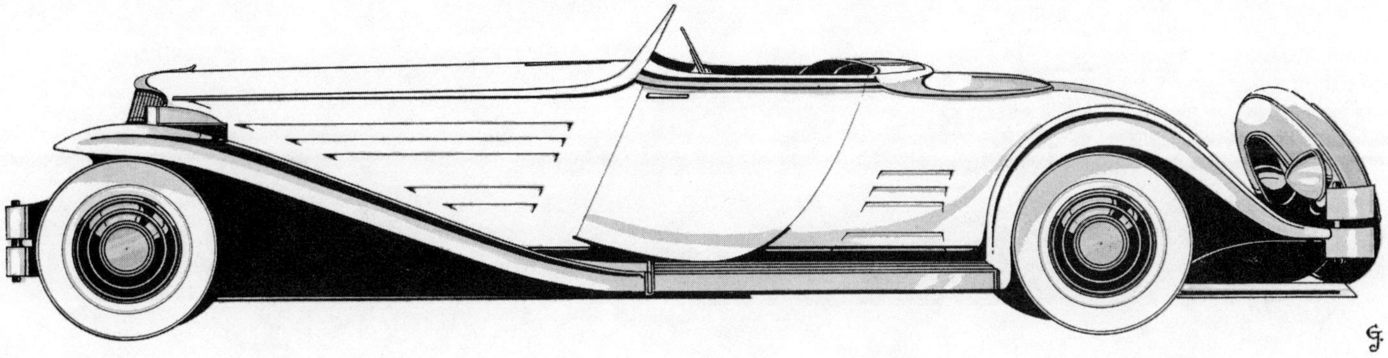
GJ.

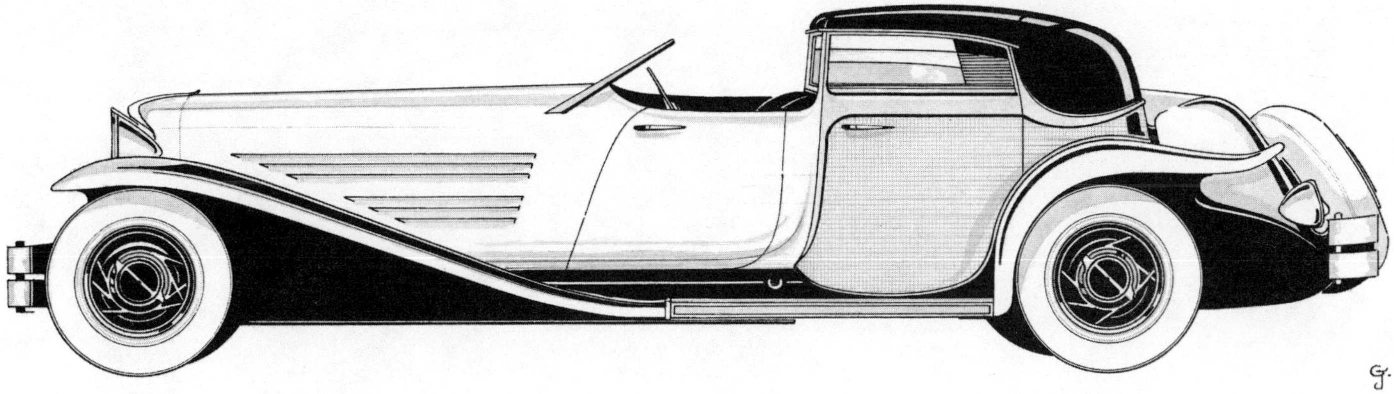
GJ.

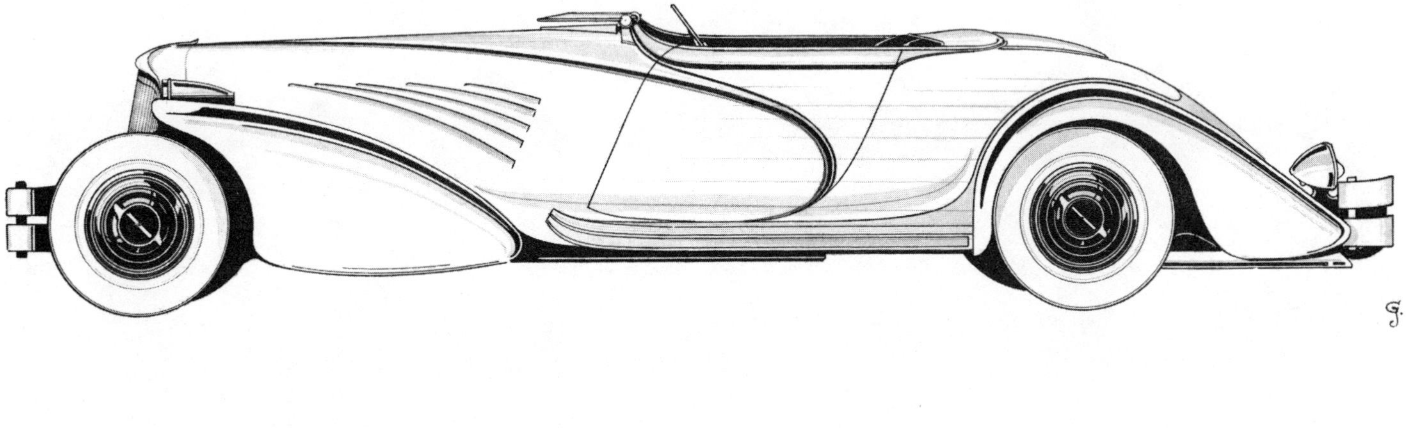
GJ.

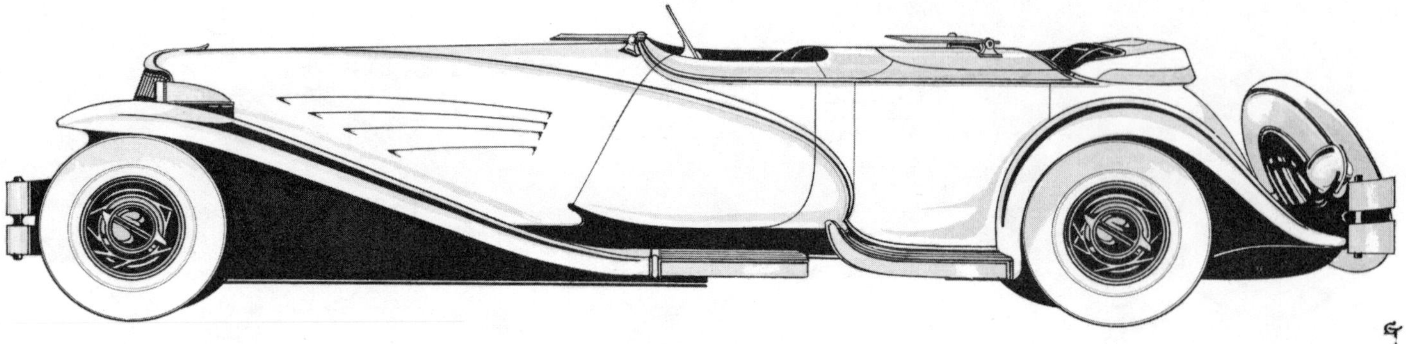

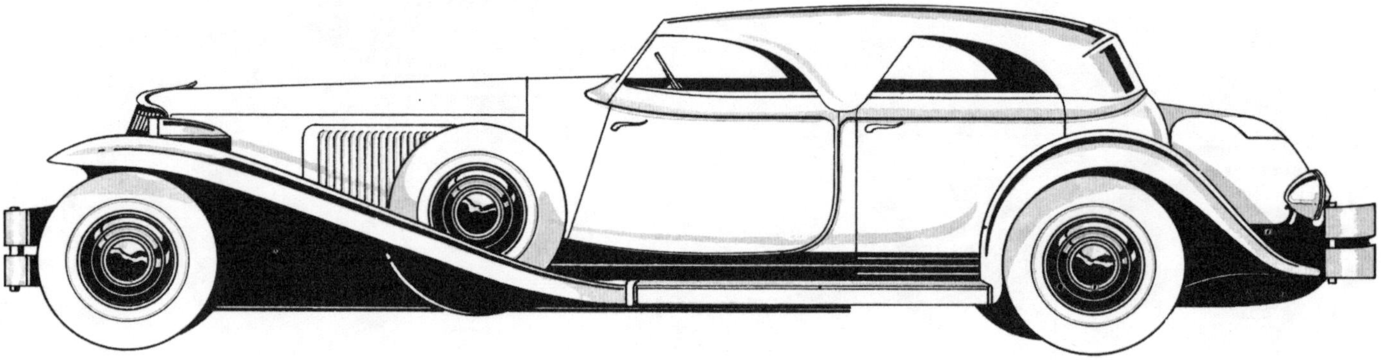

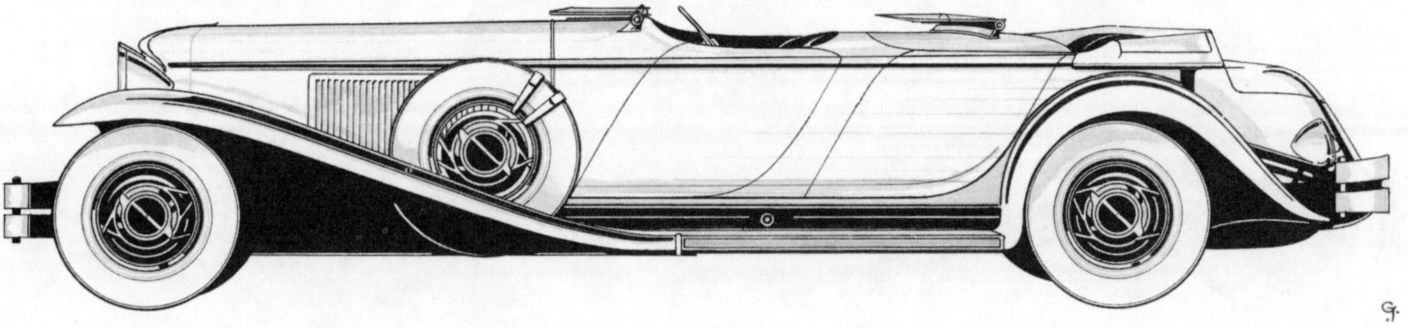

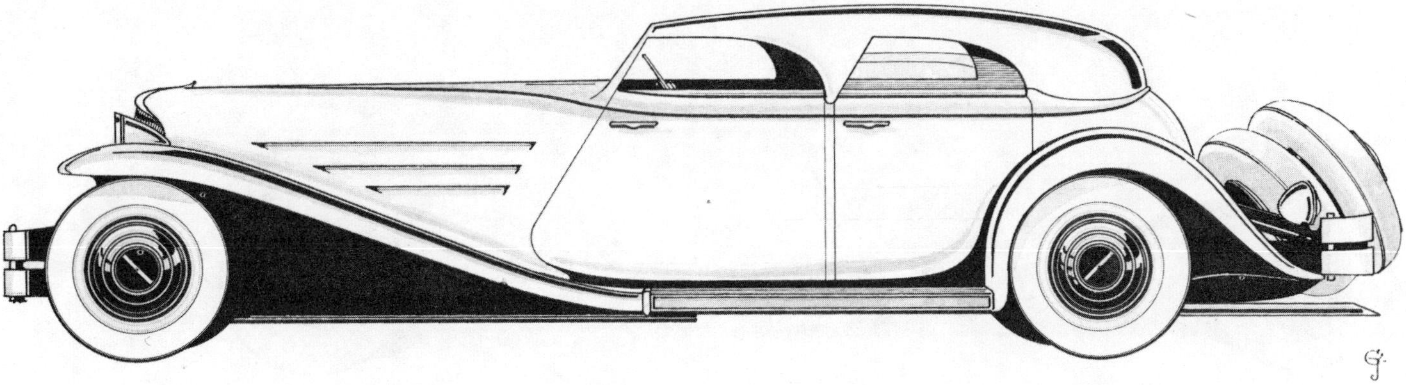

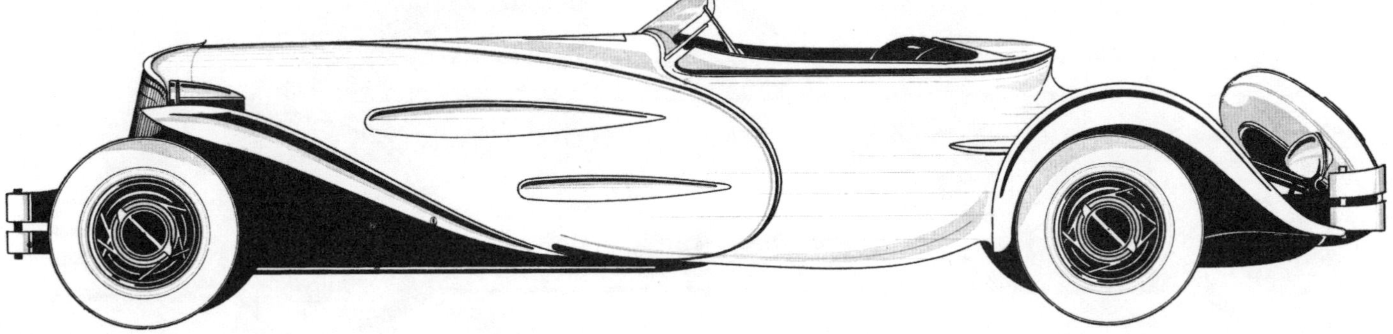

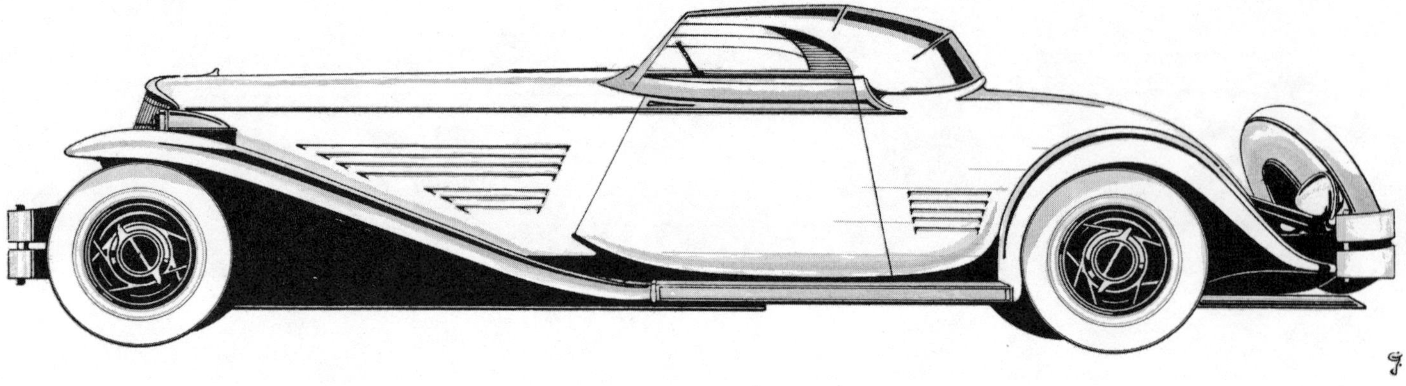

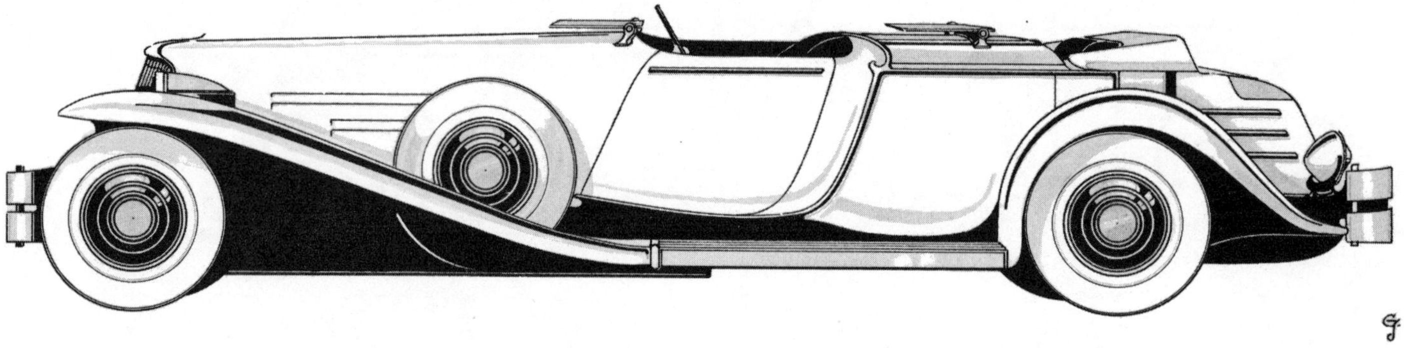

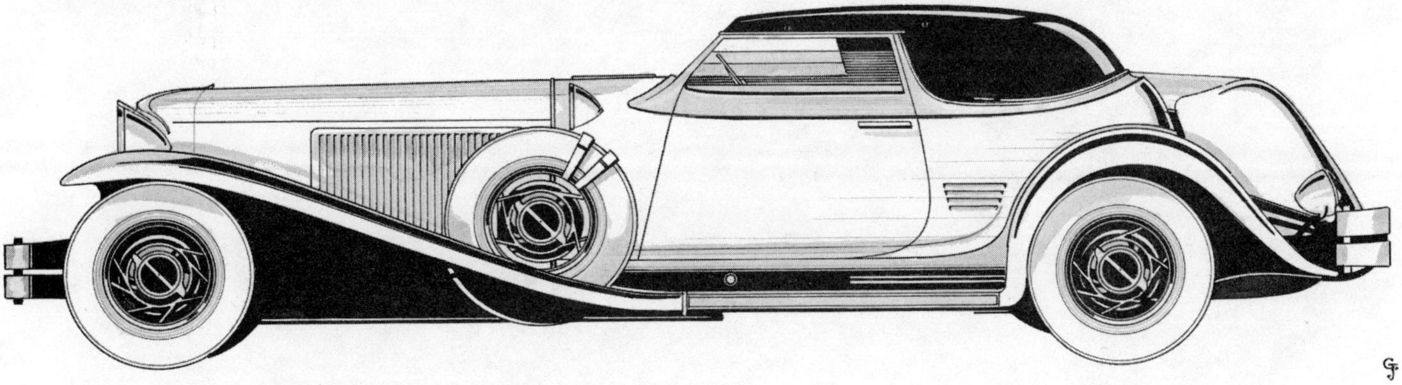

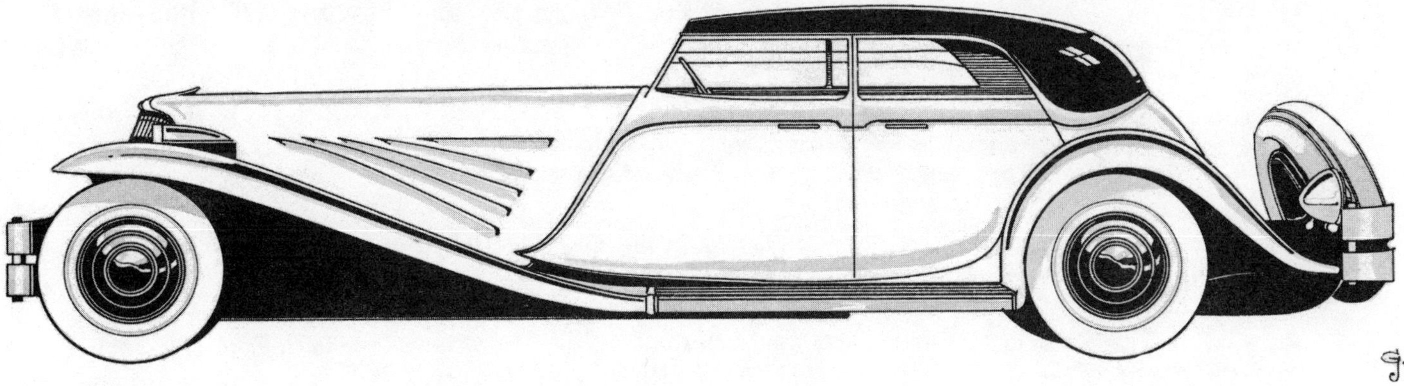

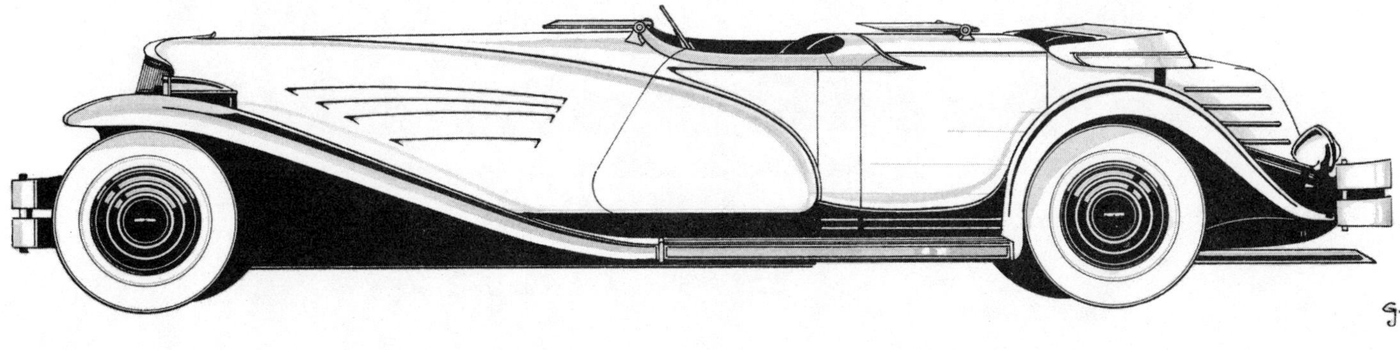

For this close-coupled touring Rudy Creteur used a variation of the streamer stripe cliche and visually extended the "read" of the hood length by the device of a unique gravel guard fixed well forward of the grille.

After one look at this dream car drawing Roy Faulkner was to buy Philip H. Wright's speedster design and hire him to supervise the building of the body for a show car.

Rollston of New York was active with the L-29, building three noteworthy specials. There was a victoria with lines reminiscent of those built for the Duesenberg chassis, a five-passenger berline and a smart sport touring for which design credit has been given Rudy Creteur. The latter, completed late in 1931, was shipped to Venezuela to satisfy an automotive enthusiast in the presidential family there. Later records of all three are obscured.

Leaving Pasadena in the spring of 1930 with sights set on Detroit, Phil Wright, the junior designer from the productive Murphy team, recalls stopping over in Chicago en route. Taking advantage of the layover he called upon the South Michigan boulevard showroom of Auburn-Cord-Duesenberg with some sketches under his arm of a new speedster too radical for consideration at Murphy's.

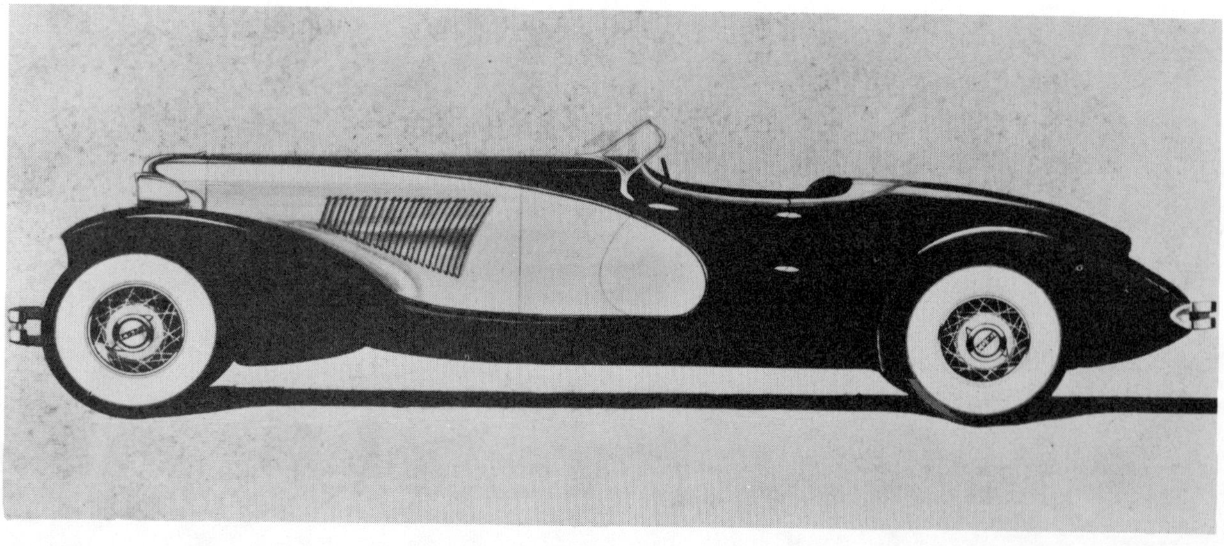

Following a cordial reception Wright remembers that his excitement began to mount with the arrangement of an early afternoon appointment that day with the Auburn Auto president, Roy Faulkner, to see the drawings. To Cord's top man the speedster design was *just right* for translation into metal as a key display car for the upcoming 1931 show season. Wright's dream car design was committed and he was commissioned to oversee its construction at the Corporation's Union City body division, where it would receive the *La Grande* body plate. Phil Wright's next stop had to wait.

Hollywood's platinum blonde darling, Jean Harlow, was shown in the press with this speedster. One report has it that the car was a token of appreciation from her husband, the director Paul Bern and that she took the car to France where it received honors at the Paris *Concours.* The speedster's lithe lines generally are credited by authorities today as the outstanding example in sport design on the chassis. Later disposition of this one-off style is mysteriously veiled.

Weymann wood and leatherette construction was unusual and interesting. Retouched highlighting of the basic forms prepared this photograph for coarse screen reproduction.

Another unique coupe was a quite continental creation made by the *Weymann American* Company, a builder noted for its unusual body structure. A system of wood framing—with special attachments to obviate the usual wooden joints and permit a flexible structure—was covered by layers of duck and curled stuffing hair and finish-covered with an imported artificial leather known as *Zapon Liss.* The advantages claimed for this Weymann patent system were lower cost and faster delivery to the patron over conventional body construction. As with most products with a primary appeal to fashion, long service life in the field was not a consideration of great import to the original owner.

The Weymann coupe—with accommodation for a third passenger in a snug curb-facing second seat—debuted at the 1930 Chicago Salon. It later appeared at the New York Salon with a price tag of $7,500. Paul Whiteman, the renowned band leader whose music was spun gold to Society in 1930, had shown life-long automobile enthusiasm through a succession of

special cars. Whiteman acquired the Weymann coupe and posed in a photograph in which the car's highlights had been retouched to the point of exaggeration. The explanation was elementary: The photo was prepared as the subject for a mass printed postcard which was eventually mailed to thousands of Cord prospects by dealers. Above Paul Whiteman's autograph on the postcard appeared his handwritten inscription "This is my second Cord. How do you like it?"

A little known *second* fabric-covered L-29 was built under quite different circumstances, according to a recent finding by Cord archivist Robert Fabris. In the form of a fastback coupe following a cabin speedster style—derived from the then well-publicized and unique Auburn Cabin Speedster[3] —it was fabricated by *Glenn Curtiss,* the pioneer aircraft builder, who personally was attracted to front-wheel drive. Mr. Curtiss' secretary recollects that a right-hand mechanic, Henry Kleckler, helped Curtiss in the building of the car, *ala* Aerocar construction. One motor historian conjects that it may have been driven only briefly before meeting with catastrophe, a theory based on the observation that its design provided the driver with severely impaired side and rear vision—design practice standard for aircraft, but certainly less than ideal when applied to a machine for the highway.

In England the established coachbuilder *Freestone & Webb* was engaged by a continental personality in 1931 to construct a five-passenger victoria incorporating several special requirements, paramount of which was a capacious area for transporting an extensive wardrobe on tour. The design was dramatized by an aero theme featuring pontoon fenders so adequately sectioned that one contained the battery and the other a spare parts and tool chest.

Still another special L-29 for which records are scant was reportedly built by *Million-Guiet* of Paris as an opera coupe employing a popular style note among European coachbuilders of the time. Doors opened all the way to the

Upon first taking delivery Glenn H. Curtiss had telegraphed the factory ". . . car exceeds my expectations, and I predict it will make many friends. Front drives are here to stay." It was to be the last year of his life. The July 1933 date on this freshly modified unit attributed to the Curtiss Aerocar company, would indicate that, while perhaps instigated by GHC, it had become a custom project most certainly completed by other hands. According to one report the car was prepared for Curtiss' son; according to another it wound up in the hands of William Stout.

[3]Destroyed accidentally in a garage fire at the height of its public renown.

American Austin lines were classic, in miniature. Its chassis was mechanically simple. Quality and efficiency were unquestioned. Austin was intended as the perfect transportation for two people. Unfortunately, a substantial backlog of supposedly firm orders vaporized for the company after the experience of early owners became known. The car had become the instant butt of pranksters' most imaginative brawn. The general public simply could not accept the car casually; every night became Halloween. At the sight of an unattended baby Austin sane citizens would feel compelled to (Continued)

lower limit of the body, conveying the illusion of an extraordinarily low ingress and egress. When the door was opened, of course, the necessary frame rail was quite present and the floor was a step up with a rocker panel spanning the difference between the bottom of the door opening and the actual floor.

One of the most noteworthy and remembered coupes built on the chassis was the product of a design exercise by the celebrated Count Alexis de Sakhnoffsky, who in spite of his title, acted as a design consultant to the *Hayes Body* firm of Grand Rapids, Michigan. This gentleman, whose design honors were based on a mastery of the french curve as applied to automobile design, conferred with various Hayes customers, all of whom were prominent car builders in the industry. One distinct credit of the period attributed directly to de Sakhnoffsky was the concept of the original American Austin coupe and roadster, a Butler, Pennsylvania, production which featured classic lines in a mascot-sized 75″ wheelbase.

The Count had won four straight *Grand Prix de Monaco* cups for motor car design on the Continent and his road-clinging coupe conception for the Cord was deliberately slanted toward extending his, by then, traditional recognition in Monaco.

The coupe would combine an American chassis with an American custom body. It would be the first grand prize winner in this category—*if* it met with approval. At Hayes a full size mahogany buck was made and the sheet metal panels formed over it. The finished car rose from the pavement six inches less than the production Cord sedan.

According to media of the day, de Sakhnoffsky crossed the Atlantic with the car on the *Ille de France,* then drove from the dock to Paris, and the Riviera, where his fifth *Grand Prix* was captured exactly as anticipated. A few days later, at the Beaulieu *Concours* the Hayes was awarded the coveted *Grand Prix d'Honneur*.

swing into wild action to relocate the little 1130 pound automobile to a sidewise position in a gateway, or up on a porch. In one instance an owner returned to find his car resting in the limbs of an elm. Instant popularity as an adult toy had struck down the commercial best interests of the American Austin.

No corners were cut in development of the one-off coupe in which Hayes would stake its reputation on the international scene.

A golf bag compartment, side accessible behind the seat through the exceptionally wide single door, left foot room to spare for rumble passengers.

Cone-shaped wheel discs were used to cover the spokes on the Hayes special — a concession to continental coachbuilder practice of the time.

Returned to the U. S. in triumph the Hayes coupe became a publicity ambassador for its builder until the mid-'thirties, when it was quietly withdrawn from display as the new *balloon* school trend in production car body design began to inflate. Later the coupe became privately owned and drifted into obscurity.[4]

---

[4]One of a scant number of custom Cords that by good fortune survive to the present day. Restored and on display in a private museum in Milwaukee. Some other existing cars: A tri-color *Murphy* phaeton, the *Murphy* town cars, the *Fuller* coupe, the *Weymann* coupe.

While the factory body types on the L-29 secured a creditable number of honors in design competition both at home and abroad, it was the individual style expressions extended among the custom body cars that brought a special aura of desirability to this fresh new American motor car.

Even among those body types provided as standard there was about the Cord automobile an aura of excitement that transcended a youthful spirit to the contemporary scene.

Cord's own body building subsidiary *La Grande* publicized a tri-color victoria-coupe design to supplement the standard types. The trim line of its gently sloping windshield was to remind officials at Auburn of a pleasant design feature somehow overlooked in the freezing of the original production body styles with a vertical windshield.[1]

---

[1]An adaptation of this body type was momentarily to be adopted as a catalog style for the Auburn car line.

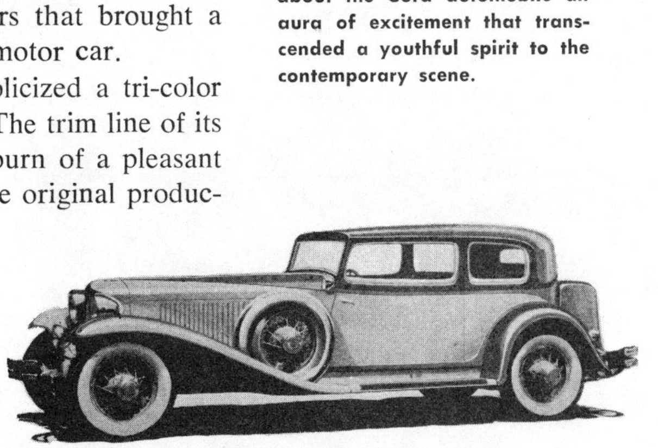

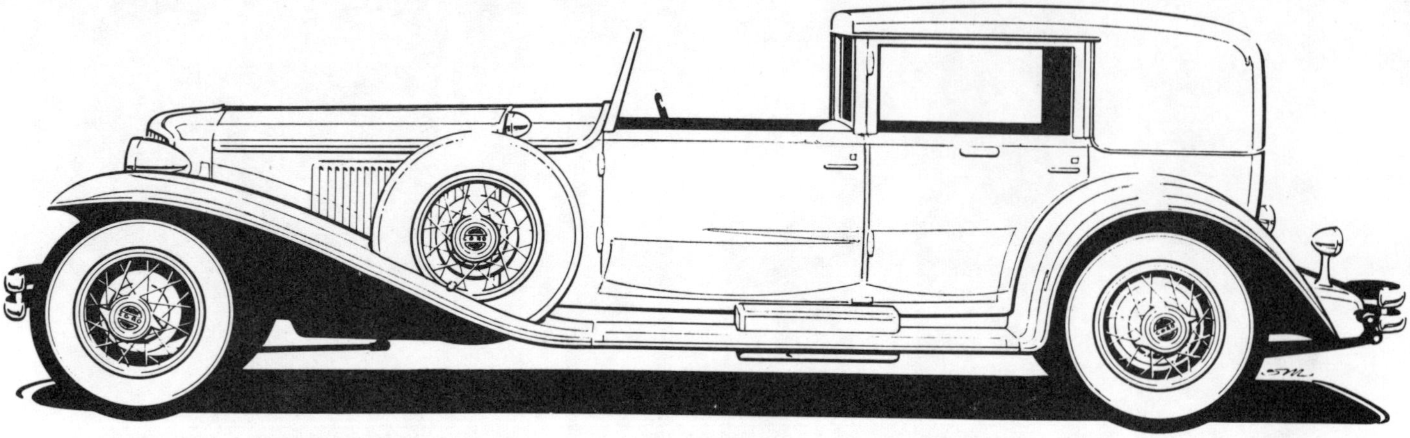
SM

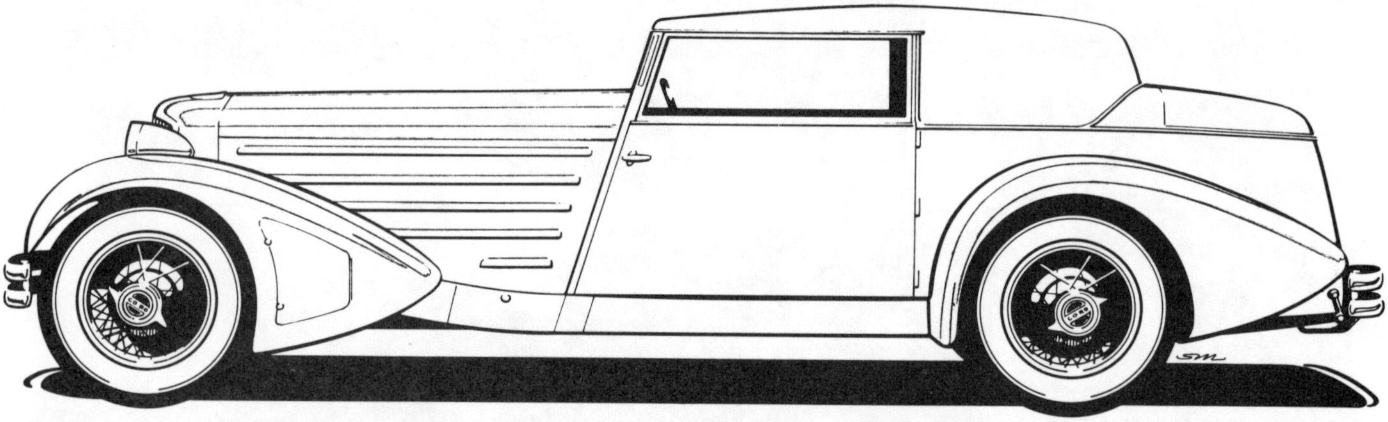
SM

SM

There was in the deep, blind-quarter, club-seating coupe the appeal of a design apart from the conventions of any production body style, and the attraction of a car immediately private and very personal. The blind victoria might be considered to have been, in effect, an owner-driven town car.

A postscript to the styling story of the L-29 reaffirms that a classic chassis never really becomes passé for design practice. In the heyday of the *Walter M. Murphy* coachbuilders one particular Pasadena schoolboy used to pedal his bicycle over to the Vernon Street dream factory and climb the steep stairs to that famous design room. He believed he would like to draw cars.

This junior enthusiast was to obtain his first drawing instruction at Murphy's where Frank Hershey, a kindly young designer, believed that *enthusiasm* was a father to *talent*. Hershey believed that was how most car designers *became* car designers. He offered this boy pointers on car styling, and progressively showed him how to work cleanly, depict form, shadow and reflection. Hershey proved to be an able instructor.

Strother MacMinn absorbed it all. Later he would go on to General Motors, then return to the coast as an independent designer and consultant in the field.

Twenty years ago the publisher commissioned MacMinn to make a series of line drawings for J. L. Elbert's classic work *Duesenberg, the Mightiest American Motor Car*.

For this new volume Strother MacMinn was asked to delineate several of the select custom body Cords in crisp new line drawings. Mac ably obliged. His *Proux* town car, *Freestone & Webb* victoria and *Million-Guiet* coupe appear opposite.

But what excited MacMinn most in the invitation was a challenge to depict the L-29 design that *he might have drawn* for E. L. Cord's original presentation at Murphy's had he been somewhat more than a kid at the time. His original victoria debuts on this page.

It may be noted that among his drawings of authentic bodies for the Duesenberg book Strother MacMinn had worked in a sketch of one coupe d'ville as an amalgam of *Hibbard & Darrin* design features. Some years later, the Hoosier enthusiast William Goodwin arranged to have his car rebodied, in the shop of one Ray Jones, to the specifications of MacMinn's composite design.

Only days to come will tell if the owner of an L-29 chassis, working with a contemporary coachbuilder, may elect to turn this new MacMinn victoria into sparkling reality.

6. *Out of the Crucible of Racing*

Success is not a prize to be won for what has been done, as much as a demonstration of ability to do more.

Propelling an automobile by its front wheels was not a brand new idea when E. L. Cord set out to develop it as a distinguishing and salesworthy feature. The very vehicle around which the great Selden patent controversy had arisen in the first decade of the motor industry in America was, itself, a front-wheel drive.

Through the years the concept had drawn attention from automotive engineers all over the world, with the work of pioneer Walter Christie now recognized as the cornerstone effort from which later designs were to benefit. But, by 1929, fwd had never become adopted anywhere generally. In theory, by the elimination of parts alone, it would, ideally, result in lower unit cost. But in practice it seemed to present engineers with limitations, or at least, special problems[5] that fostered adoption of rear-wheel drive as the common production solution among car builders.

In the days of dirt track racing in small town America every elm tree mechanic on the barnstorming circuit held the annual Indianapolis 500 Mile Race in special esteem. The men who drove there were the backyard operator's heroes; the machines these men ran were the envy of his mind's eye. Among these observers perhaps no one respected more the place of man and machine in racing as a crucible for engineering advancement than E. L. Cord.

---

[5]One of the primary recurring stumbling blocks to fwd development appears to have been the common insistence from every management that the fwd design under consideration utilize as many standard "catalog" components as possible.

Walter Christie's front-drive racing car — here shown with the legendary Barney Oldfield—was only one of Christie's contributions to the motor world. His role as creator of the modern armored motor tank — first put into service in World War I — is perhaps more generally known today.

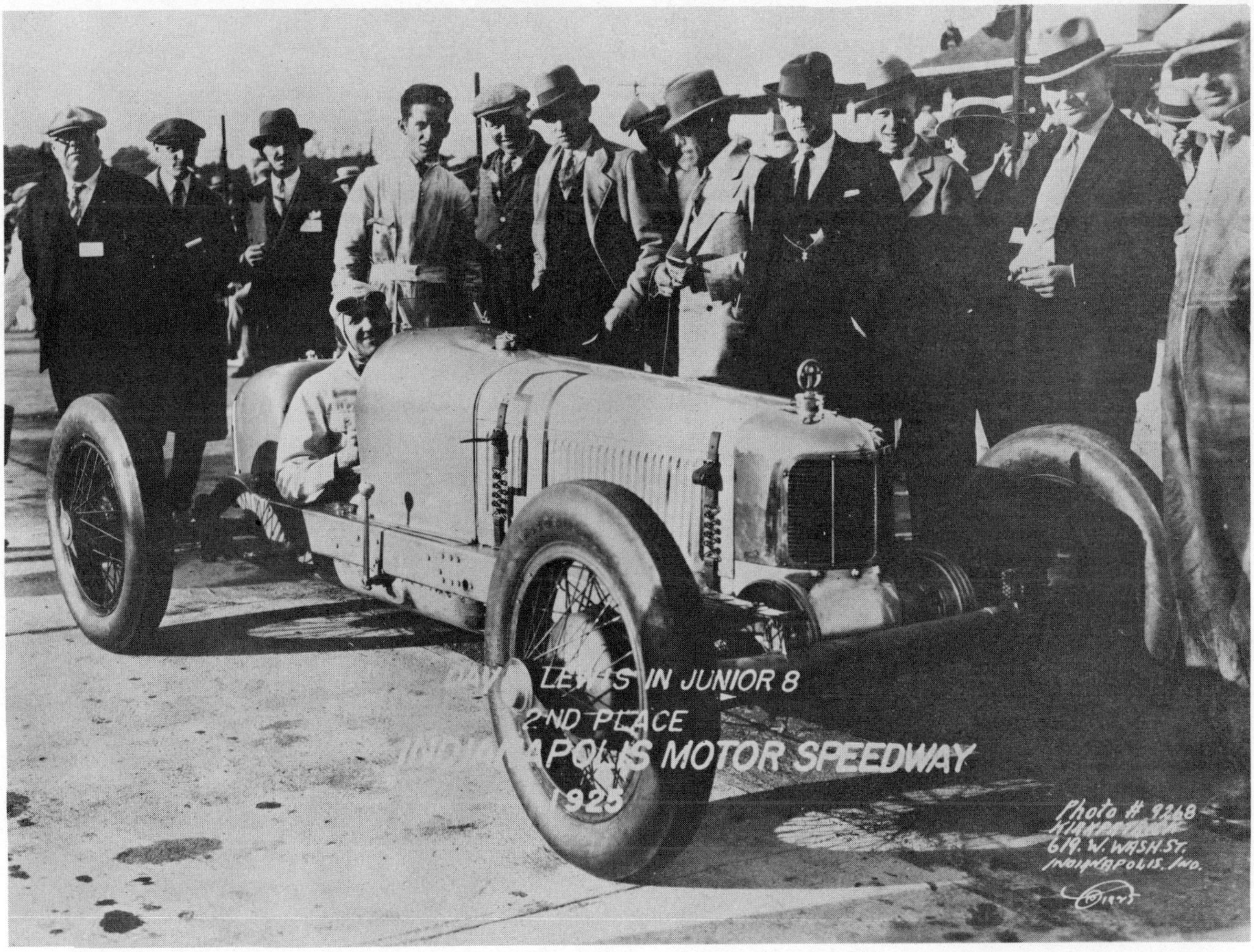

Tradition at the brickyard permitted sponsors to title their entries to commemorate branded products freely. So it was that the original Miller front-drive, without so much as a nut or a bolt from a Locomobile Junior automobile, came to be known as the Locomobile Junior 8.

At about the time Cord was proving a miracle worker at the Auburn Automobile Company the front-wheel drive idea was proving its mettle at the 500 by making the biggest news of the day in the racing world.

One of motor competition's contemporary greats, the then sole American driver to win with an American car at the *Grand Prix* (1921 in a Duesenberg), and the man then being toasted as the 500 winner for 1922 (in a Miller-powered Duesenberg) was Jimmy Murphy, who had given the track layout at Indianapolis much serious thought. After becoming convinced that front-wheel drive would make it possible for a racing car to enter turns at higher speeds at the brickyard he commissioned Harry A. Miller, then prominent as the builder of racing cars of stamina, to design and construct a fwd car, early in 1924. The ramifications from Murphy's independent action were to become greater than he could have dreamed.

Jimmy Murphy, the farsighted Irishman, did not live to tool his fwd dream car around the brickyard. That Fall, as his unusual special was nearing completion at Miller's California shop, Murphy suffered fatal injuries from a racing accident on Labor Day, in Syracuse, New York. Miller then sold the car to interests who entered it in the 1925 500 as the *Locomobile Junior 8,* a title which promoted the top of the line for the then flourishing Durant Motors, an enterprise recalled more vividly today as the Father of General Motors' last grand scale promotion than for its own motor products.

Memorial Day, 1925, marked a spectacular proving event for the car which—but for a bad luck incident during a pit stop—clearly would have captured the checkered flag.

Dave Lewis, a former Duesenberg team driver, was piloting the fwd *Junior 8* in second place when the leader, a conventional *Miller Special* hit a wall at 312 mile point. Behind him were Phil "Red" Shafer in a *Duesenberg Special,* Ralph Hepburn in a *Miller,* and, close behind, Pete de Paolo in another *Duesenberg.* At the 400 mile point de Paolo had come up through the front of the field to second place. Lewis, with a seemingly safe four-lap lead rolled into the pits for a regular stop on his 173rd lap. It was then that an unnamed member of the pit crew inadvertently changed the course of 500 history. In haste, the threads of the right front hub became swedged while changing wheels. The then necessary act of hand rasping the damaged threads away to clear cost many minutes, and ultimately the race.

Bennett Hill, an exceptional driver who had been forced to retire earlier in the race when his conventional *Miller* had broken a rear spring, took over as the relief driver. As the crowd went wild Hill managed to make up about a lap and three-quarters, and his *Miller fwd car* was entering the southwest turn of its final lap when de Paolo crossed the 500 mark, ending the event. Hill finished just 50 seconds behind the *Duesenberg* in the closest and fastest race then run in the track's history.

After the startling record made by this pilot fwd car, Harry A. Miller built a progression of similar front-wheel drive specials. Common among them was an unorthodox gear train in which the engine torque had to pass through the ring and pinion gears before going into the transmission. Inherently, the drive system made shifting at speed practically impossible.

Professional racing drivers, creatures of steel to a man, were accustomed to making procedural adjustments in catering to odd characteristics with their mounts, each of which was "special." Drivers, enthralled by the stunning performance of the fwd Miller, met the high forces on the transmission gear teeth with case-hardened brawn; against physical laws they managed their gear changes. Each car brought new acclaim to the fwd concept.

Concurrently, Tommy Milton, another Indianapolis winner and racing great, was completing an *unlike* fwd car developed independently at the Hyatt Roller Bearing Lab in Detroit. His engineer was Cornelius W. Van Ranst, who had worked with Fred Duesenberg as early as 1915, and gained further stature as chief engineer at the Chevrolet Brothers' Frontenac Motors, then renowned in racing circles for its high quality competition equipment, mostly built for Model T Ford conversions.[6]

This particular Miller-powered chassis, the *Detroit Special,* employed a more conventional drive train and was capable of smooth shifting at any speed. It too was for the promotion of Durant interests, through the active participation of William C. Durant's son, Cliff.

During this race it happened that several drivers, by substitution, were to have a crack at driving the car. Cliff Durant had been scheduled to drive but had been knocked out by illness. Tommy Milton started in his place. A

[6]A Fronty-Ford had come in 10th at *Le Mans* in 1923, ahead of many of the great marques of Europe.

From the original front-drive Detroit Special engineered by C. W. Van Ranst Auburn's FWD project was destined to directly benefit. With Tommy Milton is Sanford Moss, the Walter Christie of supercharging.

while later Leon Duray[7] took over for a short time, providing him the chance to compare the merits and performance of the *Special* with the regular "standard" fwd *Miller* with which he was already familiar as a driver. Van Ranst himself drove a few laps, and Ralph Hepburn finished the car in eighth place.

The significance of this event would later result from Duray's turn at the wheel.

Part of the Duesenberg success as a Cord subsidiary resulted directly from the fact E. L. Cord had taken over an automobile with an established reputation. This sterling racing and fine car record had proven a plus from the first days of acquisition.

Public interest generated by the outstanding performance records of the various fwd racing cars was now at a peak. Cord foresaw a fresh opportunity for head-turning interest with the special appeal of front-wheel drive in the passenger car market. He ordered his staff at the Auburn Automobile Company to go ahead on research and development of such a car.

---

[7]The stylish name with a French connotation adopted professionally by one James Stewart, an American racing driver.

7. *Putting the Horse Before the Cart*

The policy of a manufacturer is not visible. However, it is the most important thing in any automobile . . . Factory buildings, machinery, engineering laboratories and financial resources, in themselves are not important. They are only tools to work with. It is what these physical properties produce that is significant to the public.

Assigning the staff at Auburn to develop a front-wheel drive automobile from scratch struck Cord, initially, as the simple solution for getting under way. Unfortunately, the order did little to advance his project. Among these automobile engineers—whose total experience lay in the realm of conventional chassis layout—the speedy adoption of clear-cut direction for fwd chassis development called for more imagination than they could muster.

Cord found he had to set some sort of *pattern* before them before their fwd thinking would translate into action. He knew the critical importance attendant in determining a plan that later in retrospect would prove to have been *right* for development. It was the kind of challenge E. L. Cord met with the courage of his convictions.

What better fwd layout could he apply than one already, apparently, proven tried-and-true on the bricks at Indianapolis? It came almost as a reflex action for him to move to capitalize on the reputation of the leading exponent of fwd in racing circles.

As a lifelong racing fan Cord enjoyed fraternal company in the pits. And at this moment he wore the mantle of a racing patron, besides, through his control of the great Duesenberg. Cord approached Harry A. Miller and arranged immediately for the use of the Miller patents and shop services for the construction of a fwd passenger car. Cord reportedly retained Miller with salary, as well as royalties, to be based on production. As a post script to the agreement, Harry Miller, personally, was to receive one of the very first new cars to roll off the assembly line.

While it has been difficult to document the point, there has been conjecture that the name Errett Cord was considering for his new car at this stage would popularize its racing designer by being called the *Miller*. At any rate, this arrangement with Miller gave Cord a feasible starting point for his fwd project.

Back at Auburn his engineers fortified their experience by gleaning a blueprint acquaintance with front-wheel drive as conceived by the Miller shop. Harry Miller was available as a consultant; all they had to do was go ahead. Still, the traditionalists moved haltingly. It became apparent to Cord that if the project were to be spearheaded to fruition his crew needed not alone a pattern, but a knowledgeable, active, front-wheel drive engineer as a chief.

It was through a lucky turn of events that E. L. Cord was to resolve this stand-off. When the veteran racing driver Leon Duray chanced to meet Cord in Chicago, about this time, he was fresh from his experience with the Detroit Special at Indianapolis. When Cord related to his friend

A gear train solution acceptable to the racing fraternity was to prove far from ideal when applied to passenger car chassis design.

how he intended to produce the Miller fwd as a passenger car Duray was alarmed. Speaking from his personal experience he described the inherent problem of shifting gears in the Miller, and also told Cord how the Detroit Special presented no shifting limitations at any speed. He told how their power trains differed. To adopt the Miller type layout, Duray observed, would spell certain disaster.

"If you are dead serious about this front wheel venture, Errett, you ought to get in touch with Van Ranst and check out the possibilities of changing your transmission design!"

Characteristically, E. L. Cord picked up a telephone on the spot and soon had Cornelius Willett Van Ranst lined up for a meeting in Chicago.

With Harry Miller also present for the conference the Detroit Special engineer explained to Cord in clear language why Miller's front drive was impossible to shift. Technically, the gears were endowed with high inertia forces as a result of their location on the high torque side of the ring and pinion; consequently, they couldn't be slowed down enough to make easy shifting possible. To compensate, he pointed out, the gear size would have to be increased for strength purposes to such an outlandish degree it would not be feasible. Van Ranst recommended substitution of a gear layout along the lines of that he had employed in the Detroit Special.

Cord had found the *leader* for his project. Within the hour he signed C. W. Van Ranst as chief and immediately directed him to move out to Los Angeles, where the staff and facilities of the Harry Miller shop were to be at his command for construction of an experimental prototype.

C. W. Van Ranst began his work in California with an appraisal of the Miller patents and plans. He elected to adopt both the front suspension and the inboard brake mounting directly from existing designs. To mock up a trial car various Auburn components were simply adapted as an expedient measure.

A small Lycoming eight, then part of the Auburn line, was used. In order to locate the clutch up near the transmission the conventional placement of the engine was reversed. A transmission housing, meticulously developed by Miller's chief engineer, Leo Goossen, to accept standard Auburn transmission and differential gears, was the principal special fabrication required.

Van Ranst's changes only began with his departure from the Miller transmission concept. The earmarks of a pure, Miller-designed package became less and less distinct as the new director advanced the fwd design through a substantial series of original improvements. From this period forth it seemed unlikely to close observers that the car would materialize for the market designated a *Miller*. Announcement of the new FWD model as an added *Auburn* line had become a more likely conjecture.

Five feverish months of activity followed. Fitted for expedience with a modified Auburn sedan body, the first runable fwd car was ready for a trial drive early in November, 1927. E. L. Cord flew to California for the test. History was in the making when Van Ranst, Miller and Leon Duray took off for an impressionable tour with the fast-moving financier at the wheel. As they merged into traffic and headed for a steep, winding climb in the foothills above Los Angeles unfamiliar riding characteristics clearly began to present mixed feelings.

Performance in cornering was difficult to rationalize. Harry Miller, it was reported, ventured that perhaps the engine was missing in turns. Cord analyzed the almost violent lurching of the car as a power train slippage. In effect, he was right. Van Ranst, of course, knew the uneven performance resulted from use of single universal joints—which he had not advocated —in the steering drive wheels. The system had been employed in the prototype as an economy measure over the constant-velocity Rzeppa joint used in Miller's competition cars. A necessary constant-velocity drive joint, the chief engineer explained, could also be obtained by using a double universal joint at the road wheels. This time the extra expense was quickly granted.

Styling certainly was not a consideration in the first operable FWD chassis. As an expedient a handy Auburn body had simply been bolted to the straight-railed chassis. Utility was served.

To E. L. Cord, though momentarily discomforting, the trial run in this crude prototype confirmed the validity of his fwd dream. He wanted to bring an improved version to the market as soon as it could be done. Cord sent Van Ranst to Indianapolis, where he would be formally supported with a staff at Duesenberg, Inc., to design the production FWD car. First detail for redevelopment; a satisfactory, while not prohibitively expensive, constant velocity joint.

The FWD engineering project was not budgeted and deadlined, as would have been the case in the forced climate of a larger motor company. It proceeded under the strict general dictum that as many of the Miller patented features as possible were to be used and that special tooling was to be minimized by using every available standard catalog part possible in the new car. Engineering pursuits that digressed from this singular objective were simply not funded. This austere program—in essence one of not spending that not at hand—was to result in a chassis of practically classic simplicity.

As the FWD production chassis took form under the firm hand of C. W. Van Ranst, even before road testing, the Auburn Automobile Company confidently began to arrange with other Cord holdings for the supply of principal components. Lycoming, Limousine Body and Central Manufacturing were tooled to supply engines and bodies. Lesser assemblies were sub-contracted outside to A. O. Smith, Long, Dayton Wheel, Detroit Gear, Delco, Gemmer, Schebler, Houdaille and others.

A full reproduction of a leading announcement story covering the L-29, as it appeared in the trade journal MoToR, begins overleaf.

Al Leamy's simple line drawings had started a stream of work that was now fast leading to emergence of the real thing.

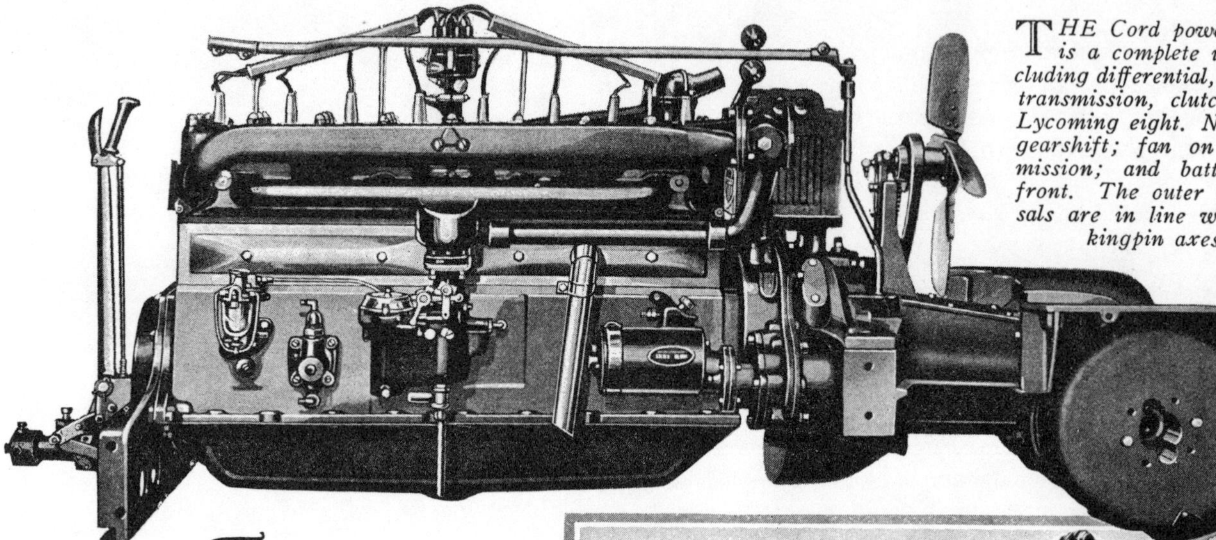

THE Cord power-plant is a complete unit including differential, brakes, transmission, clutch, and Lycoming eight. Note the gearshift; fan on transmission; and battery at front. The outer universals are in line with the kingpin axes

The Cord ...built by Auburn... A Front-Drive Car

THE first American front-drive passenger car to go into production is The Cord, manufactured by the Auburn Automobile Co., and named after E. L. Cord its president. It has a Lycoming eight-in-line engine with a bore and stroke of 3¼ by 4½ inches, and a wheelbase of 137⅝ inches.

It is offered in four body styles, sedan, (convertible) phaeton-sedan, (convertible) cabriolet and brougham. Prices have not yet been announced but are reported to be in the neighborhood of $3000.

The Cord is obviously distinguished by the fact that it is the first really new automobile design to appear on the market for many years. Due to the front-drive principle it stands much closer to the road than any rear-drive car. Overall height of the sedan is 61 inches while the (convertible) phaeton-sedan is 61 inches, both with standard headroom from cushion to roof of 38 inches and road clearance of 8½ inches at the center. Rear-drive cars have an overall height of about 70 inches.

Its lowness adds distinction, greatly accentuated, the writer believes, by an exceptionally good job of body designing. The radiator and hood lines are both different and pleasing, and bodies have been contoured in equally distinctive fashion. The hood is long, 46 inches, and the sweeping one-piece front fenders with a length of 80 inches are described as the longest on any automobile. Unusual two-unit front bumpers are attached to the axle, harmonizing nicely with the chromium rimmed differential cover and the shuttered radiator of unique outline. The rear of the car is neatly finished. The gasoline tank apron is divided into two pleasing panels with the Cord crest at the center, the bumper is a special design and there are two lamps on stanchions, one a taillight and the other a stop and back light.

All these factors, plus careful coloring, have resulted in attractive appearance. The car also possesses a certain air of smartness which is all its own. On boulevard or highway it cannot be mistaken for any other automobile.

The front-drive mechanism has been most carefully laid out and most exhaustively tested and is unequivocally presented as a thoroughly developed design, based on the patents of Harry Miller, well-known builder of front-drive racing cars.

As compared to rear-drive practice, the members forming the complete power plant are reversed. From front to rear, they are: Differential housing, transmission, clutch and engine, all bolted together to form a complete unit mounted in the frame.

The CORD *Is* Low, Smart, *with* High Maximum Speed *and* Excellent Roadability --Supplied in Four Body Styles

The appearance of the Cord is most distinctive

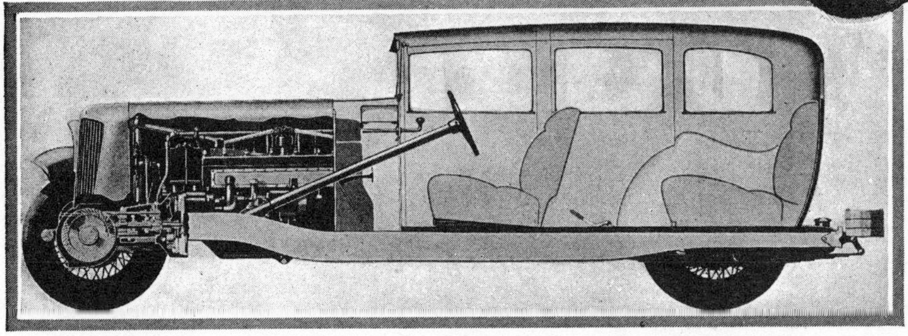

Section through Cord showing straight frame and low body

An axle shaft equipped with two universal joints runs from the differential to each wheel. The front axle is a tubular type, curved forward so as to clear the differential housing. The drop forged yokes at its ends are large and placed at an angle to permit locating the outer universal directly in line with the kingpin axis so that steering the front wheels has no effect on the delivery of power or vice-versa. There is no kingpin, the spindle yoke being swiveled on the axle yoke by two bronze-lined steel-backed bushings, and carried on a ball thrust bearing.

GREAT stress is laid on the fact that the outer universal is a constant velocity type. To make the importance of this point clear it must first be explained that when any two shafts are connected by a universal, if the driving shaft is operated at constant speed, the speed of the driven shaft will only be uniform when the two shafts are in line. If the driven shaft makes an angle with the driving shaft, the former will alternately run faster and slower than the latter during each half revolution. This variation increases in magnitude as the angle of the joint increases. Consequently if a single universal were used at the kingpin there would be an objectionable variation in driving effort when the wheels were steered from the straight-ahead position.

To secure constant velocity it is necessary to use two universal joints, since the second counteracts the effect of the first, permitting the driven shaft to run at the same speed as the driving shaft for a wide variation of angle. Thus the outer universal in the Cord is really two universals combined into a single unit, distinguished by compactness and simplicity. This patented universal is illustrated on page 144 and the caption accompanying the illustration describes its details. Drive may be described as full floating. Two taper roller bearings, mounted on a hollow spindle, carry each front wheel. A short drive shaft from the outer universal runs through the spindle and is splined to a cap bolted to the wheel hub. At the universal end this shaft is carried in a Hyatt roller bearing.

The kingpins are vertical fore and aft. Caster and camber are 1½ degrees. Toe-in is described as zero although it is understood the wheels toe out a trifle since application of power tends to make them toe in. Thus if they toe out slightly standing still they will be straight when the engine is driving. The steering gear is a Gemmer worm and roller. Drag link and tie rod are ball jointed.

The front axle is attached to dual quarter elliptic springs. The forward curve of the axle makes the customary half elliptic impracticable. The front end of the frame is kicked up so as to provide suitable clearance for drag link and tie rod. The springs point outward at an angle, thus permitting the frame to be narrower than usual at the front, and this in turn allows an unusually short turning radius, 21 feet, for a car with a 137⅝-inch wheelbase. The constant velocity outer

The Cord phaeton-sedan

E. L. Cord,

president of Auburn, after whom the car is named

The cabriolet

universals, of course, permit such sharp cramping of the wheels without introducing any difficulty.

The 58-inch front tread also assists in providing a small turning circle. The rear tread is also wider than customary, 60 inches, to allow sufficient rear seat width, since the low frame places the cushion between the wheels.

The angular mounting of the springs would twist the frame side members were it not for the fact that the front engine support is bolted directly to the two box-like frame extremities which carry the springs, spring torsion being more than adequately resisted by the engine support without affecting the frame side members. The engine, incidentally, is mounted at four points.

When one wheel passes over a bump, the consequent raising of the axle on this side tends to twist the quarter-elliptic springs. If conventional metal shackles were used, the resulting stress on both the springs and the shackles would be objectionable. The problem has been neatly solved by mounting the ends of these springs in rubber shock insulators which allow sufficient play to prevent measurable twisting of the springs.

Hypoid gearing is used to transmit the power from transmission to differential. Whereas in rear-drive practice the hypoid pinion is placed 2 to 2½ inches below the axis of the ring gear, just the opposite is true of the Cord. The pinion is located 2 inches above the ring gear axis to secure standard road clearance under the flywheel housing.

The company emphasizes the point that pinion and ring gear and differential mechanism are unusually large because considerations of unsprung weight impose no limitations on the size of these parts as it often does in the rear-drive car where these members are located within the unsprung axle. Since these units on the Cord are carried above the springs they have no affect on the unsprung weight.

The differential assembly is carried on two taper roller bearings. At each side, the driving member of the inner universal, the flange which supports the brake drum, and the short shaft running to the differential drive gear are ingeniously formed from a single forging which is carried in an annual ball bearing.

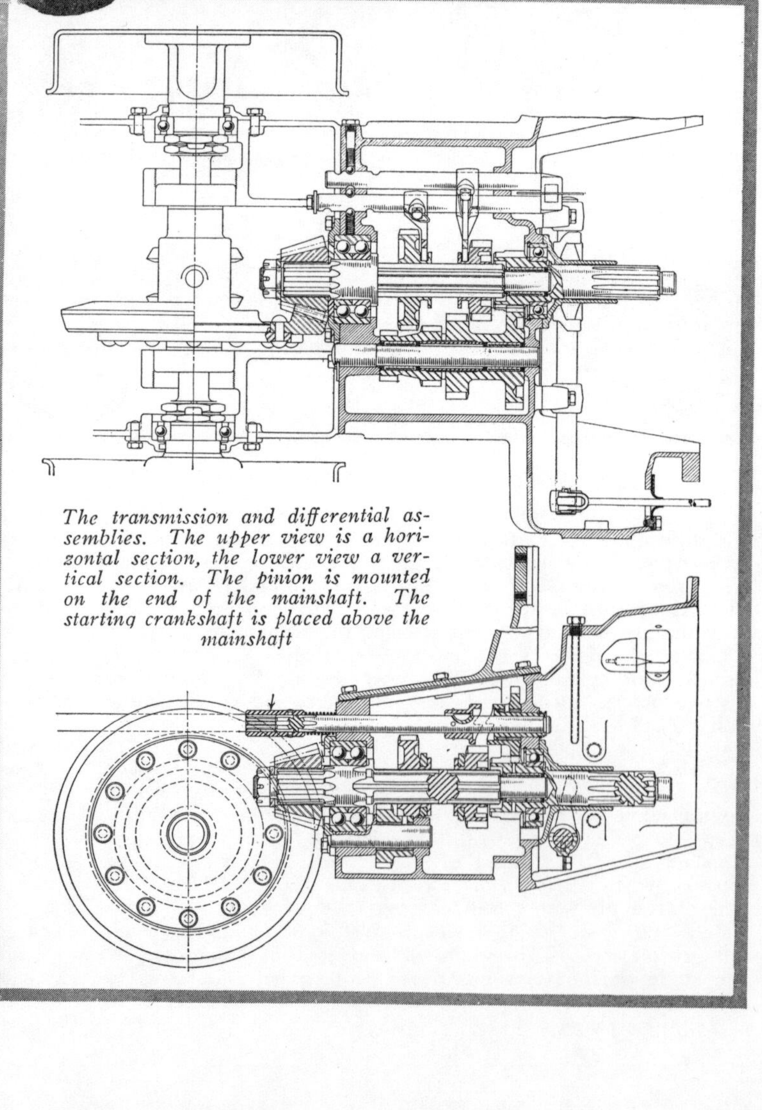

The transmission and differential assemblies. The upper view is a horizontal section, the lower view a vertical section. The pinion is mounted on the end of the mainshaft. The starting crankshaft is placed above the mainshaft

Optional gear ratios are 4.076, 4.418 and 4.818 to 1. The speedometer is driven from a gear adjacent to the differential mechanism and therefore is unaffected by a change in axle gear ratio.

The rear axle is an I-beam with a raised center portion which gives 8½ inches road clearance. Rear wheel bearings are taper roller. Rear springs are half elliptic.

The transmission, which is bolted to the rear of the differential housing, has the countershaft in the same horizontal plane as the mainshaft. The shifter shafts are placed to the right of the mainshaft. The countershaft cluster is carried on Hyatt rollers. The clutchshaft is mounted in an annular ball bearing. The back end of the mainshaft fits into a Hyatt roller spigot bearing while the front end is carried in a large, dual annular ball, an integral splined extension on the front of the mainshaft supporting the hypoid drive pinion.

Obviously with a complete reversal of the power plant mechanism special provision must be made for the hand starting crank. The crank handle attaches to a shaft reached by removing a cap near the top of the differential hand hole cover. The shaft runs through the top of the transmission to a gear which meshes with the master gear in the transmission. The cap is attractively decorated with the Cord crest.

Gears are shifted by a knob attached to a sliding rod extending from the instrument board. The rod passes between two rollers at the front, right of the engine and from thence attaches to the gearshift lever. This simple mechanism permits gearshifting in the usual manner except the so-called standard shift is not used. High is forward to the right, second rearward to the right, first forward to the left, and reverse rearward to the left.

Lockheed internal hydraulic brakes are used with 60 per cent braking power in the front—to take advantage of "weight shift" to provide maximum stopping ability.

A conventional Long single-plate clutch is used. The clutch is actuated by a shaft which runs along the left side of the engine.

The hand-brake lever is placed well forward so that the driver's compartment is unencumbered. This lever expands the rear hydraulic brake shoes by mechanical linkage.

A flat gasoline tank at the rear holds 20 gallons. Fuel is fed by an A C pump. A 1¼-inch Schebler dual carburetor is used with a dual manifold having dash-adjustable heat control. Electrical equipment is Delco-Remy. The battery is conveniently located just forward of the cylinder block. The exhaust pipe is carried down in front and the muffler is placed to the right of the crankcase. The muffler is provided with a bypass. The frame is an exceptionally interesting unit. Except for the kickup at the front, the side rails are straight all the way to the rear, thus providing an ideal foundation for body mounting. The absence of a propeller shaft permits an unusually heavy X-shaped brace at the mid-section. In addition there are two cross-members at the rear, and the engine support serve as two cross-members at the front. Frame side rails are 7 by 3 by 7/32. This frame is unusually rigid and should go far toward insuring continued body silence.

Except for minor changes incident to the application of front drive, the engine is a standard Lycoming design with such features as Nelson Bohnalite pistons, pressure lubrication, and a five-bearing counter-balanced crankshaft. Standard compression ratio is 5.25 to 1.

Bearing in mind that the power plant is turned around, the Lanchester vibration dampener is found at the rear, being fully housed in a sheet-metal cover. The timing chain, however, is placed at the front or flywheel end. Longer timing chain life should result since the flywheel

The Cord Front-Drive sedan

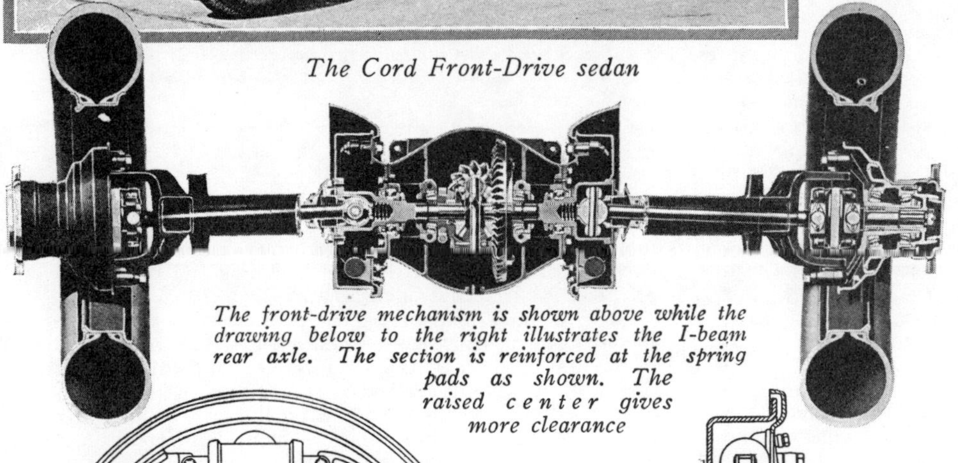

The front-drive mechanism is shown above while the drawing below to the right illustrates the I-beam rear axle. The section is reinforced at the spring pads as shown. The raised center gives more clearance

C. W. VAN RANST,

Chief Engineer of the Cord Front Drive

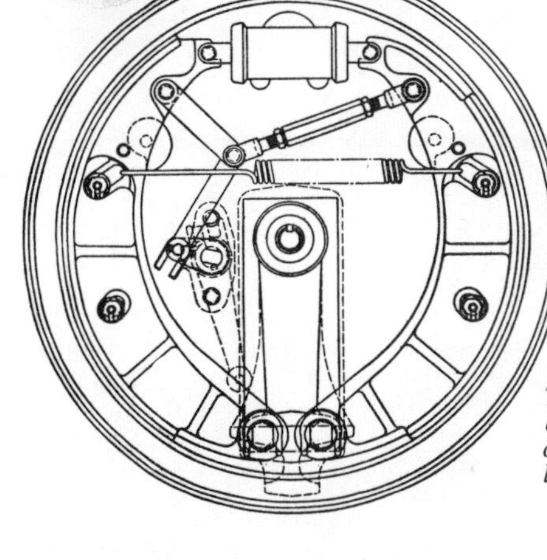

The rear hydraulic brakes are mechanically linked to the parking brake lever

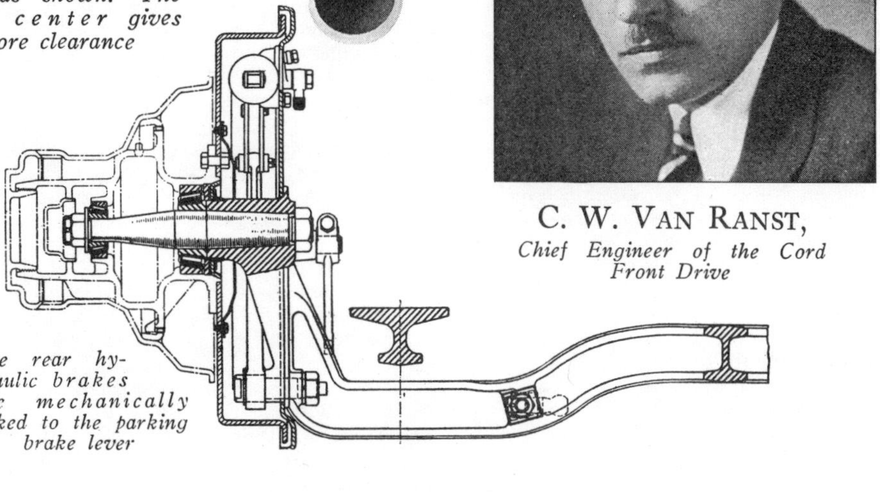

The rear of the Cord is neatly finished. Below—There are three instruments at extreme left and right, a glove compartment in the center and two banks of four control buttons

end is not appreciably subject to torsional crankshaft vibration.

The engine of course, being reversed, rotates anti-clockwise viewed from the front whereas clockwise rotation is customary. However, since the hand crank operates through a gear, its rotation is conventional.

The fan bracket is integral with the transmission cover, permissible since the shifter shafts are located to one side. The fan is driven by Vee belt from a lay shaft operated by the timing chain. The rear of this shaft drives the water pump and generator. Bijur lubrication is supplied to the fan, the fan drive pulley, the clutch throwout bearing, the water pump, and of course also to the rear spring shackles which are metal.

The radiator is a Modine with flat, finned vertical tubes. Radiator shutters, thermostatically controlled, embellish the front end of the car and there is also a water thermostat in the water outlet from the cylinder block.

INTERIORS will be finished in the finest of broadcloths or genuine Spanish leather, according to the model. Hardware is of Crest design in silver finish. Every effort has been made to give the passengers the utmost in comfort and harmony. The front seat, in addition to being unusually deep and luxurious, is four inches wider than usual. The front seat has an adjustment range of four inches and the steering column is also adjustable.

The instrument board is unique, an attractive design composed of two groups of instruments at extreme right and left, a glove compartment in the center, and a group of four control buttons at either side. The left group of instruments within convenient sight of the driver includes speedometer, oil pressure gauge, and water thermometer. The right group comprises the gasoline gauge, the oil level gauge and ammeter. The left set of four buttons operate the spark advance, the throttle, instrument lamp and left windshield wiper. The right group of four buttons controls the starter, choke, manifold heat control and right windshield wiper. Horn and lighting switch are at the center of the wheel.

The instrument dials instead of being stationary with movable hands, each consist of a cylindrical dial rotating on a horizontal axis in conjunction with a stationary pointer.

Two horns are fitted, operated simultaneously by the button on the steering wheel. They are purposely turned to different tones so that they give a most unusual warning signal which is both compelling and pleasing. The air vibrations produced by the two alternately reinforce and then oppose each other, producing a tremulous note which must be heard to be appreciated.

Courtesy lights in the running-board aprons turn on automatically when the rear doors are opened. Closed models are equipped with torchieres in the rear corners in addition to a dome light. Wire wheels are standard equipment with spares in the front fenders. Tires are 18 by 7 inches. The cowl is equipped with two ventilators.

EVEN more interesting than the constructional details of the car itself is the question, How does it act on the road? Or to state the case more broadly, What advantages does it possess over a rear-drive job?

To answer these questions intelligently it is first necessary to tabulate the major differences between front and rear-drive construction, as follows:

1. Drive is at the front. The car is pulled instead of pushed.
2. Unsprung weight is less.
3. The passengers sit several inches lower than in the usual rear-drive job.
4. The frame provides a level platform for body mounting and the absence of the drive shaft allows exceptional frame bracing.
5. Wind resistance is less.

The question of unsprung weights demands further discussion. To define it, unsprung weight is that portion of the car weight not cushioned by the springs. In a rear-drive car, it includes the complete rear axle assembly, wheels and tires, as well as half the drive shaft and more than half the weight of the half-elliptic springs, since the two latter units move up and down with the axle. By comparison the front-drive car has a simpler, lighter rear axle and the half-weight of the propeller shaft is eliminated.

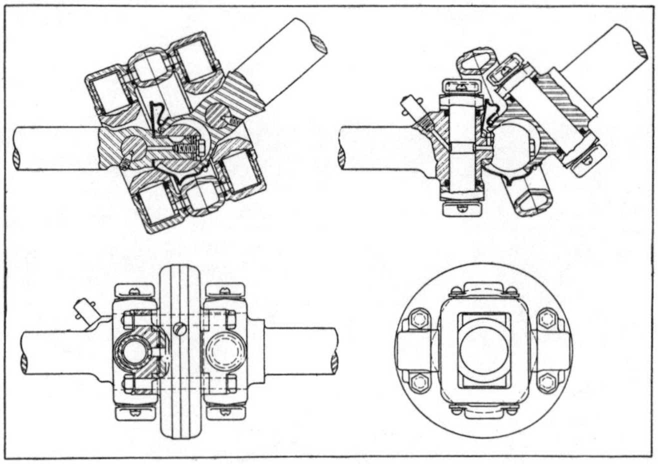

Four views of the Cord constant velocity outer universal. The driven shaft is at the left. It is really two universals in one, aligned by a dust-proof ball and socket joint. The central hollow ring carries the trunnions of both joints. This hollow chamber supplies lubricant to all surfaces except the ball and socket joint which is oiled by Alemite connection

At the front, unsprung weight on the rear-drive car includes the axle, wheels, brakes, tires and more than half the weight of the half-elliptic springs. In contrast, the front-drive front axle is relieved of the brake mechanism, the quarter-elliptic springs add but slightly to the unsprung weight, but on the other hand the front-drive front axle must carry the bumper and in addition the driving mechanism adds some weight.

WHILE the Cord and the Auburn 120 are not strictly comparable, a discussion of their weights will at least assist in an understanding of the subject. Both have the large Lycoming eight engine. The Auburn 120 ready for the road weighs 4155 pounds and the weight of the Cord sedan is 4430 pounds.

Unsprung weights for the Auburn front and rear are respectively 393 and 460 pounds; corresponding weights supported by the springs front and rear are 1732 and 1570 pounds. Similar figures for the Cord are 360 and 351, and 1840 and 1879 pounds.

Thus the ratio of sprung to unsprung weight is: Auburn front, 4.40 to 1; Auburn rear, 3.41 to 1; Cord front, 5.11 to

1; Cord rear, 5.35 to 1. The higher the ratio the better the car should ride, and the steadier it should be on rough roads at high speed, and of course no road is perfectly smooth.

One of the functions of the springs is to hold the wheels to the road. Obviously, therefore, springs of given stiffness* are able to make a rear unsprung weight of 351 pounds follow the road more closely than a weight of 460 pounds, especially when it is remembered that the ratio of weight bearing down on the springs to unsprung weight is 5.35 in the former case and 3.41 in the latter. A similar argument holds at the front end where the ratio for the Cord is 5.11 and 4.40 for the Auburn.

Therefore the higher the ratio the more closely the wheels hug the road, that is, the less they dance and chatter. Therefore on a road of given roughness at a given speed if the ratio is high the wheels will bounce less than if it is low. Likewise the car with a high ratio may be driven faster over a given rough road with the same feeling of security.

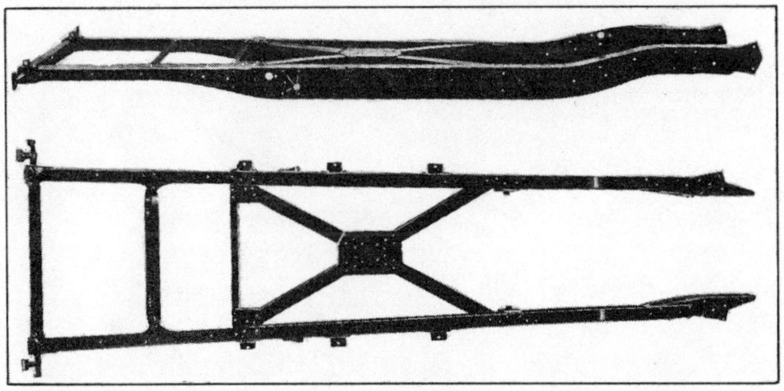

The frame of the Cord Front Drive is heavily braced

Likewise when 351 pounds of unsprung weight starts skyward after hitting a bump it disturbs the passengers less than when 460 pounds moves upward.

Because of these considerations, recalling that the wheelbase is 137⅝ inches, and noting that the car is equipped with Houdaille shock absorbers, it is to be expected that the Cord rides very well, as demonstrated by a trip of about 75 miles which the writer made over various roads from smooth, new concrete to rather bumpy gravel.

Whether the car rides better than any rear-drive model is a question the writer cannot answer, for it is impossible to recall accurately the impressions of months gone by made in various cars on totally different roads.

However, the writer believes that it handles much better on loose gravel than any rear-drive car. Even when the gravel is piled up in furrows, it may be steered from one side of the road to the other without any suggestion of skidding, due mainly to the fact that the front wheels are pulling in the direction they are pointed, whereas with the rear-drive the rear wheels are pushing in one direction while the front wheels are pointed in another.

THE company also stresses the fact that the car acts in similarly fine fashion on wet or icy pavement and muddy and sandy roads. It seems as though it should, although a clear, warm June day in Indiana eliminated the first three from consideration.

On rough roads at high speed the car is much steadier than any rear-drive the writer can recall. That tendency which a rear-drive has to slide sidewise a foot or so on a bad bump was entirely absent, due both to the front drive and also to the lower unsprung weight which enabled the wheels to hold to the road more effectively.

The front-drive principle plus the low seating of the passengers enabled the taking of turns at higher speed than with a rear-drive job, and at least on those rough turns the writer happened to come upon, chattering and skidding of the rear end was noticeably absent. The car steers easily; in the writer's opinion as easily as a good rear-drive job.

To answer a frequently voiced question, the throttle may be closed instantly at any speed without any perceptible effect on the action of the car. On the other hand, the car can be pulled out of a skid by opening the throttle.

IT was not possible to secure accurate comparative wind resistance figures but it is understood that its frontal area is about 4 square feet less than a comparable rear drive, and due to this difference a simple calculation shows that its maximum speed should be about 5 miles per hour higher than a comparable rear drive with approximately proportionate gain in fuel economy at high speed. The maximum speed is stated to be 90 miles per hour.

The difference between front and rear-drive cars can be rather accurately summed up by stating that insofar as the writer's comparatively brief experience is concerned, the front-drive possesses none of the disadvantages of the rear-drive.

This statement can be variously interpreted, depending on the viewpoint of the individual concerning the roads he drives and the speed at which he drives them.

*Spring flexibilities on the Cord and the 120 Auburn are approximately the same, the rate in pounds per inch of deflection being: Cord front, 300; rear, 160; Auburn front, 360-380; rear, 160-180.

8. Style for an Unaccustomed Form

We operate on the theory that the public knows what it wants cars to do and how it wants it done . . . This policy places an unceasing obligation upon our designers, engineers and workmen. It requires that we anticipate changes and improvements which people want. It means we must be leaders, not followers.

After C. W. Van Ranst and his staff had translated every detail of the chassis for the FWD project into blueprints at the Duesenberg engineering department the group moved to Auburn, in August, 1928, to oversee the hand assembly of several prototype chassis.

Concurrently, several designers who had contributed substantially to the metamorphous of the Auburn car styling, led by Albert Leamy and supported by John Oswald as body engineer, were evaluating a sheaf of design roughs which had been accumulating since the first days of the Miller passenger car idea. This data in various forms reflected details that individual minds in the company had proposed toward the FWD body design. Cord himself, Oswald recalls, had recommended a body molding treatment similar to a particular *Hibbard & Darrin* creation from Paris which had been displayed at the 1927 New York Salon. Another note simply observed that large window area would tend to exaggerate favorably the proportionate lowness of the car.

At a vertical blackboard the men were assembling engineering measurements of the FWD car in full size. John Oswald recommended the frame be dropped to 16″ to get the lowest workable chassis. While the industry average among cars then in production was 20″ the relatively uncomplicated rear section permitted a somewhat lower chassis and 16″ would present marked contrast.

One of the FWD rough idea sketches done by Al Leamy featured a Duesenberg Model J type radiator shell which differed principally by sweeping forward at the bottom to conceal the fwd works. Leamy's legend identified the drawing as the FD car, but a streamer-stripe on the hood characterized the drawing as an Auburn proposal, lending credence to reports that the unnamed FD project was advancing during this phase of its development under the guise of becoming an additional series of this established badge.

On the original experimental car using a dropped Auburn body the improvised radiator shell had reflected more a carryover from Miller racing cars than an element to which serious design thought had been applied. E. L. Cord had strong ideas about the front end appearance for production. He expressed the desire that it be distinctive even to the casual observer by visibly revealing its fwd nature. He asked Leamy to see a modified drawing of this frontal treatment in which the lower section would be changed to display, rather than conceal this special character.

Al Leamy then cut off the radiator shell to remove the sweep in his drawing and melded it into a prominent circular fwd differential cover form which set off the unorthodox drive dramatically. When Cord saw drawings of this revision he approved the Leamy design for production.

Cord ordered the fender valance detail kept high in the front to show as much of the universals and drive as possible. Specifically, he wanted the fenders to have the compound form at the highpoint of "inverted tablespoons"—broadened at the crown with catwalk clearance correspondingly reduced—to distinguish them from the current fender design of the Auburn line.

The modified Duesenberg grille motif and the broad open fenders combined to give the FWD car a handsome, bold look of sheer function, at once unique and inviting, yet pleasantly suggestive of its pedigree from the stable of its more costly big brother from Indianapolis. It would prove to be a classic design solution.

Replete with Auburn's streamer stripe molding this early FWD drawing indicates design direction firmly. A revamping of the lower grille to emphasize F-D would constitute the only real deviation yet to follow.

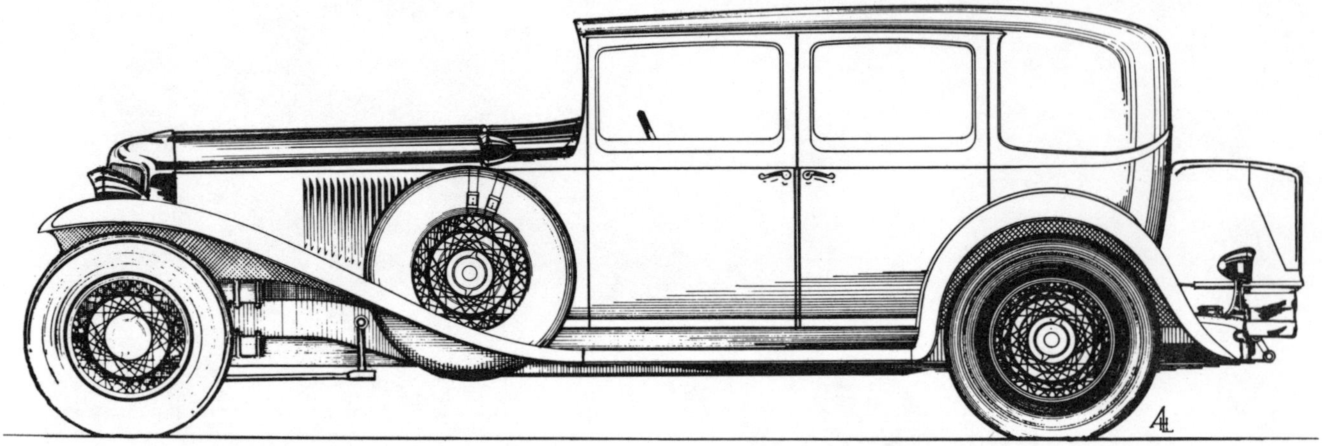

E. L. Cord's single-minded desire to create standard body types with a fashionable flair began with the blind-quarter sedan, shown here in initial orthographic projection. The top overlay — to be adopted for production — was yet to come.

With the front end theme resolved the design men proceeded to finalize body lines. Incorporating all available chassis data and many suggestions from the body design rough file—including that special molding treatment from the *Hibbard & Darrin* special—Leamy's general concept became fully detailed. Oswald then developed a full-size body layout which was ready for E. L. Cord's final study in October. It is reported that Cord liked what he saw and gave Van Ranst the go-ahead to build a working prototype. The traditional intermediate step in body design in the industry —model making—had been effectively skipped.

"They never knew what a clay model was at that time at Auburn," recalls Oswald. "None of the bodies I engineered for Auburn ever began as a model of any kind. They were surface developed on a paper draft."

John Oswald, in turn, received authority from Van Ranst to proceed with the construction of prototype sheet metal directly from the accepted full size paper sketches. Production was now the near objective.

A production convertible coupe for the FWD was a natural follow-through, for Auburn had pioneered this body style as a production type only seasons before.

F~D Cabriolet.

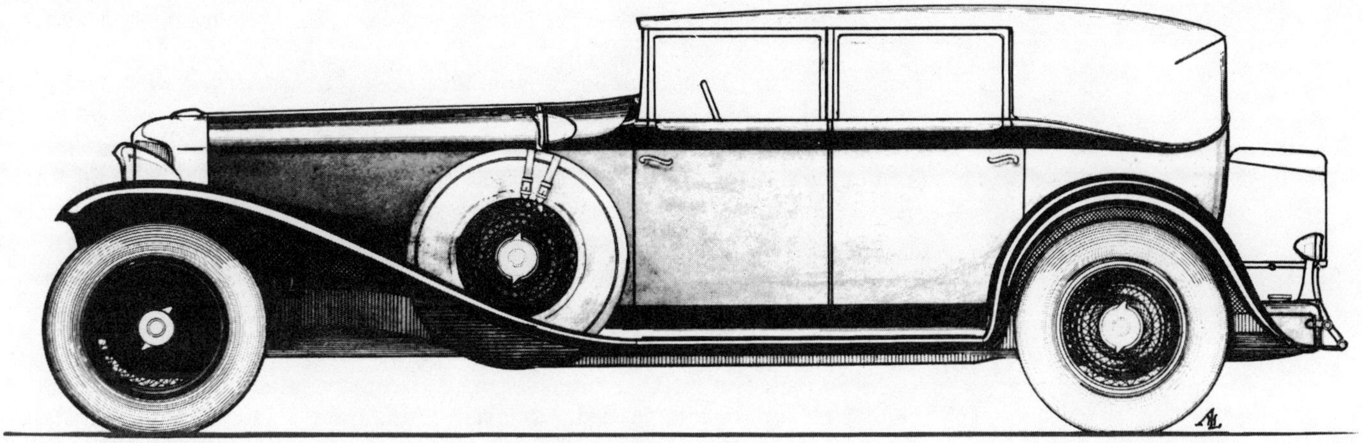

The all-weather convertible sedan which had developed solely in the realm of the coach-built body debuted as a production Auburn style in 1928.

At Auburn's downstate subsidiary, Central Manufacturing in Connersville, the body engineer was supported by several veteran metal shapers. Working from his detailed plan and elevation sketches which had hurriedly been drafted directly from the blackboard drawings the crew hammered out the new radiator shell design on a Pettingell motorized hammer. Working closely with Oswald, improvements in surface development were made in progress as the flat drawings took on a third dimension in steel.

As the sheet metal body panels were completed they were shipped back to Auburn where the first body shell was assembled on a hastily constructed buck in a small shop in the rear of the plant. As this initial production prototype body took form it became apparent to everyone present that the captivating proportions of the new FWD car would never be confused with the ordinary, even in plainest, four door form. Soon the long, narrow hoods, body panels, doors and fenders—enough for one each of the body types—were standing ready for assembly.

With top stowed the body type was clearly as represented, a true phaeton sedan.

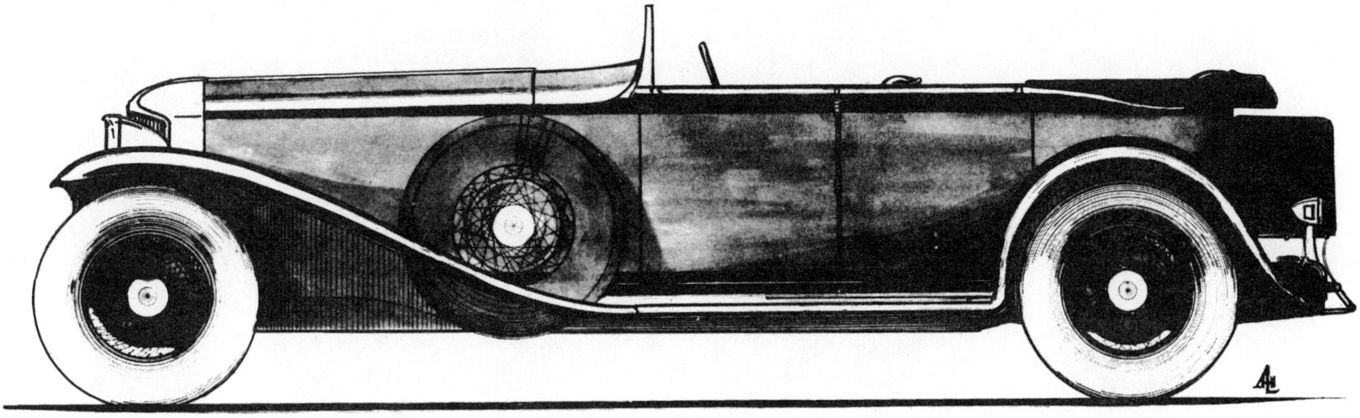

The story is told that through the tempo of a rush program, data had not always been exchanged between chassis and body construction crews, with the result that the chassis and first body failed to mate when they were initially brought together. The body would not drop into place because the engine extended too far to the rear of the chassis. Extra accommodation for the power plant was resolved in a least obstrusive manner by modifying the central firewall area with a 6″ recess.

"E. L. Cord and I took the first ride through a cornfield close by," recalls John Oswald. "The sedan doors flew open and the car flopped around like a chicken with its head off. After examining this situation, we decided something had to be done about the frame.

"Van called in A. O. Smith Co., who was then building the frames for Auburn. They recommended a heavier frame, and Van could not see it. He had to build a lightweight car because the engine he had would not give satisfactory performance with several hundred pounds of extra weight. Something had to be done quickly.

"While A. O. Smith and Van were going round and round, Herb Snow, then the chief engineer for Auburn, made a little model of a frame that we saw at the New York show on an Italian *Lancia* display chassis. It carried a slight suggestion of an X member. Herb fabricated two models about 12″ long by 3″ wide, one having an X and the other the usual ladder construction.

"There was no comparison between the two. The X frame was far superior. I then showed the models to Van and E. L. A representative from A. O. Smith was called in and they made the changes in the first of the frames for the FWD. I believe this was the beginning of the X frame in the United States."

Four chassis had been hand-assembled to receive the handbuilt bodies, one to show each of the four standard line bodies—three of which were *wildly different* for a line consisting of but four stock types! In addition to the compelling standard sedan were a blind-quarter (four-window) sedan with a fabric overlaid hard top, a convertible coupe and a convertible four door sedan. The latter production body styles had originated at Auburn only seasons before.

As it approached production the FWD was emerging as a fairly formidable performer and most certainly as an exciting new car. E. L. Cord, the man who always seemed capable of seeing through a venture from beginning to end at the outset, was witnessing the culmination of a very special project. The drive and tenacity that were a part of Cord's make-up can be illustrated by the daring pace of an incident C. W. Van Ranst recalls from the days in Auburn during January, 1929.

"Late one afternoon, just as the four production prototypes were being completed, E. L. flew in to Auburn from Chicago to make his customary visit to the office and see what progress was being made on the FWD. All the top management at the factory had just departed midweek for New York and the automobile show.

"E. L. was agreeably surprised to find that of the prototypes in progress the four door sedan was very nearly finished and ready to run. A conference with the mechanics revealed that by concentrating on this one unit, and working on through, it could be completed by late that night (Wednesday). E. L. ordered a master mechanic, whose first name was

Cord Sedan for Five

Cord Phaeton Sedan

Herb, to go home and sleep until midnight; he was then to return to the plant with bag packed ready to leave for a point unknown. E. L. ordered two five-gallon cans of gasoline stored on the rear floor of the car. Then he left for his Auburn home to catch a few hours' sleep.

"After midnight E. L. and Herb returned to the plant. The finishing crew had tested the car around the area to make sure everything was functioning properly and the FWD sedan was fueled and ready to go. At about twelve-thirty E. L. announced his plan and destination. He was going to drive non-stop, except for fuel and food, to the far west, to Phoenix, Arizona.

"A few minutes later Cord and his mechanic headed down the highway toward Ft. Wayne and points west.

"To close the story, the prototype reached Phoenix early Friday afternoon in something of a record time, during which it was not necessary to touch a wrench to the car or make any adjustments.

"E. L. had prearranged for his company airplane to meet him in Phoenix. After getting Herb set to drive the car back to the midwest E. L. took off for New York City.

"When he walked into the headquarters Auburn had set up in the Commodore Hotel at the Show Sunday it was about six p.m. When he told of the wild FWD ride to Phoenix he so recently had completed no one would believe the story. E. L. for once had to insist and went into all the details. Then his management accepted the tale and a private and informal celebration at the Commodore immediately followed to commemorate the event."

Cord's originally casual front-wheel drive idea, which may have germinated as a new car to be called the Miller, then developed and seasoned ostensibly as a new fwd Auburn line, was emerging for the passenger market in a form so unique it could only be christened to honor the man whose long-nurtured convictions had created the car.

So, upon the American automotive horizon, appeared the *Cord.*

Leaving the driveaway end of the assembly line a new car moves under its own power for the first moment as it heads out for a rigid road test before shipment.

Cord Four Door Brougham

Cord Cabriolet

9. *The Cart* Before *the Horse*

"We believe intelligent people do not want to have their intelligence insulted by wild claims and exaggerations," wrote Roy Faulkner, ". . . our modesty in presenting this new [Cord] made some other advertising, which appeared at the same time, ridiculous in its extreme."

E. L. Cord had not been completely alone when he recognized commercial possibilities for town and country in the spirited performance of fwd cars at the Indianapolis 500 Mile Classic during the mid 'twenties.

As motor annals record, another front-wheel drive American car—one that looked a lot like a slightly shorter cousin to the Cord—bowed in the press early in the summer of 1929, preceding the formal debut of the L-29 by about one month. Photographs depicted a sleek sedan with notice that the car would shortly be ready for delivery. It was called the *Ruxton.*

When Cord announced its fwd a few weeks later certain of the motoring public at large were confused. Actually, the two automobiles had been developed independently of one another. For the record, Cord was first in production and delivery by a country mile.

Ruxton, as it soon surfaced, had simply put the cart before the horse by announcing a car yet unproduced. The production Ruxton was still on the engineering drawing boards when the publicity about the car broke. Cars did not materialize for delivery till June, 1930, a year after this premature debut.

Now at your service ·· America's first Front·Wheel·Drive motor car

For several months now, there has been talk of a motor car notably new and utterly different, a car in which would be incorporated, for the first time in the history of American automotive design, the principle of the front-wheel drive, and so possess the many cardinal advantages inherent in an automobile of its kind . . . Today, this car rides the boulevards, the target of admiring eyes. It is so low that you can look over it, but none can overlook its suave grace of line, its distinctive colorings by Joseph Urban . . . It is fleet yet surefooted, restful and quiet and commanding. It carries on its radiator, as a hallmark of its excellence, the griffin of ancient heraldry, and bears, proudly, the name of Ruxton.

RUXTON

COLORINGS CREATED BY JOSEPH URBAN · EXCLUSIVE FABRICS BY SCHUMACHER

the product of New Era Motors, inc. · 17 east 45th street, New York City

THESE QUALITIES, SO COMMONLY PROMISED, ARE ACTUALLY ACHIEVED IN THE RUXTON

1. A CAR SMARTLY LOW, because a 10-inch saving in height has been effected through the elimination of the conventional rear axle and the restrictions it automatically imposes.
2. A BODY SURPRISINGLY QUIET, because there is neither chattering differential nor vibrating driveshaft to transmit noises through the body.
3. SAFETY AT HIGH SPEEDS, because the rear wheels are never trying to catch up with the front ones, and the center of gravity is unusually low.
4. RESTFUL RIDING COMFORT, because the rear axle carries but the minimum of unsprung weight, and the rear springs have only one function to perform—the perfect cradling of the body.
5. UTTER SMOOTHNESS IN TRAVEL, because the power pulls evenly from the front instead of pushing, with spasmodic jerks, from behind.
6. UNFAILING TRACTION, because pulling power is applied directly to the working wheels.
7. MAXIMUM POWER, with the minimum of loss in transmission, because this power only travels 6 inches from the 100-horsepower engine to the front axle.
8. PERCUSIVE PICKUP, because power that has such a short distance to travel is almost instantly applied, and at the lightest touch of the accelerator.
9. GASOLINE AND TIRE ECONOMY, because of perfect car balance, simplified design, the minimum of power loss, and the absence of skidding.

The story of the car without a factory begins in 1928 when an original fwd sedan was completed at the *Budd Company* in Philadelphia. William J. Muller, a venerated racing mechanic to the greats at Indianapolis, had been developing the fwd street idea for two years. As an automobile body builder to the industry Budd had produced the model unnamed on speculation. Management at Budd felt that after the striking design became known an established manufacturer would step forward and negotiate for the package rights to produce the unusual car as its own—with bodies, presumably, to be built by Budd in any event.

When not a single automobile manufacturer reacted as anticipated, a multimillionaire investor with substantial stock in Budd interests, Archie M. Andrews, moved upon the scene and vowed to see the sleek car through to production himself. He acquired the rights to the car—which had been known only as the *Question Mark*—from Budd early in 1929. It was Andrews' high hope that Hupp Corp., of which he was a major stockholder and director, could be influenced to build the car. A conservative directorate did not go along. Andrews had to look elsewhere.

Undaunted, in loose association with the Gardner automobile interests in St. Louis, he then created New Era Motors, Inc., to promote the car, which then was about to be christened the *Dolphin*. Then, suddenly, Andrews switched the name in an effort to placate one particular would-be investor.[8] Andrews adopted the hand-built, Studebaker-powered experimental car as his number one Ruxton. It was this Budd prototype that had appeared through the summer of 1929 in publicity photos taken at his Calaveras street home off Christmas Tree Lane in Altadena, California. A finished production model, or even the factory to produce one, still did not exist.

Where to build the Ruxton? That became the continuing question. Time passed. Andrews let out parts orders with independent suppliers but advised that shipping instructions were to follow. It happened that through stock control, New Era Motors had access to the Moon car assembly plant where the main production at the moment was the new Windsor White Prince. Unfortunately, this facility in St. Louis had no capability for parts manufacturing, since the Moon, Diana and Windsor were built there strictly from completed sub-assemblies shipped in from outside contractors.

After failing to arrange production at the Hupp Corporation, Andrews went to Indianapolis in October and approached the venerable Marmon company. It has been reported that here he was received with favor. Fate, in the form of Black Friday interceded. Marmon retreated.

With paper losses Andrews was still solvent and continued to infuse the Ruxton with capital and hope. He then looked about again, this time screening car makers to whom he had made loans. Among them Andrews nailed down the ultimate builders for his dream. Kissel Kar in Wisconsin presented a potential for manufacturing and machining parts that Moon had lacked. After advancing Kissel much-needed capital, the tooling for the Ruxton was set up in the Hartford (Wisconsin) plant and major components were rushed underway.

Baker-Raulang in Cleveland, the successor to the Baker and the Rauch & Lang, two veteran electric car builders turned body builders, undertook

[8]Later Mr. Ruxton failed to participate in the project at all.

Except for a common four door sedan Cord and Ruxton body types proved complementary. Cord issued a convertible coupe and convertible sedan while Ruxton promoted the open roadster and built a token number of open touring cars. Body production covered the landscape: the Edward G. Budd Mfg. Co. built the sedan; roadsters were the product of Baker-Raulang; Kissel Kar reportedly built the few tourings.

the production of a handsome roadster body to complement the four door sedan body being built by Budd in Philadelphia. Except for a few cars assembled at Kissel for early samples, parts were shipped to St. Louis for assembly at the Moon works.

The Ruxton was judged by contemporary experts to have substantial merit in engineering and design, but hard times proved the wrong moment for the car to catch hold. The personality of Archie M. Andrews may also have contributed to its downfall. The cold, unfeeling intensity he exhibited in his promotion did not always meet with the reception he sought. This may have contributed to that negative response at Hupp, and may have compounded his dealings with other companies to follow along the bumpy, circuitous road to Ruxton production.

If, supposing, Errett Cord had taken over the Question Mark from Budd in 1928, or if some other experienced automobile manufacturer had become interested, the story might have had many more chapters. As it happened, the New Era ended in bankruptcy in December, 1930—an ironic, paralyzing end brought about by a freeze of the Ruxton tooling and parts by court order at the Kissel plant when Kissel Kar went into the hands of receivers.

There was nothing anyone, even Andrews with his great dedication to the car, could do to keep the project in motion, for overnight he was figuratively, the proprietor of a dairy without access to a cow.

An estimated 500 Ruxtons had been built and their owners were pleased with the car. About half were sedans, and the other half, though largely roadsters, also was comprised of a few touring cars and at least one elegant town car.

The rise and fall of the Ruxton had proved to be a sad commentary on the state of the American market in 1929-1930. But more astute car makers, applying greater perspective to their new products, were to do better. One of them was the Auburn Automobile Company.

A graphic mechanical description of the Ruxton, as it was originally published in the Radco Automotive Review appears overleaf.

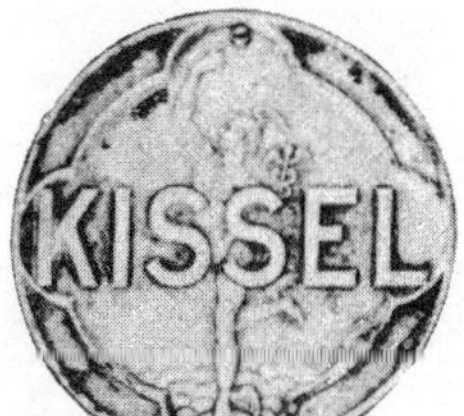

Ruxton Front Drive Unique

The Ruxton five-passenger sedan. Note the absence of running boards

An unusual amount of clearance in the front compartment is made possible by moving the hand brake forward on the left side and extending the gear shift lever through the dash

With a five-passenger sedan and sport model roadster already completed as stock models, New Era Motors, Inc., manufacturers of the Ruxton front-wheel drive automobile, announce improvements which have been made over the earlier models and have released complete details of design and construction principles.

The Ruxton has a 130-in. wheelbase with a road clearance of 10 in. on all models, including the present five-passenger sedan, which has been in service for several weeks. The chassis frame is 6 in. deep, 5-32 in. in thickness and is supported by nine cross members made possible by the front-wheel drive, which allows rigid re-enforcing from the front to the rear of the frame. Eight of the cross members are of the channel type and one is tubular. The entire frame and all cross members are of carbon steel.

Both axles are of molybdenum steel, the rear of tubular construction and the front of I-beam. The cars are equipped with six Budd disc wheels, the extras carried in fender wells on each side of the car. The tires are full balloon, 31 by 6.00.

Semi-elliptic springs of chrome vanadium steel are used on both front and rear. The front springs, 37 by 2 in., are shackled at the front end, and the rear springs, 55 by 2, are shackled at the rear.

Houdaille hydraulic shock absorbers are included, both in front and rear. The fenders are one-piece, heavy metal construction, with wells in the front pair to carry the extra wheels. On account of the low-hanging body, no running boards have been used. Leather mud splashers are used on all fenders, however.

Four-wheel hydraulic brakes of Lockheed manufacture, are standard equipment. The rear brake shoes may be given extra and separate control through a hand brake situated at the left side of the driver; 15-inch drums are used on all four wheels.

Motor

The motor of Continental manufacture is an 8-cylinder high compression, L-head cast en bloc in line with a removable head. It has a 3-inch bore, a 4¾-in. stroke and a total displacement of 268-60 cubic inches. The power plant develops in excess of 100 h.p. The S. A. E. rating is 28.80. The engine is suspended at four points. The two front supports are rigid to the frame, while the two rear supports are resilient rubber cushion mountings.

The pistons are Nelson Bohnalite, three-ring design and fitted with one

SPECIFICATIONS (Condensed)

Power

Engine—Eight-cylinder, L-head, cast en block and in line; removable head; 3-in. bore, 4¾-in. stroke. Piston displacement, 268 - 60 cubic inches. Horsepower, 28.80 (S.A.E. rating), but actually develops in excess of 100. Improved 4-point suspension mounted in rubber. High compression cylinder head. Manifold heat control.

Crankshaft — Counter - balanced. Five bronze-backed, babbitt-lined bearings. With Lanchester vibration damper.

Pistons—Nelson Bohnalite. Three rings, one oil return.

Connecting Rods—Drop-forged steel; babbitt bearings bonded to rods.

Valves—Exhaust, heat - resisting alloy steel. Intake nickel-chrome steel.

Camshaft—Driven by silent chain.

Chassis

Wheelbase — 130-in. on all models. Frame, 6 in. deep, 5-32 in. thick. Nine cross members, eight channel, one tubular. All frame members and cross members of carbon steel.

Axles—Rear, tubular. Front, I-beam. Both of molybdenum steel.

Drive—Drive, to front axle. All gears chrome steel.

Springs—Chrome-vanadium steel, semi-elliptic. Front 37 by 2 in.; rear, 55 by 2 in. Houdaille hydraulic shock absorbers, front and rear.

Wheels—Disc wheels by Budd. Two extra wheels standard equipment, and carried on each side.

Tires—Full balloon; 31 by 6.00.

Fenders—One-piece, heavy metal construction. Wells in front fenders for carrying spare wheels. No running boards, but fenders fitted with leather splash guards all-round.

Lubrication

Full pressure oiling, driven by gear pump to all main, connecting rod and camshaft bearings and valve mechanism. Oil filter, Crankcase, 8 quarts.

Fuel

Engine-driven fuel pump. Cárburetor, Zenith, dual type.

Controls

Gear Shift—Standard, three forward and one reverse. Operated by means of a unique hand grip, conveniently and accessibly located on instrument panel, instead of through the conventional gear-shifting lever.

Brakes—Lockheed hydraulic service Brakes, 15-in drums on all four wheels. Hand brake to both rear wheels, with lever at left of driver.

Steering—Gemmer roller type.

oil ring. The connecting rods are drop-forged bonded with babbitted bearings. The camshaft is driven by a silent chain. The exhaust valves are of heat-resisting alloy steel and the inlet valves are of nickel chrome steel.

The motor carries a full pressure oiling system driven by a gear pump to all main, connecting rods and crankshaft bearings and valve mechanisms. The crankcase capacity is eight quarts. An oil filter is stock equipment. Gasoline is supplied to the carburetor by means of a fuel pump with a 16-gallon fuel tank in the rear. Additional stock equipment includes a gasoline filter and an air cleaner. The carburetor is a Zenith 1¼ in. dual type.

Transmission

ONE of the problems confronting engineers in the design of front-drive automobiles where an eight in-line motor is used is the extreme distance from the dash to the front axle made necessary by mounting the clutch transmission and differential assembly at the front. The problem was solved in an unique way by Ruxton by combining the transmission and differential assembly as shown in the illustration.

View of the right front showing the spring suspension and the shape of the carrying member of the front axle

The transmission gears are divided into two sections, one ahead of the differential assembly and one to the rear. The worm of the final drive is mounted between the sections on the main shaft, which permits of a direct drive from the clutch assembly when in high gear. So far as the actual transmission is concerned, it varies but slightly from the conventional three speed type save for changes noted.

The Ruxton Transmission

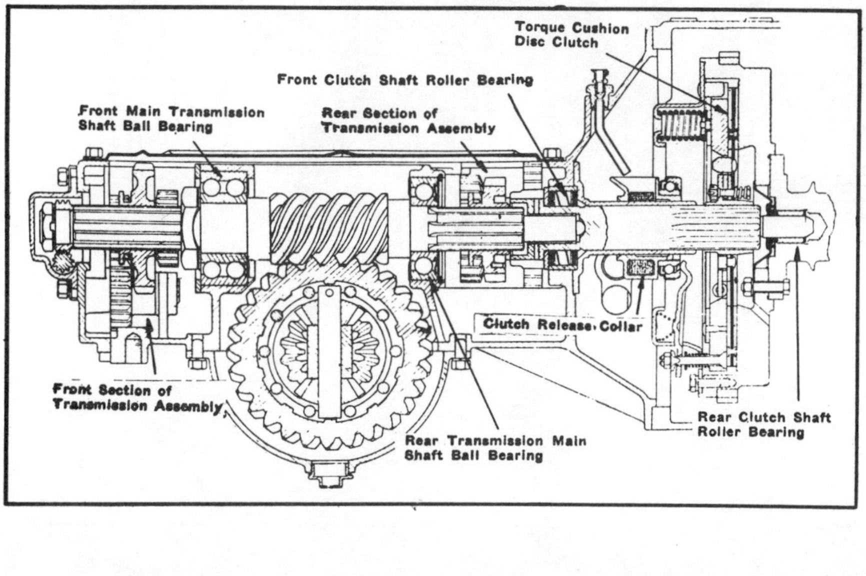

Another interesting feature which varies from conventional design in the transmission is the mounting of the gear clusters. Instead of the clusters being mounted one above the other, the arrangement of the transmission and differential within the same housing makes it necessary to mount the gear clusters on parallel shafts in a horizontal plane. The reason for this is obvious since there is no room below for the secondary.

Instead of the full bell type housing common in the rear wheel drive cars, a flat rectangular chamber split in the center by the driving axle is used. The lower half, however, is in a separate cylindrical housing. Access to the upper unit is gained through a top plate held in place by lag screws.

10. For the Love of Cars

The car I designed was deliberately different—just as the little flivver I built was different. It is the only way to win attention if you can't be big.

In motor car annals the ideas and actions of one man never emulated more exactly the aspirations of the original Horatio Alger figure than those of Errett Lobban Cord. Here was a rural boy making good at practically all he elected to tackle, while the flair for novelty inherent in the engineering features and design of his automotive products displayed to the world what great fun he was having in the process.

Through thick and thin his accomplishments seemed the very epitomy of what every man wished he could emulate. It came easily for most other young men to identify with Cord, for his interest in cars had begun and was sustained as informally as their own. He belonged to that generation who had grown up as the automobile itself was growing up. Contemporaries could relate quickly to Cord's prosaic, quite unspectacular principle: *do with what you have.*

Errett Cord began life in Warrensburg, Missouri, in 1894. His father was a Scotch grocer. The family moved to Los Angeles when he was young and there he graduated from high school. Like every mechanically-minded boy he liked to tinker with automobiles. Young Cord also had a natural sense of form and color. Legend has it that at seventeen he bought a Model T Ford for a few dollars, rebuilt its engine, constructed a rakish speedster body—and sold it to a man in Hollywood for a sizeable profit. The next year he bought, remodeled and sold a score of similar cars, averaging a profit of $500 each.

Owning a car was still a major excitement in the second decade of this century. While the Mercer Raceabout and the Stutz Bearcat were apples of every young man's eye the ubiquitous Ford chassis — which accounted for 50% of the motor industry's production — became the substitute dictated by reality. To this scene young Cord brought a knowing hand, fine esthetic capacity and keen commercial sense.

Errett Cord's Model T Ford custom conversions precursed a spreading speedster craze. Country roads everywhere became ablaze with homemade speedsters. A few years later a whole field of body builders would propose a "new" car for the price of a rakish do-it-yourself body kit. Making Model T look like something other than what it really was had become big business.

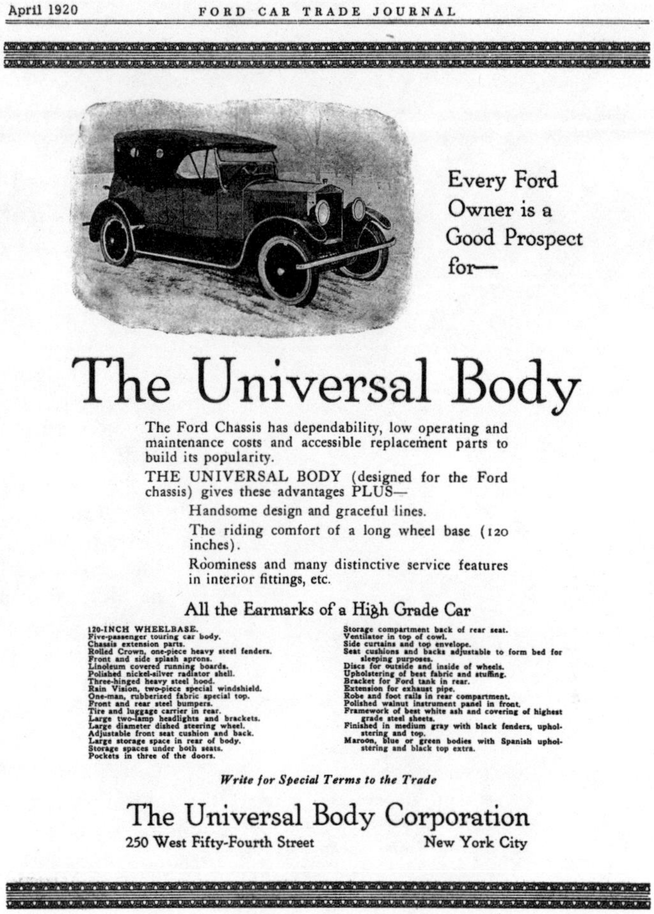

By the 'twenties fashion's top limit was well established in the hands of the imported Rolls-Royce. Shamelessly body builders paid tribute to this supremacy by offering a Rolls-type radiator for the lowly Ford. Roamer and other car makers would copy the same marque for their full lines.

The capital assembled from these car deals was invested in a service station and garage. He continued to make deals on the side. As a barnstorming race driver and race mechanic, through dabbling continuously in used cars, in every phase from rental to stage lines, he advanced through the college of hard knocks. Cord was a speedy learner in this trade school of trial and error in which nothing was sacred.

After he lost all he had made, and more besides, on a trucking line servicing mines in Death Valley and parts of Arizona, Errett Cord packed up his young family and decided to try his lot in the middle west.

In a few years to come even the sky would not be the limit.

11. *Individualize and Sell*

What satisfied yesterday seems mediocre today.

Cord moved to Chicago, arriving with his wife and two tiny sons the day after Thanksgiving, in 1919. With his experience selling Model T speedsters and other special interest cars having sharpened his wits as a salesman he applied at one of Chicago's best known automobile distributors. He was turned down.

"Cord didn't want just to sell automobiles. He wanted to represent this one particular car—the Moon—because he believed in it and because he had looked a long way ahead," reported *Forbes* magazine of an interview with Cord.

" 'A few days later the man who turned me down went to Florida. Without saying a word about my previous experience, I applied for the same position, but this time I saw the sales manager. He hired me. When the boss came back from Florida I was second high man on the list, so he didn't fire me.'

"In going to the sales manager, after the owner of the agency had turned him down, Cord made a move that would prove characteristic in days to follow. He had refused to stop trying when everything seemed against him, and he won out."

Cord individualized the Moons with special paint and extra fittings like spot lights and lower tops. He became sales manager of the agency within the season. He was 25. Continuing the tactic he originally had used on old Fords Cord went on, in the next several years, to sell more Moons than anyone alse ever had. The stake he built up from this supersalesmanship was applied to buy into the agency, which then had secured the entire Illinois and Wisconsin territory. His reputation as a merchandiser spread through the motor industry.

When E. L. Cord arrived on the scene at Moon the company had just adopted the gothic radiator line of the R-R. Under Cord it was to become the largest selling of production cars flattering the Rolls. Except for its commanding appearance the Moon was a somewhat ordinary "assembled" car from St. Louis.

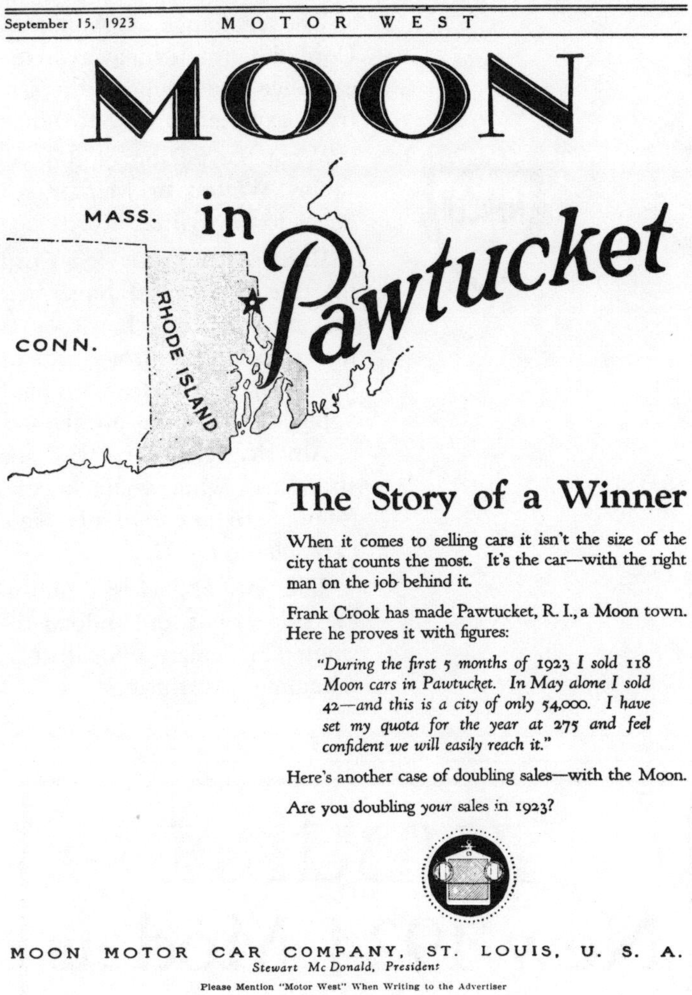

The momentum E. L. Cord had brought to the Moon company through his super-selling of this product was continued by the organization after he had moved to Auburn. A Cord charisma had infiltrated even the Moon company's periodical advertising. In the fall of 1925, perhaps in part to counter Cord's favorable strides up at Auburn, the Moon company began a fresh try for the gold ring with the introduction of a companion car called the Diana — featuring a radiator unabashedly inspired by the great Belgian Minerva.

By now E. L. Cord had set his sights on real money. In looking around he had a chance to talk with Ralph Austin Bard, whose bank controlled the little Auburn Automobile Company, a pioneer but obscure firm then mired in debt and strapped with obsolete inventory.

Bard had heard of Cord's fantastic record with the Moon and together they went out to take a tour of Auburn. Down from Chicago on the first inspection Cord looked over the former Eckhart Carriage Works that served as a part of Auburn's factory only to laugh out loud, it has been reported, at every decrepid detail.

Sales were needed most. But the public acceptance of the product had so wained and cost efficiency in production was so unknown that the situation was clearly hopeless. With its warehouses brimming with spectacularly dull, brand new leftover models Auburn had only produced 175 new cars for 1923. Pricing had been about $200 above the Buick in the same specification class. The company needed only to lie down to be dead. And, beyond those individuals directly involved, no one cared.

Auburn had never basked in the sunshine of grand repute like the *Winton* or the *Mercer*—superior automobiles then also in their final days —for it had never risen above being "just another car".

The challenge at Auburn would have turned other men away. E. L. Cord did not turn away. He sensed means by which he could bring acceptance and credit to the sadly lacking Auburn operation. He even knew from experience how to make the public clamor for the product.

What the person of this young man might have done at the helm of a failing Winton or Mercer is a story that will never be told, for it was never to be written. Cord was ready to cast his lot with the senile Auburn.

Bard readily provided Cord with the free hand he had asked for—and the title General Manager went along with it. Cord's one stipulation was that he would work without salary, providing he was allowed an opportunity to buy control—at a price which would let the bankers out with a profit—*if* he put the company back on its feet. The formula that would apply: 20% of the profits and options on the stock at $20.

American industry was about to witness the first grand scale demonstration of what would become the secret of Cord's dynamic successes to follow: *An uncommonly vigorous capacity for concentrating every effort to reach a set goal.*

The only appeal in Auburn's existing product was *price.* So Cord made the price right and unloaded some hundreds of the leftover models on a single car dealer, who, in turn, was able to push the cars to the public at ridiculously low prices.

September 15, 1923 — MOTOR WEST — Page 11

AUBURN

New 1924 Models

New Low Prices

A Wonderful Dealer Opportunity

The new 1924 Auburn Line is attracting new buyers—just as it won Auburn distributors who viewed it several weeks ago. Reports from various parts of the country point to record-making increases in sales. Auburn is truly going strong!

There is something contagious about enthusiasm. And especially when founded upon an honest product, honestly made, rightly priced and generally appreciated.

New sales opportunities and larger profits are being opened up by the new 1924 line of Auburns. New values in automobiles are established. The Auburn Franchise is exceptional!

To those dealers who are looking ahead, Auburn offers outstanding advantages. Each Franchise is fully protected, written for dealers as well as the factory, and carries intensive factory co-operation far out of the ordinary.

Look over the prices below and write us for complete information.

Auburn Automobile Company
Auburn, Ind.

	OLD PRICE	NEW PRICE
6-43 Touring	$1165	$1095
6-43 Sport	New	$1325
6-43 Touring Coupe	$1535	$1495
6-43 Sedan	New	$1595

	OLD PRICE	NEW PRICE
6-63 Touring	$1725	$1595
6-63 Sport	$1985	$1850
6-63 Sedan	New	$2345

All prices f. o. b. Auburn

AUBURN ESTABLISHED 1900

Please Mention "Motor West" When Writing to the Advertiser

"There is something contagious about enthusiasm" observed one of E. L. Cord's early ads (preparing for a clean-up sale of pre-Cord design Auburn models). The same ad foreshadowed a policy that would become a benchmark of Cord advertising: "honest product, honestly made, rightly priced". By the fall of 1923 E. L. Cord was well on his way to certain renown.

Then, at just the right moment, he seemed to call to mind one of Henry Ford's often trumpeted tenets for commercial success: *when a product doesn't sell, improve it and lower the price*. Once again Cord called upon his customizing proclivities and added interest to the sub-assemblies on hand with sporty new colors, lower tops and other little alterations readily fabricated for more appeal. The new cars were then assembled and dumped into the market at more fire sale prices. In effect, Cord scrapped the existing inventory with a promotional flair.

About this time Cord also persuaded the Lycoming people to begin work on a straight-eight engine. He didn't believe that an automobile with a straight-eight engine had to be an expensive car as it traditionally had been.

Under his stewardship Cord's new Auburn began to roll ahead almost immediately. There was no massive overhead staff through which motion might have been lost. Cord required no board for decision making. He knew what he wanted and he knew how to give the orders that would bring results.

There was an ingenious aspect to this quick, impulsive man. Once asked where he was going, and what he was headed for, Cord was startled.

"It seems to me every fellow starts off wanting the same things. We want something for our stomachs, and a roof over our heads. We want to take care of our children. So I want to make money, and I want to have some fun."

Our aim is to originate and build improved, fine cars better than any cars have ever been built before, and sell them for a great deal less than commensurate quality cars have ever been sold before.

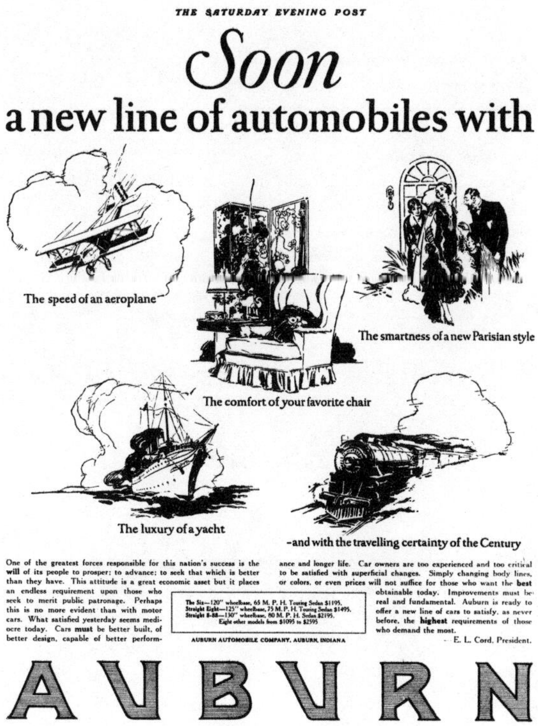

12. *For an Indelible Identity*

Be different if you can't be biggest.

It seemed unlikely that with all of his vigor and profanity Cord could turn Auburn, a very weak sister of the motor industry, around. But he threw himself at his job with the energy of a supercharged turbine. He brought about operating economies and stepped up plant efficiency.

His whiz bang disposal of the unsold Auburn backlog resulted in a reported half million dollars to go toward paying the company's debts and finance the development of a new model without further borrowing.

Into the new model went fresh ideas of weight, power, lines and speed —leaving their mark on every Auburn to be built thereafter. Cord sought and secured a distinguishing design note to incorporate into the new Auburn. The streamer-stripe molding he decided upon was the catchy sort of thing that would set small boys—and some not so small—straight about Auburns for ever after.

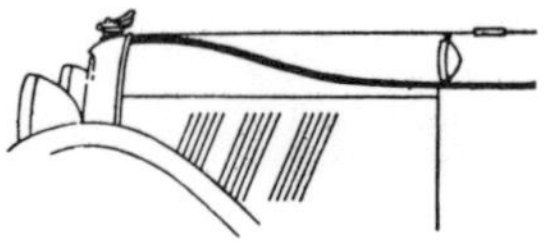

Legend has it that Cord paid an unknown designer $50 for the idea. The demarcative line keynoted again Cord's youthful verve for something different. A recurring sense of the unusual within the frame of good taste would later assure public recognition for each of his motor enterprises to come.

Cord's tuning of the Auburn company for a new model, while superselling a lackluster existing inventory to clear the decks and the air, was so expeditiously handled that his success became big industry news. In the first year of his management, 1924, Auburn made 2,226 cars and the deficit was reduced to negligible bounds. In 1926, the profit was appreciable. In 1927, he put the stock on a four dollar dividend basis plus eight per cent in stock.

Cord's master hand personally touched all phases of product development. To promote the finished automobile he wrote his own ads, applying an underlying theme of forthright logic. Some were classic.

As it became increasingly apparent within the industry that young Cord's tenure at Auburn was miraculously guiding the enterprise, from a once certain grave into a position of unquestioned repute, Wall Street became entranced. The rise of E. L. Cord was to be the American success story of the day.

LONG BEACH PRESS-TELEGRAM — SUNDAY, FEBRUARY 20, 1927

Auburn Automobile Company's Earnings Nearly One Million

Net earnings of the Auburn Automobile Company for the year ended December 31, 1926, after all deductions, including provisions for Federal income taxes, were $949,132, or the equivalent of $11.17 a share on the 84,929 shares of stock outstanding, a record year in the company's history.

Net of $949,132 for last year compares with net of $755,685 in the year ended December 31, 1925, when per share earnings were only $8.89, figured on the present capitalization.

The year brought about great improvement in Auburn's already strong financial position, current assets as of December 31 last totaling $4,714,571, as against total current liabilities of $838,-172, more than doubling working capital. More than half of the latter item was represented by cash, which totaled $2,360,953.

It Is Not What You HAVE But What You DO With It!

South America has larger water falls than Niagara. But harnessed Niagara works for homes and industries. Acres of buildings, miles of machinery and even mountains of money can give an automobile factory impressive SIZE but still not give the public the BEST car. It all depends upon the USE made of them. Measured by its physical properties and financial success, Auburn today is one of the "big" automobile companies. Just because Auburn has acquired control of several important parts companies, and in other ways strengthened its position, Auburn will not advertise that Auburn is NOT an assembled car. The fact is that EVERY automobile is more or less "assembled". HOW much it is assembled is immaterial. Important is, how GOOD a car is it for the money? Auburn will make its own parts when it means a better finished product. Auburn will continue to buy from parts-specialists when THAT is better business. Auburn pledges the public to USE its increased SIZE to continue to lead in the economical manufacture of BETTER motor cars.

E. L. Cord
President
Auburn Automobile Co.

YOUR NEXT CAR
AUBURN
POWERED BY LYCOMING

6-66 Roadster $1095; 6-66 Sport Sedan $1195; 6-66 Cabriolet $1295; 6-66 Sedan $1295; 8-77 Roadster $1395; 8-77 Sport Sedan $1495; 8-77 Cabriolet $1595; 8-77 Sedan $1695; 8-88 Roadster $1995; 8-88 Sport Sedan $2095; 8-88 Cabriolet $2095; 8-88 Sedan $2195; 8-88 7-Passenger Sedan $2595. Freight, Tax & Equipment Extra

AUBURN AUTOMOBILE COMPANY, AUBURN, INDIANA

13. *Forging an Empire*

Auburn's policy is to make dealers, not break them, the company that makes its dealers makes itself.

While the public held him in awe, and jealous competitors cursed him, Cord privately admired those automotive pioneers who had shaped the American industry from scratch in the days of his own childhood. He held in special esteem the monumental movements of that flamboyant visionary, William C. Durant, who created General Motors, only to lose control a few years later. The story is well known how Durant then set out to bring to prominence in the industry a newcomer named *Chevrolet,* with which, in new merger with General Motors, he managed, by stock exchange, to assume his old driver's seat at GM all over again.

After the initial surge of effort to restore solvency in the mid-'twenties Cord hadn't been preoccupied with Auburn. He began lining up suppliers within the fold and creating an empire like a young Durant.

With the rise of Detroit as the motor center pioneer Indiana automobile builders and their suppliers had found some traditional sources of credit turning thumbs down. The suppliers were struggling through hard times.

A full reproduction of the detailed 1929 prospectus for the Auburn Automobile Company, issued by A. B. Leach, members of the New York Stock Exchange, begins on the next page.

When Auburn began to breathe anew with a steady pulse these subcontractors were attracted to the Auburn aura, Auburn stock then began to become a strong trader in the market.

Like Bill Durant, who had brought Oldsmobile, Buick and Cadillac together, Cord held a fine commercial appreciation for automotive names already seasoned and respected by the public. Soon he brought the revered racing car engine builder Fred Duesenberg into the fold. Later he arranged to use the famous front-wheel-drive advocate Harry A. Miller's patents for his Cord.

Shortly after acquiring Duesenberg, Inc., which dominated the market in its lofty price class, Cord added the Lycoming Company which produced his motors, and the Spencer Heating Company, a boiler maker. The Stinson Aircraft Corporation, followed, along with the Central Manufacturing and Limousine Body companies, both of which served Auburn.

Cord had sought a factory with assembly line capabilities in the grand sense. He found it in Connersville, Indiana. It was the complex of the Lexington Motor Company, formed in 1920 to build the *Minute-Man Six,* and later used to make the grand, short-lived *McFarlan.*

When he acquired this 82 acre complex in 1927 Cord secured a one story assembly building nine hundred feet long. After a rebuilding program costing two million dollars the facility was comprised of 20 modern buildings arranged so all materials moved through the entire factory in a regular forward flow. A million and a half square feet of floorspace was set up for a production of bodies and assemblies for 250 completed cars a day.

Cord observed in one of his periodical advertisements that the purchase of an automobile was an investment in machinery to manufacture transportation, and that *no salesman can 'talk' quality into a car that has not had quality built into it.* Production reached 14,517 for 1927.

THE INSIDE STORY OF AUBURN

AUBURN
ESTABLISHED 1900

A. B. LEACH & CO., INC.
NEW YORK CHICAGO
SAN FRANCISCO

E. L. CORD, *President*

"Success is obligatory."

"The only limitation of a business in America is the limitation of the men running it."

"When you buy a motor car, you are buying machinery to manufacture transportation."

"I believe the passport to public patronage is the value of the *car itself.* That is why Auburn says 'compare and drive the Auburn and if the car does not sell itself, you will not be asked to buy."

"Success is not a prize to be won, for what has been done, as much as a demonstration of ability to do more."

"No salesman can 'talk' quality into a car that has not been built into it."

"Brains are the most important ingredient in a motor."

"A company's *product* can be no better than its *policy.*"

"A business must *succeed* or it cannot *serve.*"

"It is not necessary to change a car radically if it is built right."

"The car-builder is the custodian of the car-owner's investment, and he should do nothing to jeopardize or depreciate the owner's investment."

"Only those survive who continue to deserve to."

"Auburn's policy is to make dealers, not break them."

"The company that makes its dealers makes itself."

—E. L. Cord.

One of the Fastest Growing Automobile Companies in America

AUBURN AUTOMOBILE COMPANY

- **AUBURN** INDIANA **PLANT**
- **CONNERSVILLE** INDIANA **PLANT**

LYCOMING MANUFACTURING CO.
WILLIAMSPORT, PA.

- **SPENCER HEATER CO.**
  WILLIAMSPORT, PA.

DUESENBERG, INC.
INDIANAPOLIS, IND.

LIMOUSINE BODY COMPANY
KALAMAZOO, MICH.

CENTRAL MANUFACTURING COMPANY
CONNERSVILLE, IND.

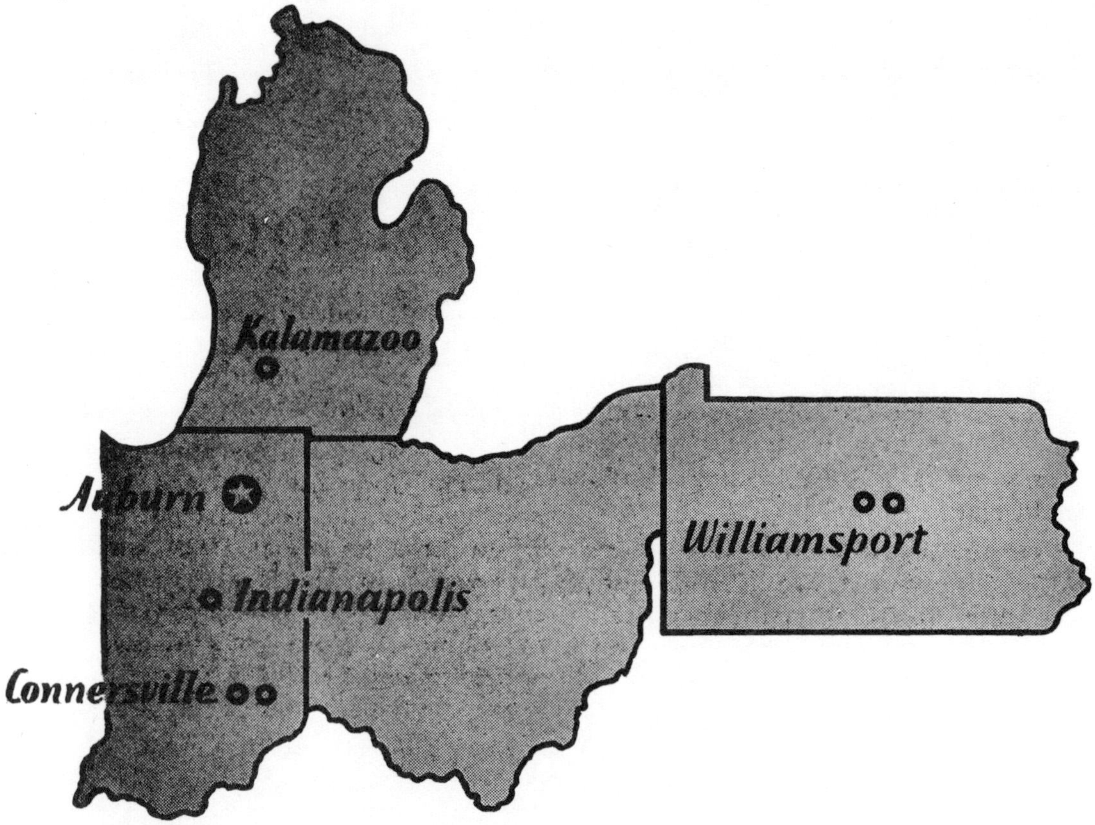

A SELF-CONTAINED
AUTOMOBILE MANUFACTURING
ORGANIZATION

The First Auburn Automobile

LONG before the majority of today's automobile owners were born, the seeds for Auburn's growth were planted. The Company's present solid foundation was laid by the Eckert Brothers in 1876, when they opened their carriage and wagon shop at Auburn, Indiana.

The first Auburn Automobile was built in 1900. Since then, 1600 different makes, built by about 600 manufacturers, have been on the market. There were approximately 147 makes in 1902, 84 in 1920, while today there are only about 27. Auburn is one of the very few names known to the automobile trade continuously since 1900.

Before Mr. Cord became connected with the Company in 1924, Auburn's best production year barely exceeded 5,000 cars. As late as 1924, only 2600 cars were built. Due largely to Mr. Cord's energy and vision which paved the way for Auburn's rapid growth, production approximated 14,700 cars in 1928.

This is the Auburn car that was being marketed when E. L. Cord joined the Auburn organization.

Below is the first Auburn model introduced by Mr. Cord. It embodied many new features such as the first real streamline stock car, metal side quarters, and a body lower by 8 inches. He also championed long wheel base (in fact 130 inches) when most manufacturers were pushing models of 115 inches. This car was a pioneer in the Straight Eight field—only three other manufacturers had yet introduced Straight Eights. The previous Auburn models had a $1250 reputation. Mr. Cord's first model listed at $2350, and 5600 of them were sold in 1925, compared with 2600 cars sold in 1924.

THE AUBURN INDIANA PLANT

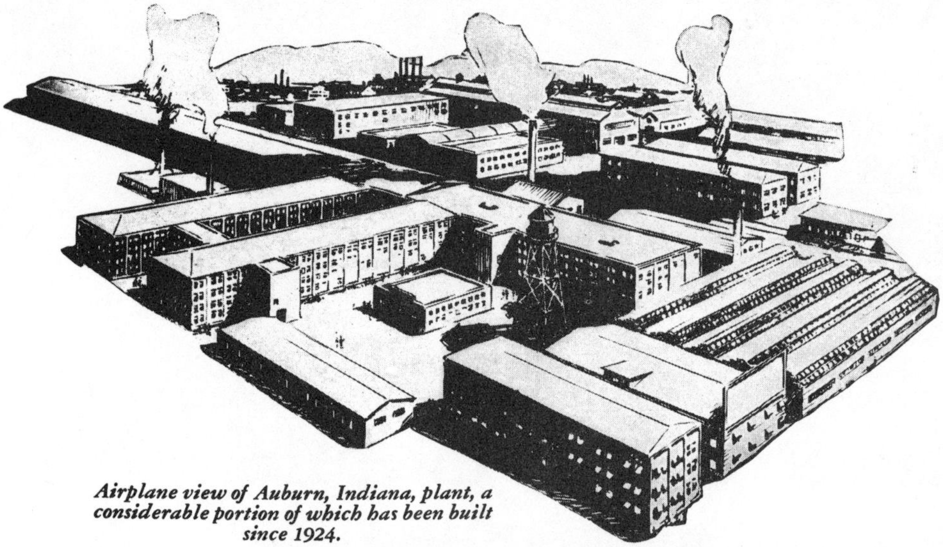

Airplane view of Auburn, Indiana, plant, a considerable portion of which has been built since 1924.

The beginning of an automobile, four hours and 45 minutes before the completed car leaves the end of the assembly line.

Riveting running board hangers to frame.

Engines as they arrive from Lycoming.

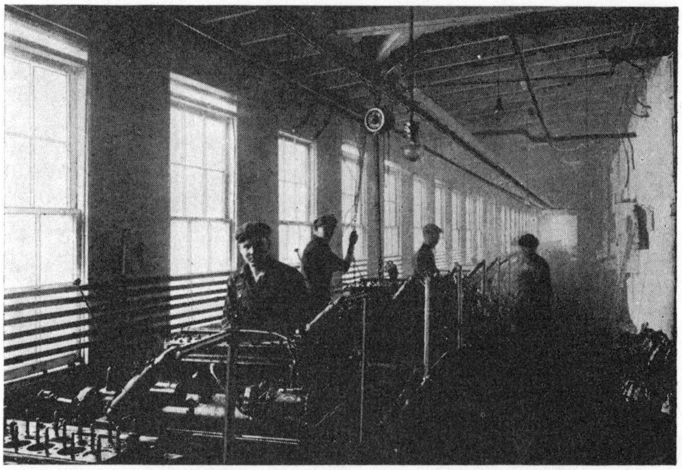

Engines receiving final block test requiring 7 hours' continuous running under load.

Bodies receiving first rub-down preparatory to applying filler coat.

One of the two final assembly lines where chasses receive all parts except bodies.

All production is handled by the most up-to-date methods, equipment, and labor saving devices. In 1924, there was only one assembly line and no automatic conveyors—today there are two final assembly lines and the entire plant operates on schedule required by over two miles of automatic conveyors.

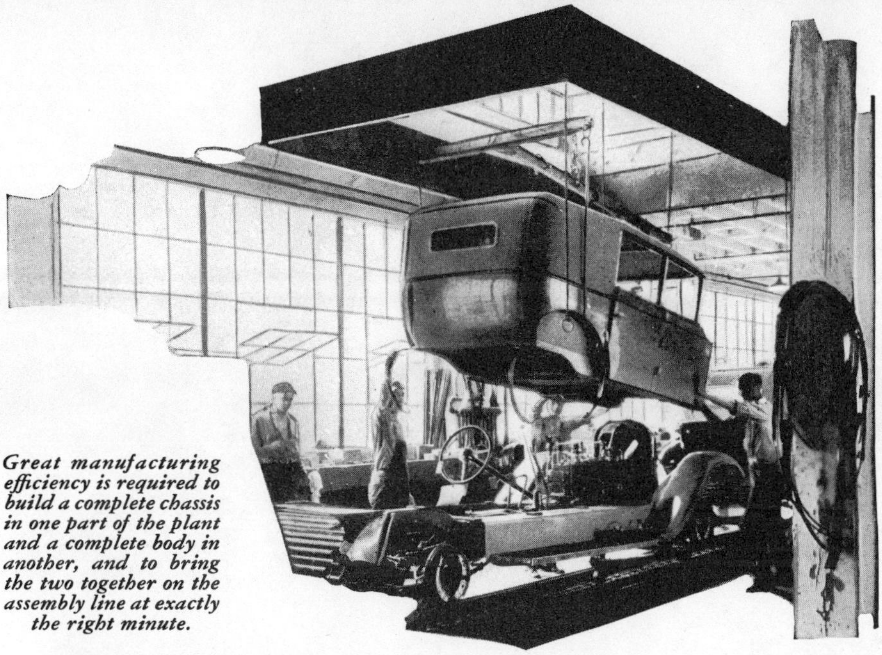

Great manufacturing efficiency is required to build a complete chassis in one part of the plant and a complete body in another, and to bring the two together on the assembly line at exactly the right minute.

HARRY DUNN
Purchasing Department

For 1929, Auburn has introduced a complete new series of Sixes and Straight Eights that authoritative trade publications credit with being exceptional values at unusually low prices.

E.O. PENRY
Production Department

The model 120 Sedan has 130-inch wheel base and 125 h. p., Lycoming Motor, Bijur Chassis lubrication, four internal expanding hydraulic brakes and the strongest frame under any car. Price, $1895.

The 120 Speedster. A fast sport model and duplicate of strictly stock car holding many world's records. Price, $1895.

Auburn was the first to introduce the custom type of convertible Phaeton Sedan as a production model. Its success was so pronounced in 1928 that it was impossible to fill all the orders, although this is Auburn's highest priced model. Model 120 above, 130-inch wheel base and 125 h. p. Price, $2095.

The model 8-90 four door Sport Sedan for $1395 puts this 125-inch wheel base Straight Eight under the price of the majority of the better Sixes. It has Bijur chassis lubrication, hydraulic brakes and hydraulic shock absorbers.

With 120-inch wheel base, 60 h. p. and 7-inch frame, this is claimed to be the longest, strongest, roomiest car in the market under $1000.

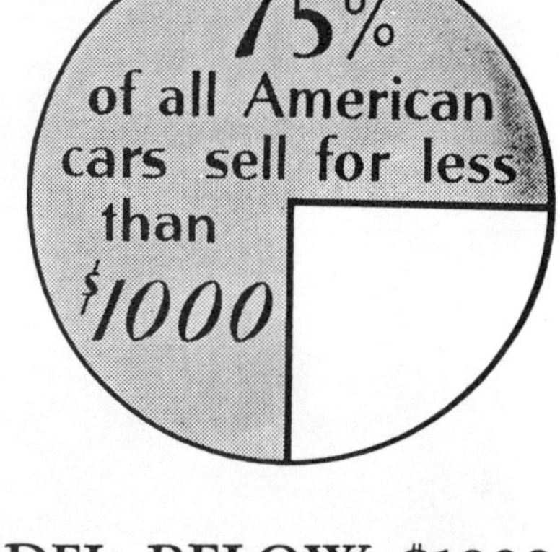

AUBURN NOW ENTERS MARKET WITH A MODEL BELOW $1000

THE CONNERSVILLE PLANT

Above—Interior view of new body assembly building, 796 feet in length. Below—On the drafting boards.

B. & O. Railroad grading crew laying 1½ miles of spur track to serve the plant. Two other railroad connections enter the other end of the property.

The Connersville property is one of the best arranged and equipped plants for economical production in the industry. It was originally designed with a view to future expansion without interrupting production.

A part of metal stamping department in the body plant.

Applying and soldering metal.

Wooden frame-work ready for the metal covering.

Metal finishing department.

Door hanging and final assembly prior to receiving priming coat.

Ellis W. Ryan, Vice President, in charge of operations at Connersville.

Final Paint and Trim Line. Bodies, entering one end of building in the primed state, are carried 1⅜ miles on automatic conveyors through the successive steps of rubbing down, filling, drying ovens, final lacquer, final rubbing and interior and exterior trim. After being completely finished, they are taken overhead on another conveyor to the point of assembly on the final chassis assembly line.

LYCOMING MANUFACTURING CO.

Airplane view of machine shops.

JOHN H. McCORMICK
Pres. and General Mgr.

W. H. BEAL
Vice-Pres. and Sales Mgr.

This Company, controlled by Auburn since 1927, is the second largest exclusive manufacturer of automotive power plants in the world. Numbered among its most important customers (in addition to Auburn) are: International Harvester Company; Gardner Motor Car Company; Stewart Manufacturing Company (manufacturers of Stewart Trucks); Republic Truck Company; Henney Motor Company; John Deere & Co.; Crossley, Ltd. (English subsidiary of Willys Overland); St. Didier S. A., Paris, France; Locomobile Co. of America; Elcar Motor Car Co.; K. Hattori & Co., Tokyo, Japan. The Plant is equipped throughout with the most modern and up-to-date machine tool equipment. Exceptionally able management of long experience in motor production is in charge.

Motor block castings passing through milling machines.

Multiple spindle drills doing 37 boring and tapping operations at once.

Motor block castings being bored for crank, cam and generator bearings in one operation.

Final motor assembly line.

Expert machinist balancing crankshaft.

After engines are block-tested for 8 hours under load, they are torn down, examined and reassembled before shipment.

{Left} View of cupolas from charging platform. Samples of each "heat" are taken for chemical and physical tests to insure uniformity of castings.

Finished moulds ready for pouring.

Hand ladles are used for pouring small castings.

Electric cranes operating on overhead tracks carry the molten metal in large ladles from cupolas to core boxes on foundry floor.

The Finished Product. A crank case casting being inspected before being sent to machine shops.

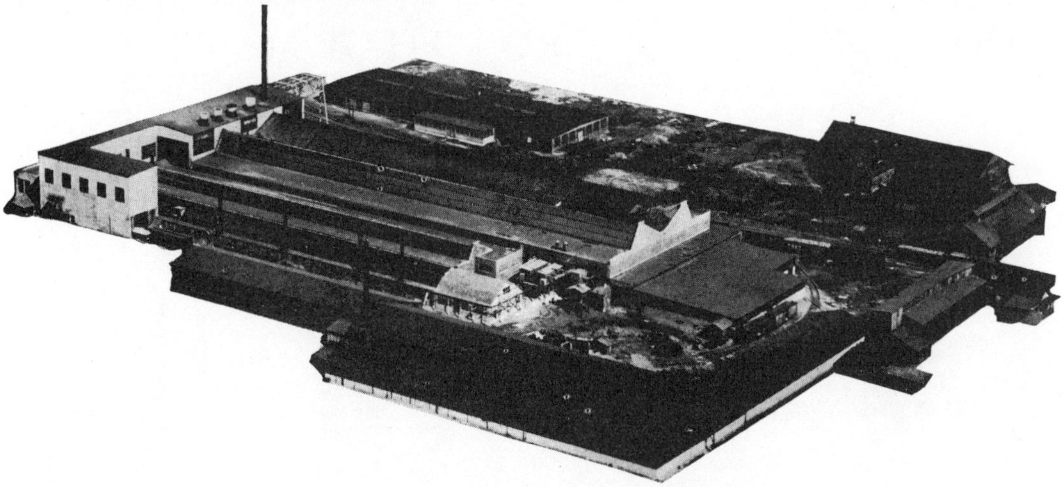

Airplane View of Foundry

Equipped throughout with mechanical conveyors, the Lycoming Foundry is one of the most modern plants of its kind in America. With a capacity of 250 tons each 10 hours, the entire operation is mechanical except in a few isolated instances. Capacity operations, with many departments running over time, have been carried on for the past several months.

1924

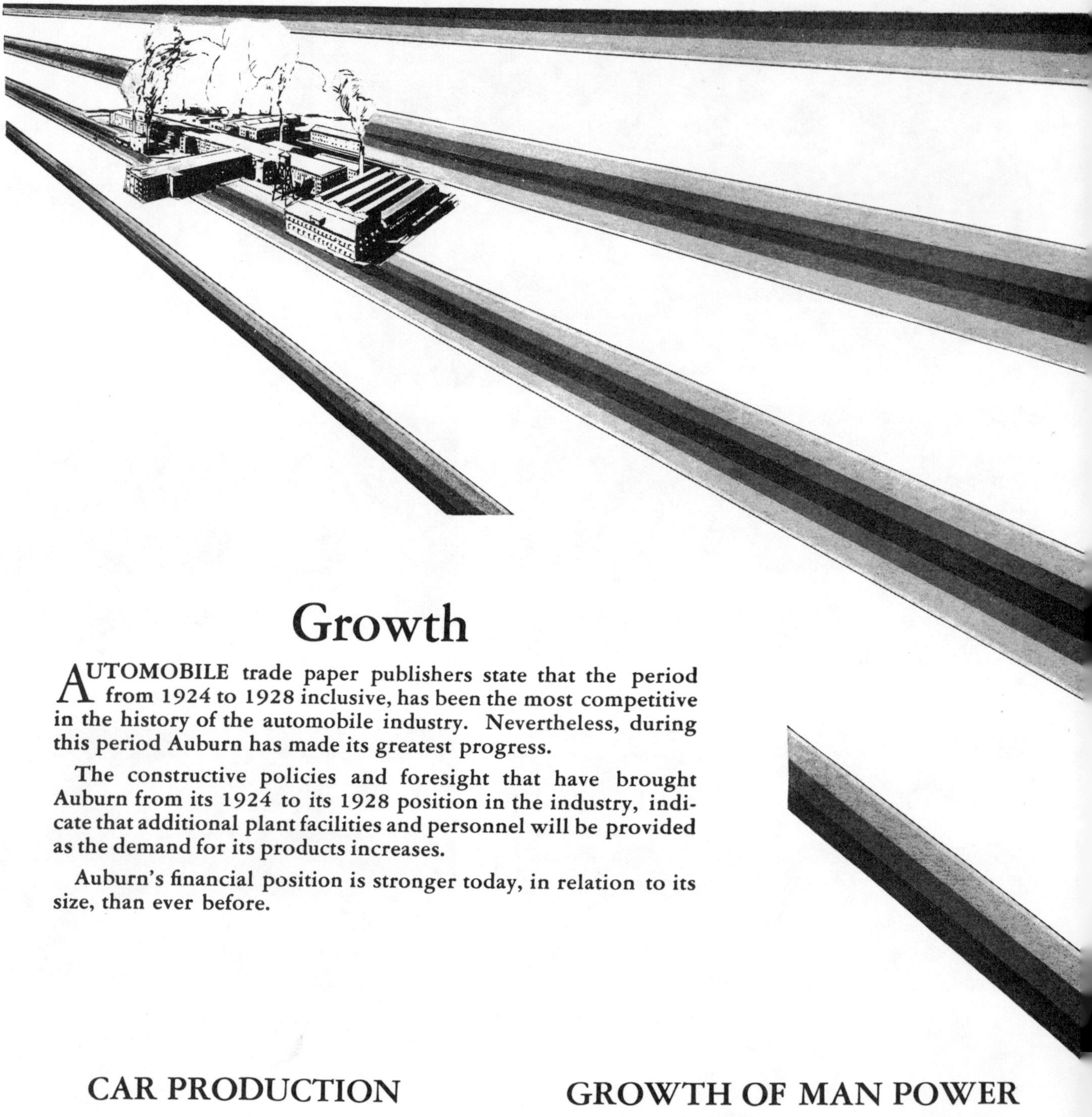

Growth

AUTOMOBILE trade paper publishers state that the period from 1924 to 1928 inclusive, has been the most competitive in the history of the automobile industry. Nevertheless, during this period Auburn has made its greatest progress.

The constructive policies and foresight that have brought Auburn from its 1924 to its 1928 position in the industry, indicate that additional plant facilities and personnel will be provided as the demand for its products increases.

Auburn's financial position is stronger today, in relation to its size, than ever before.

CAR PRODUCTION

1924 - 2400
1925 - 5600
1928 - 14700
1929 - 45000 (Estimated)

1924 1926 1928

GROWTH OF MAN POWER

Number of Employees
1924 - 450
1928 - 6300

1924 1926 1928

1928

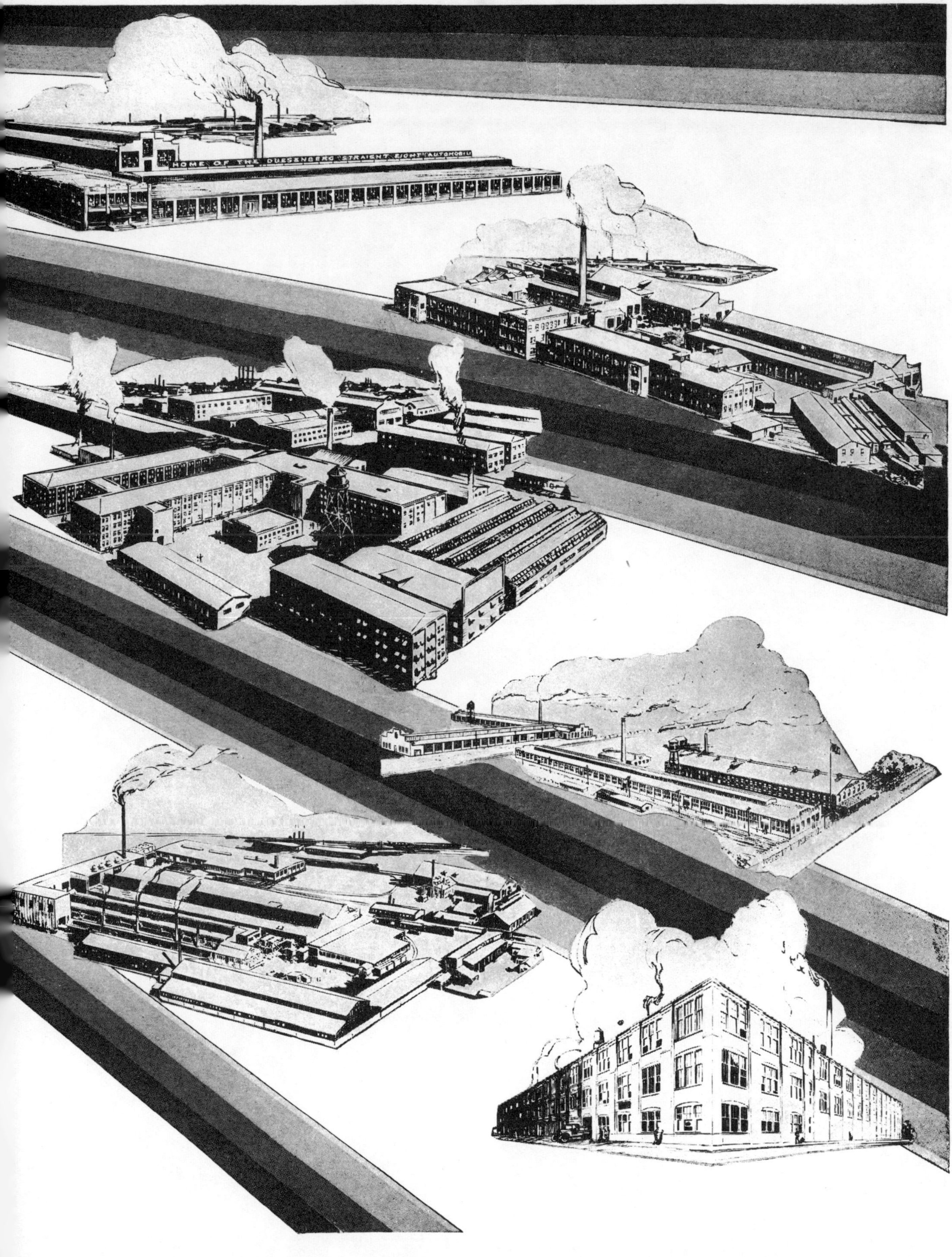

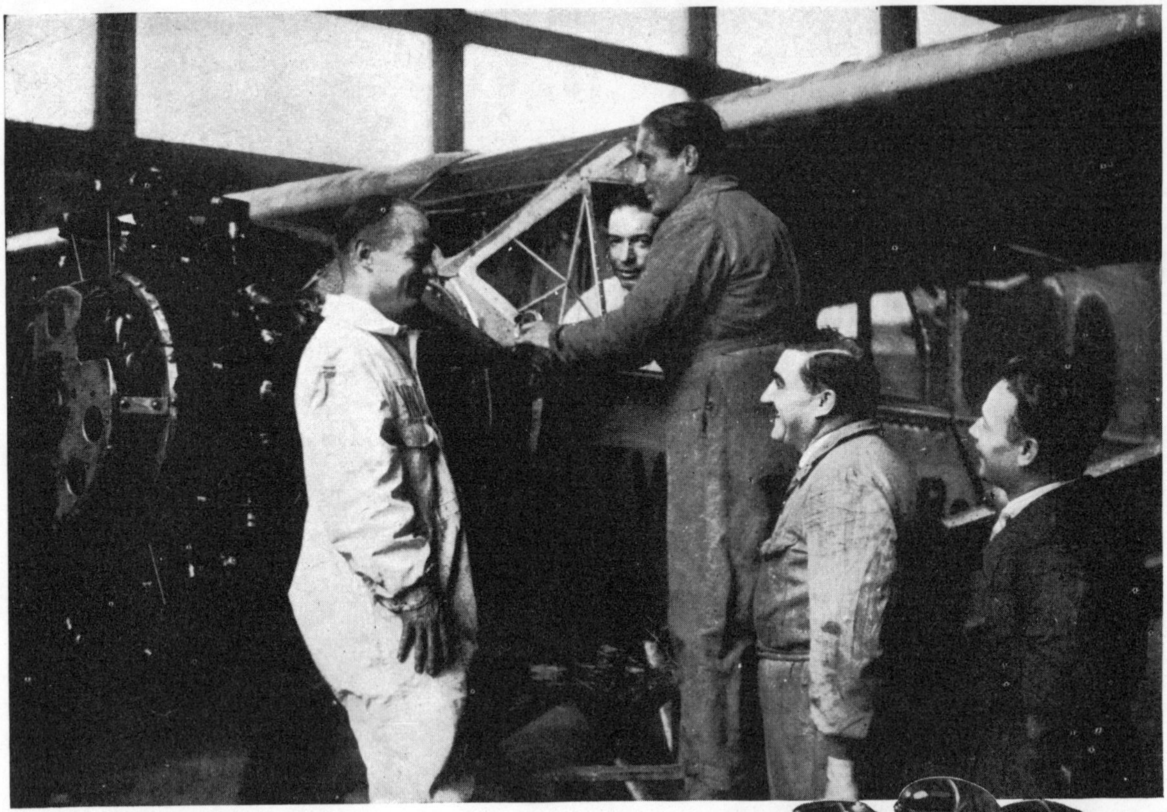

T. H. {DOC} KINKADE
{In white overalls}
Internationally famous aircraft engine expert who has recently assumed Lycoming's contact with aircraft manufacturers.

VAL CRONSTEDT
In charge of engineering, Lycoming aircraft engine division. An engineer and designer of long experience on both aircraft engines and aircraft.

Three-quarter rear view of Lycoming 185 h. p., 9 cylinder radial air-cooled aircraft engine.

Aircraft engine mounted in wind tunnel. Each engine, before leaving the factory, is coupled to the dynamometer and tested in this wind tunnel. An air speed of 160 m. p. h. is developed by the blower, producing the same air conditions as encountered in actual flying.

On left is shown dynamometer and water-brake. To the right may be seen large blower motor and generators.

Control panels for accurate measurement of horse power, temperature and fuel consumption.

ANTICIPATION OF FUTURE REQUIREMENTS OF AIRCRAFT INDUSTRY

FOR the past 18 months Lycoming has carried on an extensive development program, involving the engineering and tooling for production of several types of aircraft engines. Early in 1929, the Company expects to be in production on the model pictured on the opposite page. The management believes a market exists for 2500 to 3000 of these units annually. Many changes in types and designs of aircraft engines will no doubt follow with the rapidly expanding aircraft industry. The Company's personnel is sufficiently versatile, and its equipment adequately adapted to meet such requirements. It is believed that no other aircraft engine has been developed under more favorable circumstances. Designed primarily for reliability and strength by one of the country's foremost aeronautical engineers, it has had, from a production standpoint, the added advantage of the cumulative experience of the entire Lycoming engineering organization. The resulting product incorporating many new features, has been brought to the production stage in the Company's new laboratory, especially constructed for this purpose and equipped with the only highly specialized equipment of its type in commercial use. Laboratory equipment alone involved an expenditure of over $100,000.

DUESENBERG, INC.

H. T. AMES

Gen'l. Sales Manager, Duesenberg, Inc., long experienced in distribution of high grade cars.

Final assembly and body trim building.

Left, Administrative building; Right, Part of machine shops.

All materials when received at the plant are carefully inspected and tested in laboratory.

View of corner of machine shops. {Note splendid light conditions necessary for extremely accurate machine work.}

Peter DePaolo at wheel of Duesenberg race car, winner of 1925 Indianapolis race at 101.13 m.p.h., being the track record.

Tommy Milton's Duesenberg, which made a record of one mile in 23.07 seconds, 156.04 m.p.h., at Daytona, Florida, in February 1920. This record stood unbroken until Malcolm Campbell {England} made 201 m.p.h. in 1927.

George Souders, winner 1927 Indianapolis Speedway Race in a Duesenberg, average speed 97.5 m.p.h. Duesenberg cars won this event three times out of four.

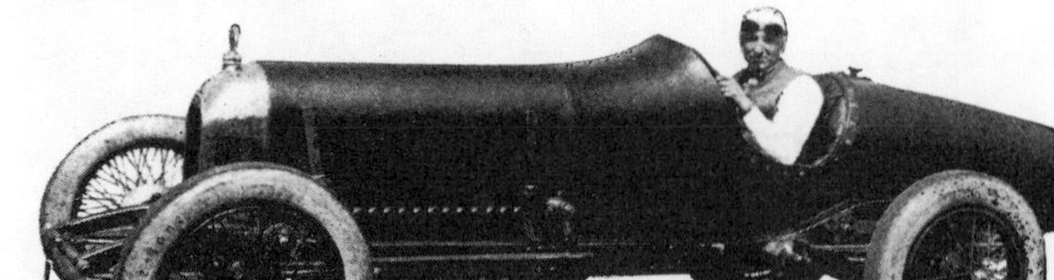

Joe Boyer in Duesenberg race car, winner 1924 Indianapolis Speedway Race. Average speed 98.5 m.p.h.

ONE OF THE WORLD'S FINE AUTOMOBILES

THE first Duesenberg engine was built by Fred S. Duesenberg in a small blacksmith shop at Rockford, Iowa, in 1898. From this humble beginning, Duesenberg has become internationally known and has contributed many of the most important developments that have brought the present day motor car to its high state of perfection. Included among his contributions are the Straight 8 Motor, first 4-wheel hydraulic brakes in America, improved type steering gears and small cylinder bore. As a dollar-a-year man during the World War, he built many aircraft and sub-chaser engines of original designs.

Backed by the above experience, Duesenberg has devoted his genius during the past 26 months to the development of a super-powered passenger car. As a result, the cars pictured herein are now in production. With unfilled orders on hand amounting to nearly half of the Company's 1929 scheduled production, the management expects an exceptional future business from America's greatest automotive achievement.

P. A. WATSON
One of the most talented production men in the Auburn organization.

FRED S. DUESENBERG
Vice-President in charge of engineering.

Custom built Duesenberg town car recently shown at New York Automobile Salon.

Front view new Duesenberg Phaeton.

Duesenberg Phaeton of distinctive design recently introduced.

(Left)
View from front end Duesenberg motor showing polished aluminum timing gear housings and double overhead camshafts.

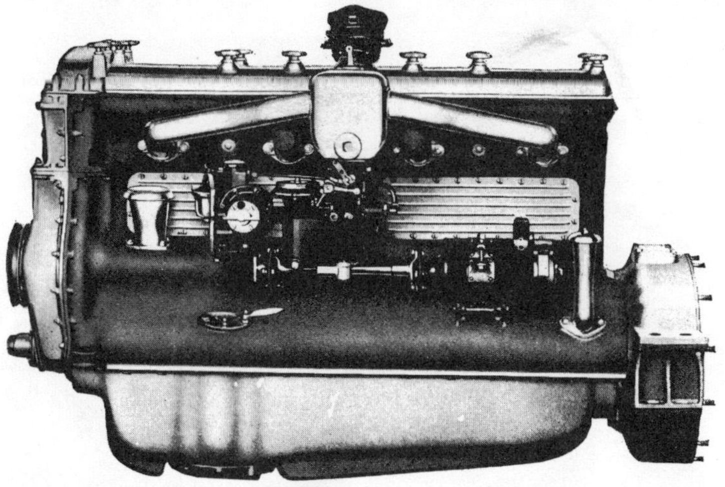

View from intake side 265 h.p. motor in which much aluminum is used to reduce weight.

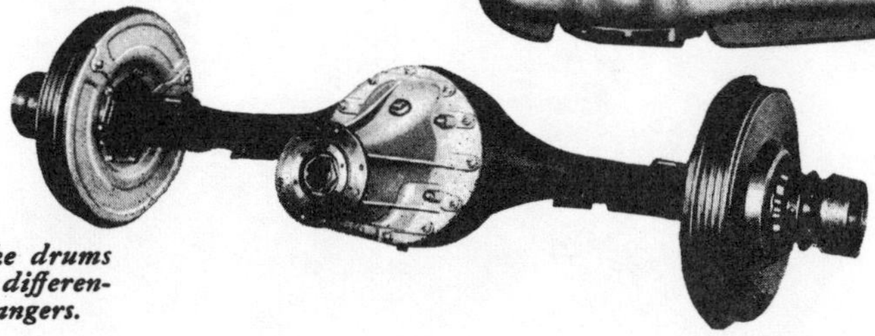

Rear axle and brake drums showing duralumin differential housing and hangers.

LIMOUSINE BODY COMPANY

J. D. BOBB
President and Gen'l. Mgr.

BY control of this Company, acquired in 1927, Auburn obtained an important adjunct as a body source. To this Company goes the credit of producing several of Auburn's distinctive body styles, for which the Company has been noted. For many years builders of high grade bodies, Limousine's entire production has for the last two and a half years been taken by Auburn. Among other models, the Phaeton Sedan and Cabriolet Roadster bodies, which are receiving unusual public approval, are built in this plant.

Beginning of a body frame.

Partially finished Phaeton Sedan bodies ready for priming coat.

Final metal soldering, finishing and assembly line.

AUBURN'S DOMESTIC SALES—5½ TIMES GREATER IN 1928 THAN IN 1924

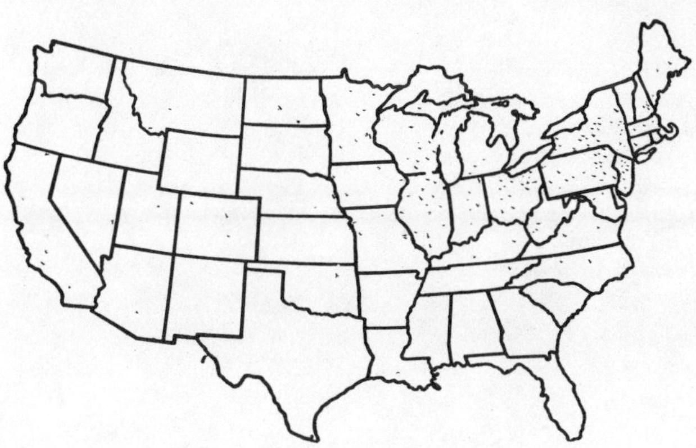

DEALERS AND DISTRIBUTORS, 1924

R. H. FAULKNER
Vice-President and Director of Sales

N. E. McDARBY
Sales Manager

DEALERS AND DISTRIBUTORS, 1928

AUBURN'S dealer organization, built practically from scratch in 1924 to its present size and buying power, has been, in no small degree, the result of an unique situation in the industry. It is significant, that at one time or another, Auburn's principal executives have themselves been automobile dealers. They know the problems of distributors and retailers. To this understanding is largely attributed the fact that over 85% of Auburn's dealers are successful. Unit sales during 1928 were 5½ times greater than during 1924.

The announcement of Auburn's 1929 program, under which it expects to sell 45,000 units, included Auburn's entry into the low priced field. The new model, selling for less than $1000, has opened many new avenues of outlet through a large number of new retailers, who until recently, handled competitive lines.

It is necessary that as the number of dealers increases, the number of cars per dealer must increase also. Otherwise, a factory would prosper at its dealers' expense. Auburn has seen to it that its dealers share in Auburn's growth and success.

Auburn has built a strong, well financed dealer organization, due principally to the fact that over 85% of all Auburn dealers have been unusually successful. The purchasing power of the present dealer organization is ten times stronger than that of 1924.

ADVERTISING POLICY

E. L. CORD believes, "one of the big things in advertising is the DOING of it." Auburn has followed the policy of "laying its cards on the table face up" to the public. It has found the public eager for information, responsive to suggestions and open to conviction. Each advertisement begins in the engineering department and is completed in the production department, because the Company believes that the best advertisement is the one that has the closest relationship between what the advertisement says and what the car does. All Auburn advertising has aimed to create confidence in the car itself. It is written to sell a car that will justify the claims made.

H. G. HERSH
Advertising Manager

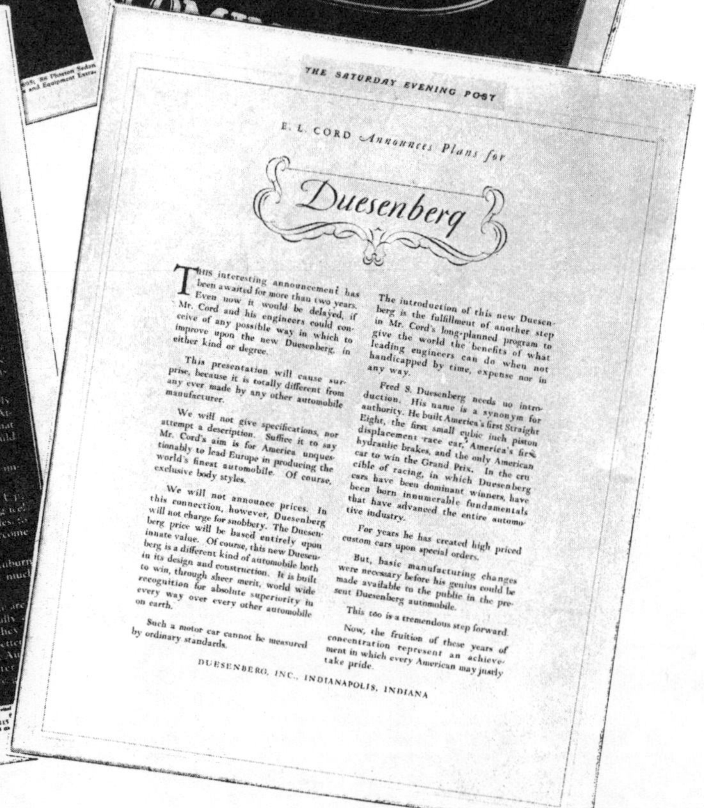

EVIDENCE OF AUBURN'S POLICY TO PROTECT THE OWNER'S INVESTMENT

AUBURN
Protects The Owner's Investment
Continuity of Design Prevents your Losing Money

By Looking At These Pictures—
Of Auburn cars shown here, you probably could not tell which one was built in 1925 or in 1928. And, the 1929 Auburn will have the same similar design. While, year after year, Auburn cars are constantly improved, built better and greater value given per dollar, yet their design is perpetuated. Packard also follows this policy. Because, if a car has a distinctive and exclusive design originally that is fundamentally right, it is not necessary to penalize owners by changing it radically.

25 — 1926 — 1927 — 1928 — and 1929 will continue this same design

An Important Statement of Policy That Stabilizes Automobile Values

The public actually loses millions of dollars every time motor car manufacturers obsolete their previous models by radical style changes in the design of their new cars. This colossal economic waste is unnecessary.

When the design of a motor car is one thing today and then is changed to a totally different thing tomorrow, it upsets values.

It does not alter the intrinsic value of yesterday's car but it lowers its market value. It makes it an old style car in appearance.

Now the unfairness of this is, that the shape of a radiator or the curve of a fender have absolutely nothing to do with the performance, endurance and value of any motor car.

But these superficial things when radically changed can have everything to do with your pocketbook.

Manufacturers should constantly improve and refine their cars but these changes should be the natural development, in logical sequence, as the result of a definite engineering policy and manufacturing program.

The Auburn car built four years ago is a more cherished possession today, and commands a higher resale value, because the new Auburn car is a perpetuation of the same distinctive design.

Auburn does not obsolete the car you bought yesterday by antiquating its design, nor by repudiating its engineering today. Built right originally, it permits of progressive advancements without annulling the value of its predecessors.

This policy protects the owner's investment.

If one manufacturer introduces a new design-fad, and for expediency reasons others imitate him—then next year if the one changes design again, the imitators must imitate again. At one stroke the owners of such cars have had their investment depreciated. Style is *desirable*, but not when it *destroys dollars*.

Individuality in design, retained for years, *accumulates in worth*. It admits of variations and betterments without upsetting values.

The automobile business should be reciprocal, because it is the consumers' dollars that keep the manufacturer in business. Therefore, the car-builder is the custodian of the car-owner's investment and he should do nothing to jeopardize or depreciate these investments. E. L. Cord

Auburn is building for stability, for sound, steady growth so that the Auburn buyer of today will feel an even greater allegiance to Auburn tomorrow.

The car builder cannot hold public confidence by jumping from pillar to post, but only through building a car that is basically better, and then by keeping it better.

STRAIGHT EIGHT
Closed Car
$1595

76 Sedan $1395; 76 Sport Sedan $1295; 76 Cabriolet $1395; 76 Roadster $1195; 88 Sedan $1695; 88 Sport Sedan $1595; 88 Cabriolet $1695; 88 Roadster $1495; 88 Speedster $1695; 88 Phaeton Sedan $1895; 115 Sedan $2195; 115 Sport Sedan $2095; 115 Cabriolet $2195; 115 Roadster $1995; 115 Speedster $2195; 115 Phaeton Sedan $2395.

AUBURN AUTOMOBILE COMPANY, AUBURN, INDIANA

Dealer's Name and Address

AUBURN'S ability to introduce distinctive models without destroying used car value by radical changes in design, has been very marked during the past four years. The product has been constantly improved, but has been sufficiently in advance of the trend to eliminate the necessity of repudiating its previous year's engineering and design by making radical changes resulting in costly and uneconomic loss to the public.

{Below} Auburn caravan showing very slight exterior design changes since 1924.

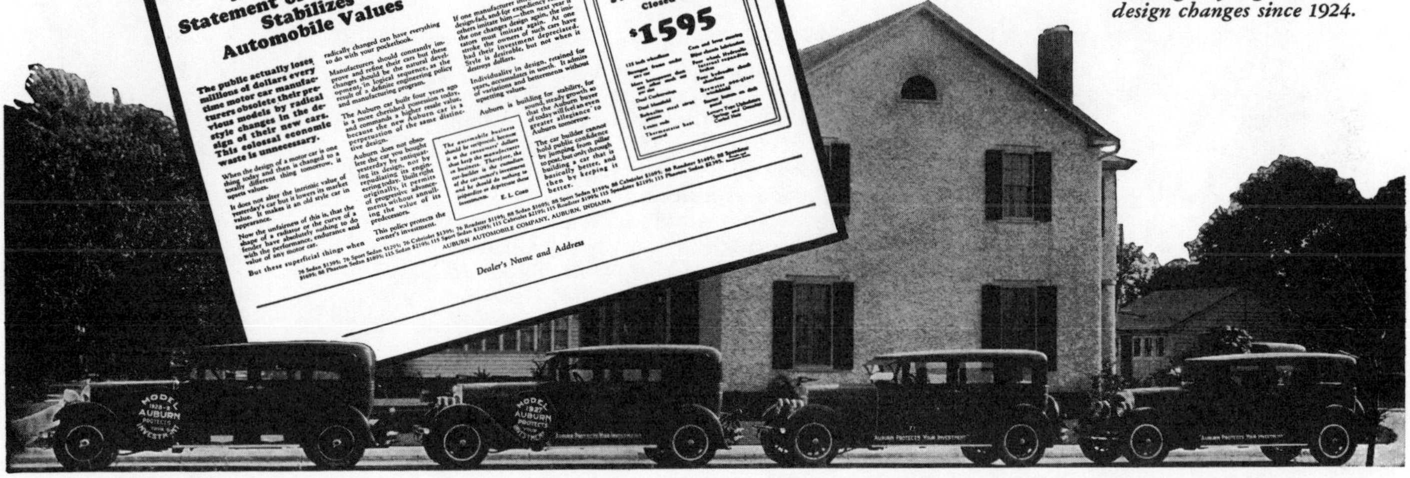

1928-9 | 1927 | 1926 | 1924-5

WADE MORTON
Contest Manager

THE purpose of continually testing Auburn cars in abnormal ways and to unprecedented extremes is not simply to demonstrate speed superiority, but to conclusively prove the car's efficiency, strength and endurance. In these highly competitive days, Auburn believes the public is entitled to the unvarnished truth about the relative value of motor cars. Its tests are carried on at public events sanctioned and conducted under the supervision of the American Automobile Association. These tests are made with strictly stock cars, which are exactly the same as those sold to the public by all Auburn dealers. Aside from the fact that Auburn's stock cars hold many world records, the public benefits from this definite and trustworthy proof of engineering, materials, construction and endurance.

Auburn Roadster on Atlantic City Speedway where many stock car contests have been held and where many of Auburn's world records have been made.

H. C. SNOW

FRED S. DUESENBERG

C. W. VAN RANST

E. O. PENRY

A. H. LEAMY

IN 1924 Auburn had an engineering staff of five men. Today there are more than 200, including such authorities as Fred S. Duesenberg, Harry A. Miller, John H. McCormick, C. W. Van Ranst, H. C. Snow and E. D. Herrick. This carefully selected engineering force is dedicated to a ceaseless search for new metals, new methods and new improvements. It is not simply devoted to production problems, but also to the betterment of the present models and to the creation of new types of cars.

ROBT. A. PEARSON

R. W. DWIGHT

JOHN W. OEHRLI

W. H. TROEMEL

LAWRENCE CAMERON

R. J. WATERBURY

JOS. M. STOUT

HARRY A. MILLER

ENGINEERS

J. H. McCORMICK

H. A. WEAVER

VAL CRONSTEDT

E. D. HERRICK

W. H. BEAL

F. M. BENDER

MR. CORD says, "A salesman cannot talk quality and performance into a motor car." Basic engineering work and proving-ground testing in excess of contemporary practice are responsible for the quality and stamina of the Auburn car. Auburn is extending its research and experimentation to unusual limits. New fields are constantly being invaded and explored, new problems solved and new results obtained. In this fundamental way, the Company not only exerts every possible effort to make the present Auburn car an outstanding value, but also to underwrite its future status in the industry.

W. B. BARNES

L. J. MAY

CLOYD DICKERSON

BURTON L. HUESMAN

J. C. BERRY

C. F. McCULLOUGH

EARL WINCHESTER

EXPORT

EXPORT 1924

EXPORT 1928

Export Sales Increase 1488% from 1924 to 1928

THE rapidly increasing foreign demand for Auburn cars is accepted as a distinct tribute to this American product. Export sales have increased every year since 1924. The year 1928 shows an increase of 30% over 1927. In 1924 there were six foreign sales outlets for Auburn; today there are more than ninety, as listed below. The list of foreign dealers is impressive numerically, but even more important are their character and high financial responsibility. Ten have a net worth of over two million dollars each, and as many more of over one million dollars each. Only 7/10 of 1% of Auburn's 1923 total was exported, whereas 17% went abroad in 1928. The year 1929 promises a further increase in foreign dealers and sales.

EXPORT SHIPMENTS	
1924	163
1926	1189
1928	2196

Foreign Distributor Organization Shows Remarkable Growth in Four Years

1924

Buenos Aires, Argentina
Melbourne, Australia
Amsterdam, Holland
Hamburg, Germany
Manila, Philippine Islands
Brisbane, Australia

1928

NORTH AMERICA
- Toronto, Ontario
- Ottawa, Ontario
- Kentville, Nova Scotia
- Dartmouth, Nova Scotia
- St. Johns, Newfoundland
- Vancouver, British Columbia
- Fort William, Ontario
- Montreal, Quebec
- Edmonton, Alberta
- Calgary, Alberta
- Winnipeg, Manitoba
- Victoria, British Columbia
- Halifax, Nova Scotia
- St. John, New Brunswick
- Quebec City, Quebec
- Saskatoon, Saskatchewan
- Tampico, Mexico
- Mexico City, Mexico

CENTRAL AMERICA AND WEST INDIES
- Willemstadt, Curacoa
- Balboa, Canal Zone
- Havana, Cuba
- Guatemala City, Guatemala
- San Jose, Costa Rica

SOUTH AMERICA
- Montevideo, Uruguay
- Lima, Peru
- Curacas, Venezuela
- Asuncion, Paraguay
- Porto Algere, Brazil
- Bahia, Brazil
- Sao Paulo, Brazil
- Santiago, Chile
- Pernambuco, Brazil
- Buenos Aires, Argentina
- Bogota, Colombia
- Cochabamba, Bolivia

EUROPE
- Vienna, Austria
- Hamburg, Germany
- Koenigsburg, Germany
- Breslau, Germany
- Nice, France
- Athens, Greece
- Lisbon, Portugal
- Paris, France
- Saarbrucken, Germany
- San Sebastian, Spain
- Leipzig, Germany
- Berlin, Germany
- Rome, Italy
- Gottenberg, Sweden
- Reykjavik, Iceland
- Warsaw, Poland
- Helsingfors, Finland
- Constantinople, Turkey
- Prague, Czechoslovakia
- Budapest, Hungary
- Antwerp, Belgium
- Zurich, Switzerland
- Oslo, Norway
- Rotterdam, Holland
- London, England
- Cologne, Germany
- Bucharest, Roumania

AFRICA
- Algiers, Algeria
- Funchal, Madeira Is.
- Umtata, South Africa
- Kampala, British East Africa
- Cairo, Egypt
- Ponta Delgada, Azores
- Ceuta, Spanish Morocco
- Las Palmas, Canary Is.
- Gwelo, South Rhodesia
- Johannesburg, South Africa
- Port Elizabeth, South Africa
- Capetown, South Africa
- Durban, South Africa
- Loanda, Port. West Africa

ASIA
- Madras, India
- Shanghai, China
- Beirut, Syria
- Colombo, Ceylon
- Singapore, Straits Settlements
- Tokyo, Japan
- Smyrna, Turkey
- Hong Kong, China

AUSTRALIA AND PACIFIC ISLANDS
- Sidney, New South Wales
- Melbourne, Victoria
- Adelaide, South Australia
- Perth, West Australia
- Brisbane, Queensland
- Manila, Philippine Islands
- Christ Church, New Zealand

R. S. WILEY
Manager
Export Department

MECHANICAL FEATURES

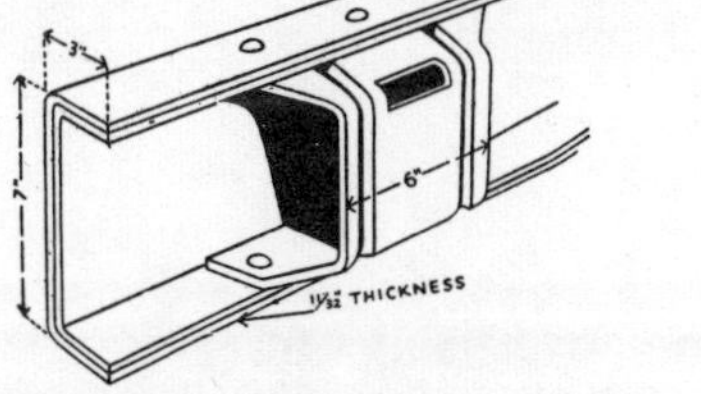

Showing double armor-plate frame and shimmy-proof motor supports.

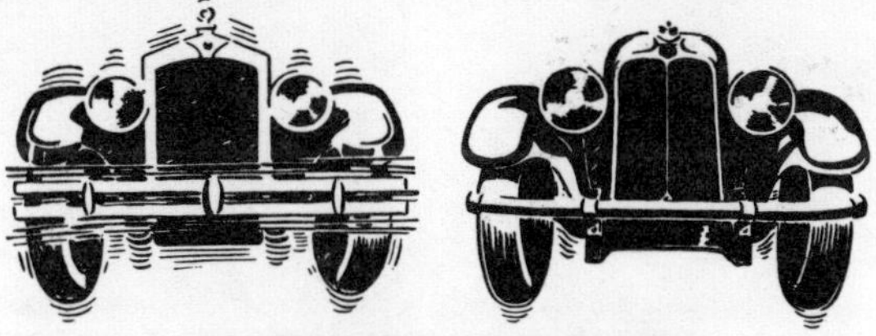

There are seven strong cross members and new type shimmy-proof supports—therefore, no wobbling. Wear and tear greatly eliminated and comfort and safety greatly increased.

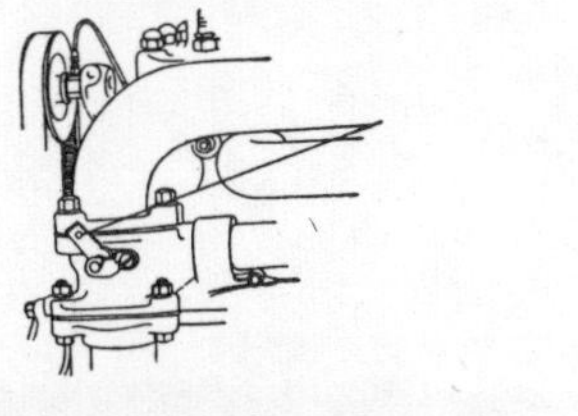

This lever on manifold exhaust operates from dash and opens and closes valve that permits warming fuel as weather conditions require, insuring greatest efficiency.

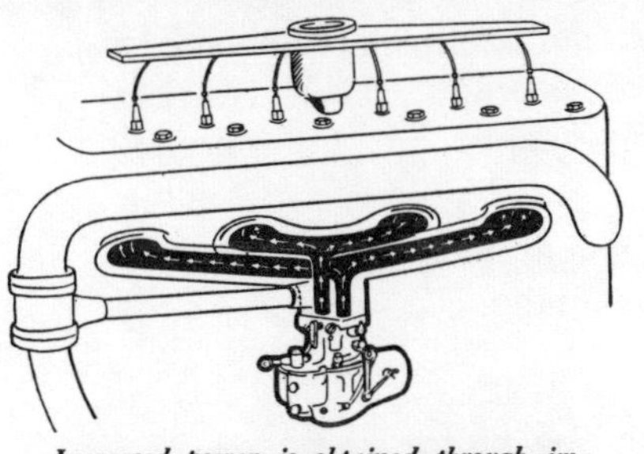

Increased power is obtained through improved Dual carburetion and manifolding; and improved combustion chamber design and improved head and port design.

Special muffler with by-pass for increased power at high speeds.

Metal side quarters, Brewster type windshield, lower and stronger construction.

Tomorrow?

BASIC engineering and development work is a continuous obligation. Therefore, Auburn's concentration upon structural improvements is never relaxed. As a result, Auburn is not at the mercy of future competition; never forced to hastily rush imitations upon the market. Instead, Auburn is prepared to do the leading by introducing changes, betterments, and even new type cars whenever the time is ripe.

—E. L. Cord.

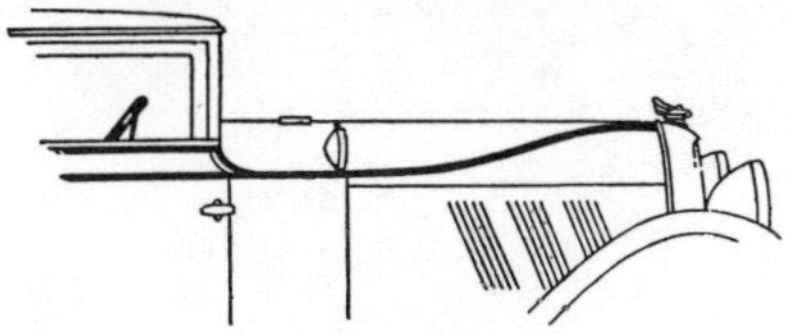

Distinction

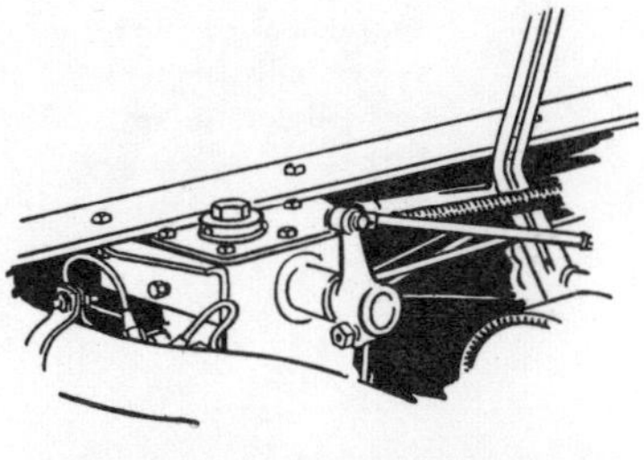

Compensating cylinder for hydraulic brakes. This pressure cylinder is in constant connection with the supply tank; always full of fluid, therefore constant braking action.

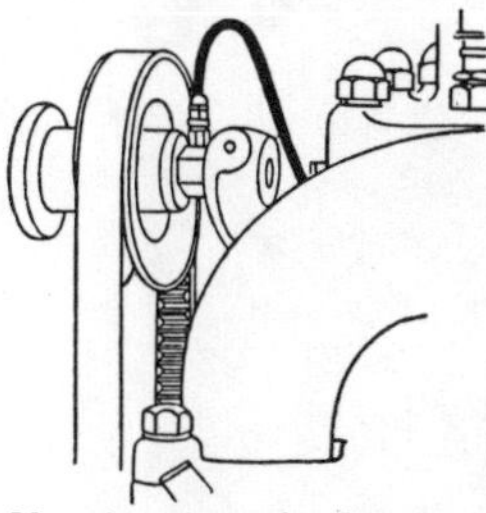

Metering pin on fan bearing, one of the 21 points lubricated.

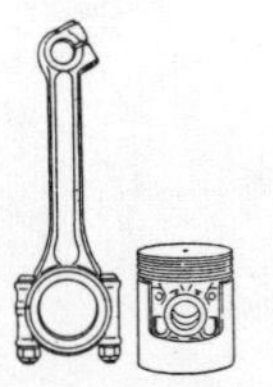

Bohnalite aluminum Invarsteel-strut pistons and Lynite rods, give maximum efficiency with minimum weight.

Race-car type of quickly demountable wire wheels.

New instrument panel indirectly lighted; coincidental lock and all controls conveniently located.

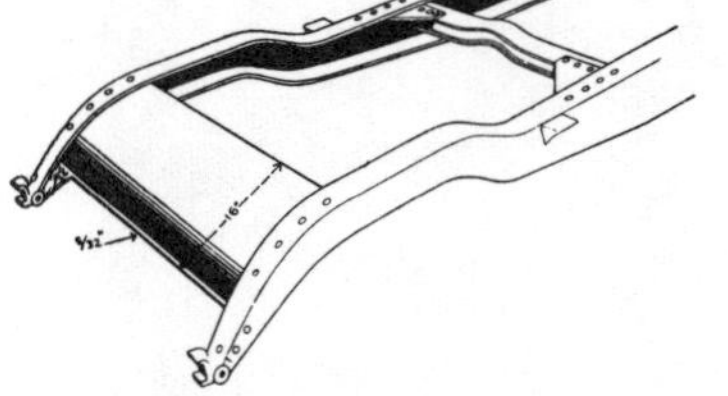

Rear boiler plate cross member, extra-wide gussets and frame one inch deeper for entire length.

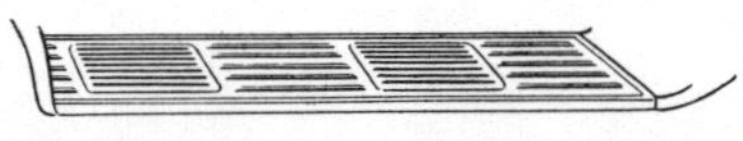

Steel running boards.

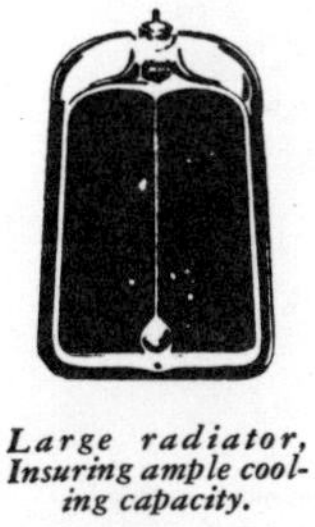

Large radiator, Insuring ample cooling capacity.

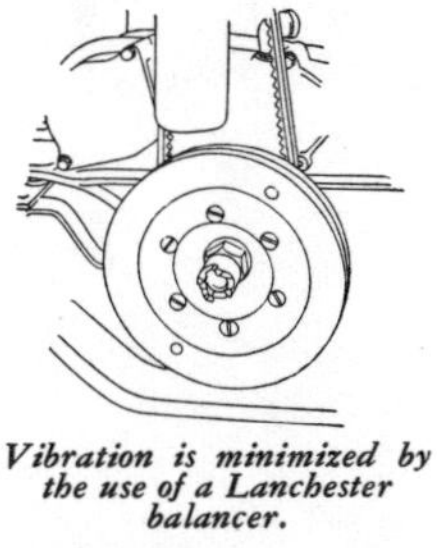

Vibration is minimized by the use of a Lanchester balancer.

Ample head and leg room.

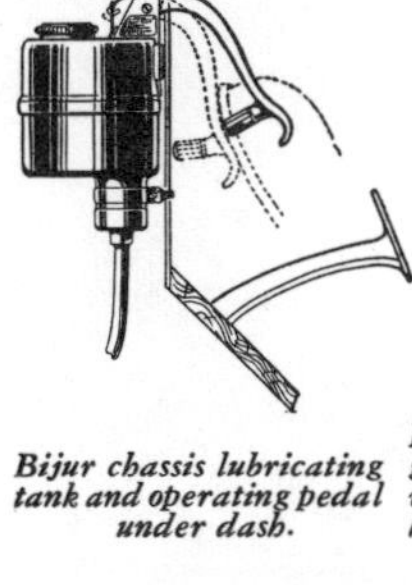

Bijur chassis lubricating tank and operating pedal under dash.

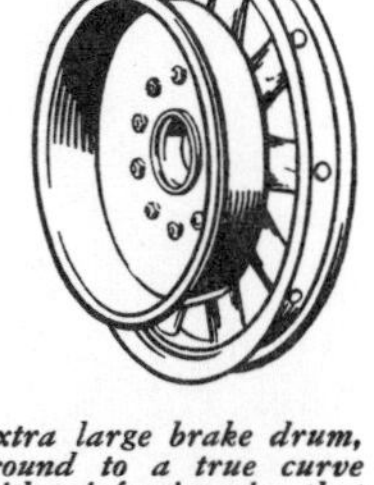

Extra large brake drum, ground to a true curve with reinforcing ring that keeps its shape permanently true.

14. A Bold Recovery

Instead of depending upon extravagant advertising, force-draft selling schemes, or cracking-whip dealer tactics, our method is: let the cars do their own selling.

Traditionally, the Auburn franchise could not compete with that of bigger manufacturers. The Auburn dealer had customarily been a garage-man who wanted a car to sell but had too little capital to play the game in style.

E. L. Cord's early experience selling both new and used cars to the public guided him remarkably in product planning: *the new car must have built-in saleability.*

The degree of next **year's success for any motor car company and its dealers, will be measured by the quality, durability and economical performance that is built into that company's product** this **year.**

The new Auburn cars became a popular value for money and the franchise much sought after. Design innovations attracted the young in heart: for 1928 the first production convertible; for 1929 the first low-

During the early days of the depression company ads were successfully slanted to attract new dealers in spite of a dark forecast. A progress report blackboard format was adopted to advise up-to-the-minute movements contrary to the national trend.

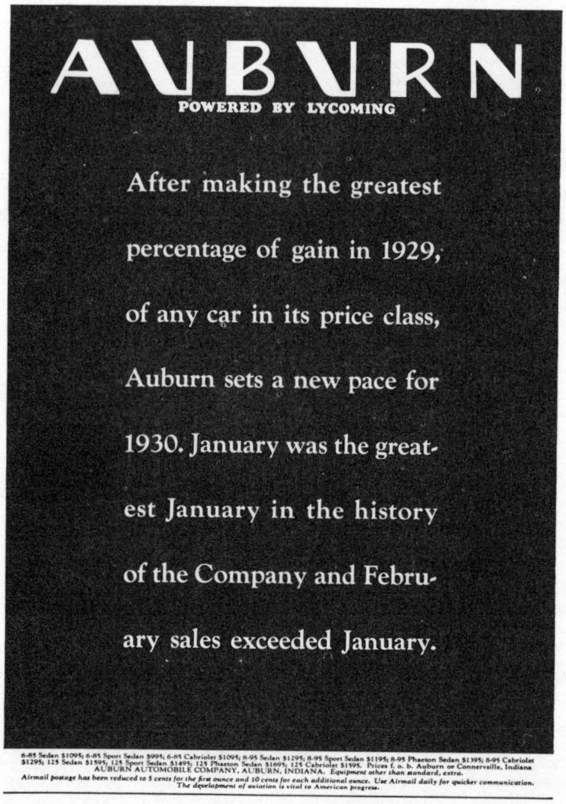

AUTOMOBILE TRADE JOURNAL and MOTOR AGE, April, 1930

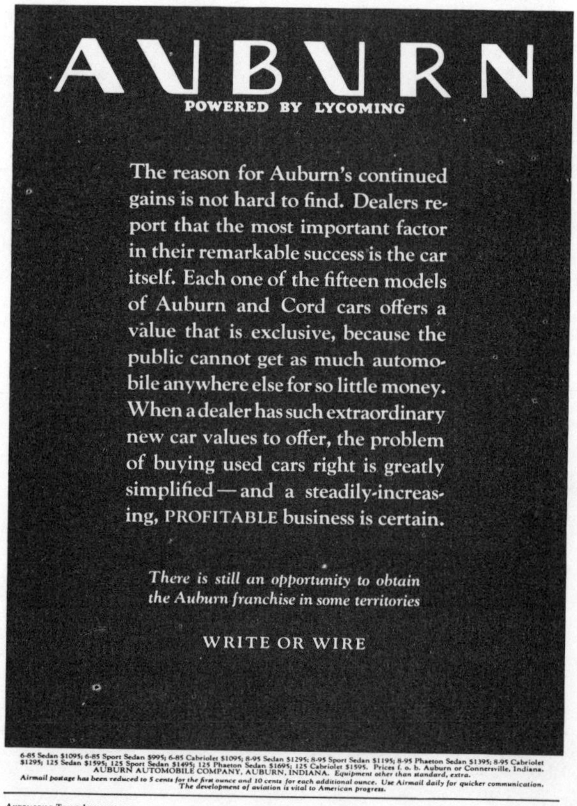

AUTOMOBILE TRADE JOURNAL and MOTOR AGE, April, 1930

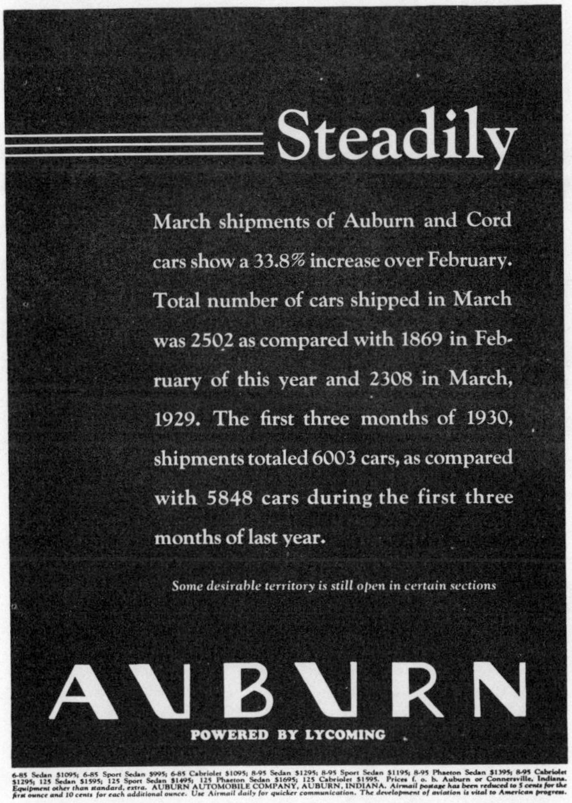

Automobile Trade Journal and Motor Age, May, 1930

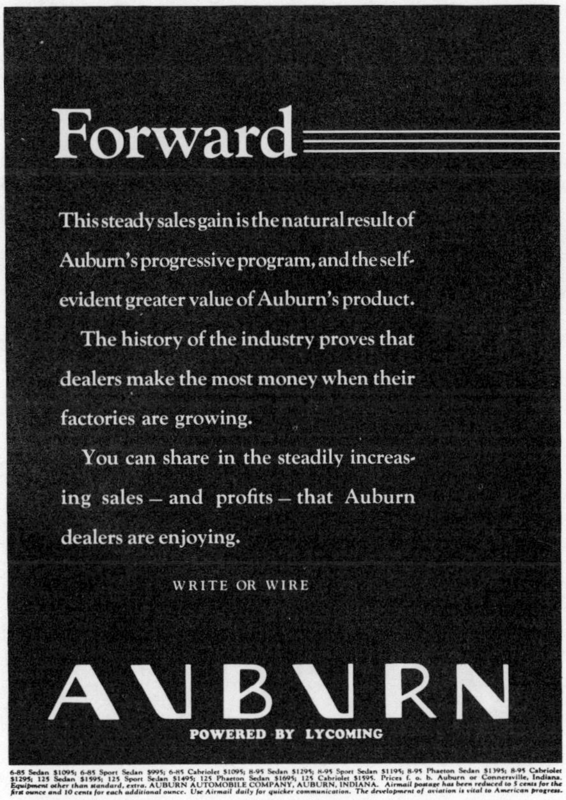

Automobile Trade Journal and Motor Age, May, 1930

The advertising program not only dispelled gloom among prospective dealers, who took up the franchise in record numbers, but attracted investors as well.

priced straight-eight. Auburn added nearly a thousand dealers, all of whom had come over from other lines.

At about the same time the Cord Corporation was formed to consolidate the interests of Cord and his associates. In addition to the plants at Auburn and Connersville, Duesenberg cars were made at Indianapolis, bodies at Kalamazoo, Lycoming engines at Williamsport and Stinson airplanes at Detroit.

While production of the long wheelbase Auburn was kept upstate at Auburn the light Auburns began to roll out of the revised Connersville plant January 15, 1929. The new Cord L-29 was assembled in Auburn, with bodies shipped in from Connersville and Kalamazoo.

By 1929 when the Cord was introduced, Auburn production was up to 23,297 units. That year the Auburn Automobile Company netted $3,600,000. The following year, first of the depression, sales dropped sharply in the first few months. To combat this Cord brought out his depression Auburn late in 1930. The car was so spectacularly improved in material and design that it looked like a lot for the money, yet was inexpensive. It was the car for shrunken incomes.

Among 1931 cars the excitement was principally an Auburn-Cord exclusive. At the New York Automobile Show the little Indiana car maker drew the largest crowds from the moment the show opened.

"The U.S. was on the downside of Depression yet here was an automobile at $945, low with racy lines," observed *TIME* magazine. "It looked rich, would do 80 mph. It answered the need of many a man who

The so-called "depression Auburn" proved one of the most brilliant products of commercial strategy in the whole history of the motor car industry. Value was spectacular and every child knew it. Buyers of the 1931 Auburn received an abundant package of quality automobile at a bargain price.

had lost his shirt but hoped his friends did not know it. It made many another man who never had it to lose, feel like a million dollars."

By the close of 1930 sales had rallied to tote up one of Auburn's big years. In 1931 it made 34,045 cars—fifteen times as many as Auburn built the first year of Cord's reign.

Select any make of car today and compare its quality with the quality of that same make five or ten years ago. Has it come down? Auburn has gone up!

Auburn stock became one of the wildest jumping jacks in the market. In 1929 it ranged from a low of 120 to a high of 154. In 1930 from 60 to 263. In 1931 from 84 to 295. Speculators made and lost fortunes on its daily movements, and Auburn paid a dividend.

TRANSACTIONS ON THE NEW YORK STOCK

TUESDAY, OCTOBER 29, 1929.

Day's Sales.	Monday.	Saturday.	A Year Ago.	Two Years Ago.
16,410,030	9,212,800	2,087,660	3,483,770	1,676,570

Year to Date.	Same Period 1928.	1927.	1926.	1925.
950,797,190	708,649,607	464,944,575	376,924,360	363,084,123

1929 High	1929 Low	Stock and Dividend Rate	First	High	Low	Last	Net Ch'ge	Closing Bid	Closing Ask	Sales
57⅞	38	Abitibi Power & Paper	40	40	38	38	−6⅛	38	40	1,800
12½	106	Abraham & S. pf. (7)*	107¼	107¼	107¼	107¼	−2¾	106	108¼	20
96	84¾	Adams Express pf. (5)	87⅛	87⅛	87⅛	87⅛	+⅛	87⅛	88	200
35⅞	24¾	Adams Millis (2)	26	26	24¾	24¾	−2¾	20	25	700
04⅞	73	Advance Rumely	8⅛	8⅛	7	7	−6⅞	7	9	2,600
19	15	Advance Rumely pf.	20	20	15	16	−7	..	16	1,300
4⅞	⅜	Ahumada Lead	1	1	⅜	⅜	−⅜	⅜	1	6,500
23⅞	95⅛	Air Reduction (†4½)	125⅛	128	100¼	120	−25	118	120	23,500
48⅞	25	Air Way El. Appl. (2½)	25	25	25	25	−3¼	25	27	3,000
11¼	2½	Ajax Rubber	2½	2½	2½	2½	−⅛	2½	2¾	7,200
10¼	4½	Alaska Juneau	5⅛	5⅞	5	5⅞	..	5⅝	5⅞	14,600
25	5	Albany Perf. W. Paper	5	7	5	7	−1	6	7	2,400
56½	18⅛	Alleghany Corporation	24¼	24¾	18⅛	20⅝	−8½	20½	21	224,100
92	80⅛	Alleg. Corp. pf. x w. (5½)	88⅝	88⅝	88½	88½	−1¼	..	..	600
254¾	204¾	Allied Chem. & Dye (6)	205	218	204¾	210	−35	210	215	32,100
125	120¼	Allied Chem. & D. pf. (7)	122	122	121	121	−⅛	120½	124	400
75½	37¼	Allis-Chalmers Mfg. (2)	46½	47½	37¼	41	−5	41	44	15,500
30½	29	Alpha Port. Cement (3)	30	30	30	30	−½	29¼	30	400
11⅛	3⅞	Amalgamated Leather	3⅞	3⅞	3⅞	3⅞	−⅝	3	4	700
42⅝	17½	Amerada Corp. (2)	20¼	21	17½	17½	−4	17½	19	11,000
23¾	4	Am. Agricult. Chemical	7¼	7⅞	4	4	−3⅜	4	5	5,700
78¾	25½	Am. Agricult. Chem. pf.	26	28½	25½	25½	−5¾	25½	29	2,400
60¼	46	Am. Beet Sugar pf.	49	49	49	49	..	45	50⅞	200
76½	30	Am. Bosch Magneto	30	30	30	30	−5	19	30	2,000
62	44½	Am. Br. S. & F. (2.40)	49	49½	44½	44½	−5½	44	46	8,200
34¾	4⅛	Am. Brown Bov. Elec.	4⅛	5½	4⅛	4⅛	−6⅞	4⅛	7	11,100
104	49¾	Am. Br. Bov. E. pf. (7)*	64	64	64	64	−1	52	65	30
184½	107¾	Am. Can (†5)	130¼	134	110	120	−16	116	120	140,100
142	136½	Am. Can pf. (7)	136⅞	136⅞	136⅞	136⅞	−1⅛	..	137	200
106½	76	Am. Car & Fdy. (6)	81⅛	87½	76	87	+6⅞	87	89	10,100
120	110½	Am. Car & Fdy. pf. (7)	113	113	113	113	..	113	114½	200
81⅝	35	Am. Chicle (2)	38½	38½	35	35	−9	35	37	2,900
55	20	Am. Com. Alco. (k1.60)	20	30	20	30	−¾	29	30	17,100
199½	80	Am. & Foreign Power	68	73	50	55	−22½	54½	57	89,500
108½	104	Am. & F. Pwr. pf. (7)	106½	106½	106	106	−1	105½	107	1,400
103	87	Am. & F. Pw. 2d pf. (7)	89¼	90	87	90	−2¼	89	90	2,000
42	21½	Am. Hawaiian S. S. (1)	21½	21½	21½	21½	−1½	..	21½	500
10	5	Am. Hide & Leather	5	5	5	5	−1	5	6	500
52¼	30¼	Am. Hide & Leath. pf.	32⅞	32⅞	31	31	−4¼	31	32	300
85⅝	43½	Am. Home Prod. (3.60)	46¼	49	43½	47	−3	45	47	9,500
54	30	Am. Ice (3)	33	35	30	35	−2½	34½	37	8,200
96	89¾	Am. Ice pf. (6)	90	90	90	90	..	90	93	600
96¾	30	Am. International (‡2)	30	41½	30	41½	−2½	41	42	71,400
8⅞	2½	Am. La F. & Foamite	3	3	2½	2½	−⅞	..	2½	900
136	99	Am. Locomotive (8)	101	101½	99	100	−½	100	101	10,500
119⅞	112	Am. Locomotive pf. (7)	115	115½	115	115	−⅜	114½	115	500
279¾	147½	Am. Mach. & Fdy. (†5)	185	185	175¼	175¼	−25¼	175	183	1,000
81¾	41⅛	Am. Metal (3)	41½	46	41½	46	−7	45	50	16,000
98¼	65	Am. Nat. Gas pf. (7)*	78½	78¼	78½	78¼	−1⅜	..	80	50
17⅞	3½	Am. Piano	4	4	3½	3½	−1½	3	5½	300
55	18	Am. Piano pf.*	19	19	18	18	−1	..	20	100
175⅝	73¾	Am. Pwr. & Lgt. (¶1)	75¼	76¼	73¾	73¾	−5¼	73¾	74	58,400
104	92¼	Am. P. & L. pf. (6)	98½	98½	92¼	92¼	−5¾	92	95	800
84¾	78	Am. P.&L. pf., A. sta. (5)	82½	82½	80	80	−2	79⅝	80	1,000
55⅝	28	Am. Rad. & Sd. San. (1½)	30	32	29	32	+4	31½	32½	141,000
64⅝	15	Am. Republics	15	20¼	15	17⅞	−4⅛	15	18	7,100
144⅝	72	Am. Rolling Mill (c2)	85¼	89¾	72	72	−13	70½	71	22,800
74¾	52	Am. Safety Razor (†5)	56⅞	56⅞	52	53¾	−4¼	53½	54	4,100
41⅞	29¼	Am. Seating (2)	30	30	29½	29½	−½	29	30	3,400
7	⅝	Am. Ship & Commerce	1	1	⅝	⅝	−1⅜	¼	1	1,800
112½	70	Am. Shipbuilding (8)*	70	78	70	70	−10	..	75	630
130¼	81	Am. Smelt. & Ref. (4)	81	84¾	81	84	−6	..	85	14,500
49	39	Am. Snuff (3)	40½	40½	39	39	−2	38½	40	2,300
79⅞	35¾	Am. Steel Found. (3)	42½	43	35¾	40	−5¼	39½	40	23,200
114	110	Am. Stl. Found. pf. (7)*	111	111	110½	110½	−½	111	112	160
85	40	Am. Stores (2½)	45	47	40	47	−13	47½	58	6,000
94¾	66	Am. Sugar Refining (5)	70	70	66	66	−6¾	66	68	7,500
111	102	Am. Sugar Ref. pf. (7)	103⅞	103⅞	102	103⅞	−½	102	104	1,100
60	28	Am. Sumatra Tob. (3)	32	33	28	29¾	−3⅛	29½	30	4,200
310¼	193¼	Am. Tel. & Tel. (9)	225	230	204	204	−28	204	205	131,100
232½	160	Am. Tobacco (8)	190	194½	182	191	−5	189	192	10,100
235	160	Am. Tobacco, B (8)	190	194¾	182	186	−9¼	185	188	41,800
121¼	115	Am. Tobacco pf. (6)	117	117	117	117	−1	117	118	200
112	107¼	Am. Type Fdrs. pf. (7)*	109	109	108½	108½	−1½	108½	109	60
199	65	Am. Water Works (c1)	70	71	65	68	−12	68	70	38,600
104	97	Am. Wat. W. 1st pf. (6)	102⅝	102⅝	102⅝	102⅝	−⅜	102⅝	103	400
27⅞	5⅞	Am. Woolen	10⅛	10⅛	8	8⅛	−3	9	10	4,200
58⅝	24	Am. Woolen pf.	25⅛	26	24	26	−2¼	20	26	1,500
46	37½	Am. Writ. Paper pf. (3)	37½	37½	37½	37½	−1½	34½	37½	100
49¼	8⅛	Am. Zinc, L. & S.	8⅛	8½	8⅛	8⅛	−2⅞	8½	10	6,300
140	75½	Anaconda Copper (7)	82	90½	75½	85	−8½	84	85	381,500
80	25	Anchor Cap (2.40)	40	40	25	35	−16	34	36	8,500
154½	102½	Anchor Cap pf. (6½)	111	111	111	111	−1	102	110	100
68⅝	30	Andes Copper (3)	34	38⅛	30	35	−5¼	37	40	11,700
49½	22¾	Archer-Dan.-M. (2)	30	31	22¾	24½	−5¾	22½	25	11,200
115	102¾	Archer-Dan.-M. pf. (7)*	104¼	104¼	104¼	104¼	−¼	104	104¼	50
95	75	Armour of Del. pf. (7)	82¾	82¾	75	75	−8	75	80	1,000
18⅝	5¼	Armour of Ill., A	5⅜	5⅝	5¼	5⅜	−1⅛	5½	5⅝	19,300
10½	3½	Armour of Ill., B	3½	3⅝	3½	3½	−⅝	3½	3⅝	32,000
40⅞	12	Arnold, Constable & Co.	12⅝	13	12	12⅛	−3¼	12	14	8,700
30	19⅝	Artloom (2)	22	22	22	22	−1	20	25	300
30⅞	25	Art Metal Constr. (1½)	25½	26½	25	26½	+1⅜	26	27	500
58¾	35	Assoc. App. Ind. (4)	40	42	35	37	−6	37	39	2,900
70⅝	28	Assoc. D. G. (2½)	28	28	28	28	−9½	..	28	22,000
107	88¼	Assoc. D. G. 1st pf. (6)	91	93	91	93	+½	93½	95	400
47¼	40½	Assoc. Oil (2)*	43¾	43¾	43¾	43¾	−¾	40	44½	10
298⅝	195⅛	At., T. & S. Fe (10)	242½	244	221	234	−17	230	235	25,000
104½	99	At., T. & S. Fe pf. (5)	102⅞	102⅞	101⅝	101⅝	−1½	101	102	1,400
209½	165	Atl. Coast Line (†10)	169½	169½	165	165	−7	165	166	4,000
86⅞	32¼	Atl., G. & W. I.	70	70⅛	67	67½	−4⅜	67½	69	5,800
62⅞	45¾	Atl., G. & W. I. pf. (4)	54¾	54¾	54½	54½	−½	54¼	55	1,700
77⅞	30	Atl. Refining (†2)	30	38¾	30	35	−5⅝	35	35½	131,300
149	80	Atlas Powder (4)	91¼	93½	80	80	−5	79	85	4,300
106½	98½	Atlas Powder pf. (6)*	100	100	99	99	−4	99	105	110
514	120	Auburn Auto (j4)	130	175	120	130	−60	135	150	3,300
11¾	4	Austin, Nichols	5	5	4	4	−1½	..	4½	4,500
42⅛	32	Austin, Nichols pf.	32	32	32	32	−3	..	32	100
65	51½	Austr. Gr. Anst. (4.49)	53¾	53¾	52½	52½	−2	52	54	200
35½	22¼	Autosales	25½	25½	24	24	−2½	24	25	11,400
45⅞	36¼	Autosales pf. (3)	38	38	36½	36½	−2	38	38¼	500
50	37⅞	Auto-St. S. Razor, A (3)	37⅞	37⅞	37⅞	37⅞	−1⅛	37¾	38	300
20	6	Aviation Corp. of Del.	7⅝	8	6	6⅛	−2¼	6⅛	6½	44,300
66⅝	15	Baldwin Loco. new	20	25	19	25	..	25	25½	20,800
125	114½	Baldwin Loco. pf. (7)*	117¾	117¾	117½	117½	−2¼	117	117½	40
145¼	112	Baltimore & Ohio (7)	115¼	117½	112	114½	−¾	113	115	85,900
80½	75	Baltimore & O. pf. (4)	78½	78½	78¼	78½	−1⅝	78	79½	200
110½	104	Bamberger pf. (6½)*	107	107	107	107	−½	105	106	80
90⅝	55	Bang. & Aroos. (3½)	63	63	55	60	−7	60	61	3,600
115	103¼	Bang. & Aroos. pf. (7)*	110	110	105¾	105¾	−4¼	110	110½	300
33¾	25	Barker Bros. (2)*	25¼	25¼	25	25	−½	24½	25½	130
49⅛	20	Barnsdall, Cl. A (†2½)	22	23	20	20⅞	−1½	20⅛	20½	61,000
106¾	95	Bayuk Cig. 1st pf. (7)*	97½	97½	97½	97½	+½	97	100	80
32⅞	17	Beacon Oil	17	17	17	17	−5	17	20	5,700
131	80	Beatrice Creamery (4)	92½	92½	80	80	−20	80	90	2,500
101	67	Beech-Nut Packing (3)	68½	68½	67	67	−5	67	68	3,500
17¾	7	Belding-Heminway	7	8½	7	8¼	−⅜	7	8½	2,900
104⅞	28¼	Bendix Aviation (2)	38⅛	39⅞	28¼	35	−7	33	35	55,800
60⅞	32¼	Best & Co.	32½	35	32½	35	−5⅝	32	36	3,600
140⅝	80	Bethlehem Steel (6)	90½	91	80	84	−10½	83	84	103,600
128	116⅝	Bethlehem Steel pf. (7)	126	126	126	126	−⅛	125½	126	2,400
61⅞	30	Bloomingdale Bros.	35	35	30	30	−10	30	37	4,100
111	100¼	Bloomingdale pf. (7)*	100¼	100¼	100¼	100¼	−5	100¼	108	30

1929 High	1929 Low	Stock and Dividend Rate	First	High	Low	Last	Net Ch'ge	Closing Bid	Closing Ask	Sales
90	25¼	Contl. Baking, A	35	35	25¼	25¾	−9⅛	25½	35	17,200
63⅞	45	Contl. Bank N. Y. (1.20)	45	45	45	45	−4	45	48	1,000
92	40½	Contl. Can (2½)	48	49	40½	44⅛	−14⅛	44	45	56,100
110¼	50	Contl. Insurance (2)	61	69½	50	59	−11	58	60	17,500
28⅜	6½	Contl. Motors (80c)	8¼	8⅞	7½	8¼	−⅜	8	8¼	49,500
47⅛	25	Contl. Oil of Del.	25	25¾	25	25¾	−1⅜	..	25¾	34,000
126⅜	82	Corn Prod. Refin. (†3½)	95⅛	98¾	90	94	−5⅞	94	94½	35,600
144¾	138¼	Corn Prod. Ref. pf. (7)*	140½	140½	140½	140½	−½	139¾	140	760
82¼	20⅛	Coty, Inc. (g2)	21	27	20⅛	23	−10	23	24	31,600
125	25	Crosley Radio (‡1)	25	29¾	25	28	−11½	28	30	9,100
79	40	Crown Cork & Seal	42	42	40	40	−12	38	52	1,600
121¾	80	Crucible Steel (5)	86¼	89	80	80	−6	80	83	4,200
116¾	109	Crucible Steel pf. (7)	109⅞	109⅞	109⅞	109⅞	−⅛	109¾	112	200
5½	¾	Cuba Cane Sugar	¾	1⅛	¾	1⅛	+⅜	..	..	400
17	9	Cuban-Amer. Sugar	10	10	9	9	−1¼	9	10	3,200
95	60⅛	Cuban-Amer. Sug. pf.*	66	66	65	65	−2	66	67	170
67⅞	40	Cudahy Packing (4)	40⅛	41⅝	40	40	−3½	40⅛	41	5,100
118	112½	Curtis Publish. pf. (7)	113	113	113	113	..	112⅝	113½	100
30⅛	7⅞	Curtiss-Wright	10⅝	11⅞	7⅞	9⅜	−3½	9⅜	9½	159,100
37⅞	14	Curtiss-Wright, A	16⅛	18¾	14	18	−1⅝	18	19	34,000
115¼	108½	Cushman's Sons pf (8)*	110½	110½	110½	110½	..	110½	114	40
121¼	58⅛	Cutler-Hammer (3½)	73	76	60⅝	71	−18	71	75	300
126½	63	Cuyamel Fruit	100½	100½	94	94	−11¼	..	95	1,700
69⅛	21¼	Davison Chemical	33¾	33⅞	21¼	25	−10⅛	25	28	15,600
46⅞	27½	Debenhams Sec. (a2.31)	29¼	29¼	28⅝	28⅝	−½	28¼	30	500
128	116	Deere & Co. pf. (7)*	119	119	117½	117½	−2	117½	119	270
226	141½	Delaware & Hudson (9)	152	152	141½	144¾	−25¼	144	145	5,800
169¾	120¼	Del., Lack. & W. (†7)	138¼	145½	138¼	145½	+8½	145½	150½	10,200
77¾	54	Denver & R. Gde. W. pf.	56	56	54	54	−3	45	54	600
64⅞	33	Devoe & R., A (†3)	33	33	33	33	−3¼	32	38	1,500
115½	112	Devoe & R. 1st pf. (7)*	113	113	113	113	..	100	112	40
164	125½	Diamond Match (8)*	126	137	125¼	135⅛	+6⅝	135⅛	136	860
11¼	6½	Dome Mines (1)	8	8	6½	7	−1	7	7½	3,800
54¼	12	Dominion Stores (1.20)	22½	23	12	14	−11	16	25	8,200
126½	71	Drug, Inc. (4)	71	72¼	71	72¼	−19	72	80	12,100
4⅞	2⅜	Duluth, S. S. & Atl.	2½	2½	2½	2½	..	2⅜	2½	100
7½	3⅜	Duluth, S. S. & Atl. pf.	3⅜	3⅜	3⅜	3⅜	..	3⅜	4	100
92	25	Dunhill Internatl. (‡4)	27½	32	25	32	−7	32	36	4,200
28⅞	14	Duplan Silk (1)	14	14	14	14	−2	..	13	500
102	92	Duplan Silk pf. (8)	95	95	95	95	−1	95½	98⅞	10
231	80	Du Pont de Nem. (†4½)	138	138	80	116	−34½	115	120	103,600
119¾	112	Du Pont de N. deb. (6)	115	115	112¾	112¾	−1½	111	113	1,800
39½	19	Eastern Roll. Mill (1½)	23	23	19	19	−8	18	24	1,000
264¾	162	Eastman Kodak (†8)	183½	186	162	170	−11½	170	180	27,800
76⅝	28	Eaton Axle & Spring (3)	29	33	28	30	−5	30	30½	9,300
39⅝	11⅜	Eitingon-Schild (2½)	11⅝	11⅝	11⅝	11⅝	−5⅝	11⅝	17	1,500
112½	61	Eitingon-Schild pf. (6½)	61	61	61	61	−8⅞	61	66	300
174	50	Electric Auto-Lite (6)	75	78½	50	50	−45	50	60	28,300
115	106¾	Elec. Auto-Lite pf. (7)*	107	107	107	107	+⅛	106¾	110¾	20
18¾	3¼	Electric Boat	4⅝	4⅞	3¼	4⅛	−1⅝	4½	5	9,500
86⅞	32½	Elec. Power & Lt. (1)	34	35⅞	32½	34⅞	−⅞	34¾	34⅞	96,200
109¾	103	Elec. Pow. & Lt. pf. (7)	106½	107⅝	106	106	−1½	106	107	3,300
104½	73	Elec. Storage Bat. (5)	80¼	84½	73	80	−3⅞	80	80¼	15,200
10½	3½	Elk Horn Coal	6	6	6	6	−⅝	6	8	100
24	7¾	Elk Horn Coal pf.*	13	13	12½	12½	−1½	12	13⅞	250
22½	3½	Emerson-Brant., A	4¼	4¼	3½	3½	−2½	3¼	5	700
13	2⅜	Emerson-Brant., B	3	3	3	3	−1	2½	2¾	100
79⅝	31	Eng. Pub. Service (¶1)	36	38½	31	34	−9	33	36	26,100
123½	90	Eng. Pub. S. pf. (5)	97	97	93	93	−3⅛	90¼	93	600
109	84¾	Eng. Pub. S. pf. (5½)	84¾	85	84¾	85	−8	..	85	200
41	31¼	Equit. Off. Bdg. (2½)	37⅝	37¾	36⅝	37	−1¼	36⅞	37	6,400
93½	43	Erie R. R.	50	53	43	45⅜	−9¾	45¼	46½	60,600
66½	57	Erie R. R. 1st pf. (4)	62	62	57⅛	57⅛	−4⅞	53	58	7,600
63⅞	56	Erie R. R. 2d pf. (4)	58	58	57½	57½	−3½	55	58	2,100
54	[illegible]	Eureka Vac. Clnr. (4)	40	41	39½	41	−2	41	42	2,800
27¼	[illegible]	Exchange Buffet (1½)*	25¾	25¾	25¾	25¾	..	25¾	26	10
10	4	Fairbanks Co.	8¼	8¼	8¼	8¼	..	5	9	100
35	11	Fairbanks Co. pf.*	22	22	15	15	−7	15	22	50
54⅞	29¾	Fairbanks-Morse (3)	39¾	39¾	29¾	29¾	−11	..	30	5,000
119⅞	106	Fbks.-Morse pf. (7)*	107	107	107	107	−1	107	108	30
72⅝	41⅛	Fash. Pk. Assoc. (k2½)	41⅛	41⅛	41⅛	41⅛	−5⅞	41	45	700
104	97½	Fed. Lt. & Tr. pf. (6)*	99⅞	99⅞	99⅞	99⅞	−⅛	99⅞	106	100
315	205	Fed. Min. & Smelting	205	205	205	205	−10	175	200	300
102	95	Fed. M. & S. pf. (7)	95	95	95	95	−1	94½	96	300
22⅝	5	Fed. Motor Truck (80c)	5	8	5	8	−1½	6½	9	6,300
123	63	Fid. Ph. Fire Ins. (2)	76[illegible]	77	63	63	−14	50	70	6,900
13¾	6	Fifth Av. Bus (64c)*	[illegible]	6¼	6¼	6¼	−2¾	6¼	7	80
98½	51	Filene's Sons	5[illegible]	51	51	51	−8	51	59	700
90	60	First Nat. Stores (1½)	6[illegible]	67	60	60	−7¾	60	64	12,600
20¼	4	Fisk Rubber	5⅛	5⅛	4	4½	−1⅛	4¼	4½	21,100
72½	25	Fisk Rubber 1st pf.*	27	27	25	25	−3	..	26	300
82½	25⅛	Fisk Rub. 1st pf. cv.*	25⅛	25⅛	25⅛	25⅛	..	25	30	210
54	42	Florsheim Shoe, A	42	42	42	42	−3¼	42	50	700
102¼	90¼	Florsheim Shoe pf. (6)	90⅛	90⅛	90⅛	90⅛	−⅛	90	95	100
82¾	35¼	Follansbee Bros. (†3)	40	40	35¼	35¼	−17¾	35¼	37	3,500
69⅝	25	Foundation Co.	25	25	25	25	−3	..	25	300
105¾	40	Fox Film, Class A (4)	50	65	40	48	−20	46	50	54,500
110	98½	Franklin Simon pf. (7)*	100	100	100	100	..	100	102	90
33⅞	5	Gabriel Snubber, A	5½	5½	5	5	−3	5	6	4,800
83½	68	Gamewell Co. (5)	68¼	68¼	68¼	68¼	+¼	65	70	500
25	3¾	Gardner Motor	5	5½	3¾	4½	−⅝	4	5	7,400
123¼	81	Gen. Am. T. Car (‡4)	90¼	93	85	87¾	−12¾	85	90	27,200
94¾	48¼	Gen. Asphalt	51½	51½	48¼	48¾	−5¼	48	50	11,400
140	130	Gen. Baking pf. (8)*	130½	130½	130	130	−½	120	130	100
69¾	26	Gen. Bronze (2)	27	33	26	30	−5½	30	34	3,400
61	32	Gen. Cable	40	40	32¼	32¾	−7½	31	35	14,900
120½	70	Gen. Cable, A (4)	80	82	70	74¾	−11¾	74	75	9,900
107½	104	Gen. Cable pf. (7)	106¼	106¼	106¼	106¼	−⅛	103¼	106½	200
122	112¼	Gen. Cigar pf. (7)*	116½	117½	116½	117½	+1	117½	118	200
403	210	Gen. Electric (†6)	245	245	210	222	−28	219	223	136,300
11¾	11	Gen. Elec. special (60c)	11⅛	11⅛	11⅛	11⅛	−⅛	11	11¼	13,100
81¾	35	Gen. Foods Corp. (3)	42¾	46½	35	40	−8¾	39¾	40	97,500
112	70	Gen. Gas & El., A (e1½)	73	73	73	73	−4⅜	..	..	5,000
116¼	100	Gen. G. & E. pf., A (7)*	102	102	100	100	−2	..	102	100
89⅛	50	Gen. Mills (†3¼)	58	59	50	50	−11½	..	55	7,800
100	89	Gen. Mills pf. (6)	91¾	92¼	91¾	92¼	+¼	91½	93¼	300
91¾	33¼	Gen. Motors (†3.30)	45½	45½	33¼	40	−7½	40	40½	971,300
126½	119½	Gen. Motors pf. (7)	120	120	119½	119½	−1½	..	120	1,400
52	35	Gen. Out. Adv., A (4)	40¾	40¾	35	35	−10	30	40	1,300
41	21½	Gen. Out. Adv. v.t.c. (2)	24	24	21½	21½	−3½	21	23	4,300
98	25	Gen. Pub. Service (b6)	25¼	28¼	25	25	−10	25	28	11,500
126¼	70	Gen. Ry. Signal (5)	80½	90	70	77	−17½	77	80	16,000
88½	54⅛	Gen. Refractories (†4½)	60	63½	54⅛	57	−11	..	..	4,700
143	100	Gillette Saf. Raz. (c5)	104¼	104¾	100	101⅞	−3⅜	95	102	15,900
48⅛	17⅝	Gimbel Bros.	18⅝	24½	17⅝	24½	+3	23	25	8,000
94	76½	Gimbel Bros. pf. (7)	77	77	77	77	−4	76	81¾	500
64¼	26	Glidden Co. (m2)	30¼	32	26	27	−9	25	30	19,500
106⅛	100¾	Glidden Co. pr. pf. (7)*	102	102	100¾	100¾	−3¼	100¾	103	60

1929 High	1929 Low	Stock
106	81¼	L
106½	81¼	L
113⅞	40	L
84½	40	L
110⅝	80	L
95	87	L
11½	4½	L
32½	13	L
88⅝	45⅛	L
31½	14¼	L
18	7	L
100¼	88⅞	L
72⅝	28	L
154¾	110	L
108⅞	40	L
118	96	L
46	30¼	
108	71¼	
113¾	94⅛	
115½	90	
48	30	
59	21⅛	
63	40	
114¾	60	
255½	120½	
24	13¾	
82½	50	
105½	80	
26	11½	
38⅝	15	
37¾	22½	
87	60⅛	
57½	24	
35⅝	21	
39½	20	
7½	5	
89⅞	30	
104	28	
18	4⅛	
72¾	29	
125	120	
108½	59¼	
29½	15⅜	
49¼	35	
34⅞	9	
27	21½	
105	102	
69⅝	9⅛	
54½	20	
122⅞	59	
39⅞	23¾	
5⅛	1	
3⅝	1	
321	145	
28⅞	7	
43⅝	10	
3⅞	2	
87	68¼	
65¾	30	
107½	99	
101⅝	55	
149	120	
156⅞	49½	
81⅝	42	
6½	1½	
31¾	3¼	
55½	27	
81⅞	10	
61¾	40½	
100⅞	20	
67½	30	
118⅞	40	
240	186	
41⅞	15⅛	
48¼	13	
71	12¾	
236¾	142	
146	140	
148¾	64	
86½	36	
37¾	26¾	
96	91	
58	15	
210	132	
141½	138¼	
122	116	
71¾	20¾	
17	2	
41	6⅝	
3⅝	1	
144	108¼	
91¾	35	
98½	65	
62⅞	25	
156	120¼	
113	50	
49¾	38¼	
256½	175	
109¼	100	
58¾	38	
90	82¾	
379	155	
132½	80⅛	
134¾	114⅝	
14⅛	1	
115	108½	
103	96	
390	191	
186¾	70	
54½	51¼	
103¾	99	
64½	47⅜	
118⅞	85	
114⅝	82	
6⅛	¾	
45	19	
64½	8	
69⅝	17	
99½	82	
10⅞	2½	
90	75	
95¾	50⅛	
450	276	
55	31½	
108	96½	
96¾	70½	
89½	50	
40	20¼	
98¾	51	
37	22	

15. *Pace for a Hearty Soul*

A business must succeed **or it cannot** serve.

E. L. Cord's methods of control differed from those employed by the more modern-spirited business leaders who have gone out and assembled huge conglomerates in recent years. The modern technique favors a dispersal of stock ownership, with the executive power left in the hands of highly paid executives, acting under the supervision of a board representing the associated and allied banking and collaborating interests. Cord appeared to want the reins in his own hands, although he usually left day-to-day regulation of affairs to subordinates.

"Cord demanded and received unusual loyalty. Roy H. Faulkner, president of Auburn, was with the company before Cord arrived," reported *Business Week,* "Lucius B. Manning, his other right hand man was another old hand at the business and acted as vice-president of Cord Corp. Most of the brass hat jobs were filled by men developed in the same way."

The right sort of men don't work for money. They work for what money will bring, and that's what I try to help them earn—not money but the real satisfactions of life, the things worth while, Cord observed in a **Forbes** interview.

When men come to work for you with that spirit there simply aren't enough days in the week for them to work. When they come to you because you offer them more than they have made elsewhere, there's only one day in the week and that's pay day—and there's only one hour in the day and that's the quitting hour.

While Cord was famed for low salaries, *TIME* magazine once reported that he often made up for it personally. "He has been known to give individual presents of $10,000 each, compensating for low pay without raising the cost of his cars to the public."

After Cord's rise to prominence in the industry at Auburn, John H. Quinlan, the Chicago *Moon* distributor could never forget him. "Errett Cord is the greatest automobile man in the country today," he told a friend in 1931, "for he knows what the people want and the dealer needs, and he gives it to them."

"In speaking of Cord as an industrialist rather than as merely a financier," observed *TIME,*" it is worth noting that no one ever saw a stock ticker in his house or heard of a private wire to a broker.

"As a racing driver Mr. Cord may have gambled with death, but he did not gamble in stocks. L. B. Manning, whose versatile career brought him a job in a broker's office, says of the first meeting with his chief. 'I noticed him because he was so kiddish in appearance, and because he always made money while other customers lost. They would buy 1,000 shares on margin. He bought 100 shares at a time outright. And he was never squeezed.' "

Without exception Cord dealer meetings were staged in facilities having all the elegance of the salon. In Chicago dealers convened at the Edgewater Beach Hotel.

E. L. Cord exhibited through his enterprise that he firmly believed the world belonged to the living generation. He was a man in great motion, coldly practical, who made the most of everything he touched. He feared and respected nothing in the industry. In short, Cord the realist was more shrewd than most of those with whom he dealt. The slower wheel, in such encounters, seldom enjoyed being passed.

So it was that critics found all sorts of things wrong with Cord. In public some called him crazy, while in private they added: "like a fox". They called him *too astute* in transforming limitations into advantages. They said he didn't know what he was doing. They even labeled the man "too young."

Cord *did know* what he was doing—*always.* And generally he made it all work. As for being too young, his critics were apparently forgetting they were once young themselves.

16. *A Time of Joy and Laughter*

Good will, as a result of value received, is the only real success.

While the scene of Cord's enterprise was centered in the east, except for growing real estate holdings in California, he preferred the easy climate of living in the southwest.

During most of 1931 Cord spent his time in California on what has been termed a "vacation". But during the ten months that he had been away from immediate direction of Auburn—with Roy Faulkner temporarily acting as president—Cord formed the *Century Air Lines,* which operated between Chicago and St. Louis, Chicago and Cleveland, and in the west as *Century-Pacific.*

In these same months he built a home in Southern California that was to be a base of operations for a generation to come. His two sons were in their teens when their mother died in 1930. Not long after, Cord married again. His new bride was a social figure and loved to entertain. Her wish was his command. At 712 North Hillcrest Drive in Beverly Hills Cord's estate became a showplace in a land of showplaces—a brand new home of Georgian Colonial architecture on vast, manicured grounds was completed in 1932. A baby girl joined the family.

It was a proud and elegant life and Cord was young enough to enjoy every part of it. In Chicago he also maintained a swank Lake Shore Drive apartment; in New York lived expensively in a suite at the Waldorf-Astoria; and, of course, he kept a large place in Auburn.

The young man from Missouri was among the true pioneers in the aviation industry; Cord believed in air travel long before the crowd. He was convinced that the secret of air success lay in setting travel rates the general public could afford. He was convinced that one day cabin and transport planes would be daily tools for the average man almost like an automobile.

When Cord originally bought his own airplane he hired a pilot. After observing and asking some well-thought-out questions he asked to take the second controls as the pilot watched. Pretty soon the pilot was going along for the ride, for Cord never stopped till he became a licensed pilot—and owned an airplane factory of his own.

Just to give himself something to do that would be fun, and provide a market for the new radial airplane engines he was having Lycoming produce, and to publicize his new Stinson trimotor aircraft, Cord launched Century and Century-Pacific Air Lines which covered 1800 miles of air routes a day and carried perhaps 20% of the country's passenger traffic.

As it had been Cord's custom his first step was to find what type of service people wanted and what they would pay for it. Next he arranged for Century to give it to them. He set his rates directly in competition with the railroads. They were based on greater volume of passenger traffic than then existed. He believed the rates would open up new business.

The Hillcrest Drive estate in Beverly Hills — designed by the noted architect Paul Williams— was to become home for the E. L. Cord family for a generation to come.

It so happened that his lines paralleled routes of *American Airways,* a subsidiary of Aviation Corporation, the third largest in the field. Century made the going tough for its older competitor by speeding up service and drastically reducing fares. The situation finally became such that Aviation Corporation, then weaving a master network of lines across the country, wished to get rid of its bothersome competition.

E. L. Cord sensed a long-distance chance to put across one of those coups which seemed to arouse in him a small boy's thrill of adventure. *Why not* sell Century-Pacific Lines to Aviation? The offer was accepted.

> "E. L. Cord, two-fisted fighter of the automobile industry, is out of the running as an independent operator of air lines and his former competitors are indulging in deep, refreshing breaths of relief," reported *Business Week* on April 13, 1932. "Aviation Corp., announces the acquisition of Mr. Cord's Century lines through a stock transfer. Mr. Cord becomes a director of Aviation Corp."

A portfolio of contemporary institutional Cord Corporation advertising begins overleaf.

Aviation was not immediately aware that it had made an elementary mistake in giving the unstoppable Mr. Cord their stock.

POLICY *determines*

A Statement to Car Owners and Automobile Dealers from
E. L. CORD

THE policy of a manufacturer is not visible. However, it is the most important thing in any automobile.

The divisions of Cord Corporation have plants in seven cities, scientific laboratories and acres of the most modern manufacturing facilities.

But factory buildings, machinery, engineering laboratories and financial resources, in themselves, are not important. They are only tools to work with. It is what these physical properties PRODUCE that is significant to the public.

The thinking that directs and co-ordinates their combined activities determines, more than anything else, how good an investment the purchaser makes.

Due to the public interest in the annual automobile shows being held over the United States, and because Cord Corporation divisions build many different automotive parts, as well as four complete lines of automobiles, we believe the policies responsible for Cord products are vital to the public.

The automobile divisions of this corporation have built their success by placing the VALUE OF THE CAR itself above all other considerations.

Our sales policy starts there and ends there.

Instead of depending upon extravagant advertising, force-draft selling schemes, or crack-the-whip dealer tactics, our method is—let the cars do their own selling!

We operate on the theory that the public knows its automobiles.

Buyers know WHAT they want cars to do and HOW they want it done. No salesmen can TALK quality or performance into a car. It must be BUILT in. Therefore, all we ask of the buyer, is to COMPARE—and DRIVE!

This policy places an unceasing obligation upon our designers, engineers and workmen. It requires that they anticipate changes and improvements which people want. It means they must be leaders, not followers. It means they must be first to offer these improvements. At the same time they must build newer, better products, of greater value, for less cost to the consumer.

To accomplish this, sixteen million dollars have been spent in engineering and development programs. The many outstanding results of this pioneering are now offered to car owners.

You are invited to attend the Automobile Shows, and to use this policy as the basis for judging the improvements introduced by the divisions of Cord Corporation.

PRODUCTS

AUBURN TWELVE . . . . 160-Horse Power—133-Inch Wheelbase

AUBURN STRAIGHT EIGHT . 100-Horse Power—127-Inch Wheelbase

CORD FRONT-DRIVE . . . . . America's Only Front-Drive Car

DUESENBERG . . . . "The World's Finest Motor Car"

DUAL-RATIO . . . . Makes Possible "Two Cars In One"

LYCOMING MOTORS Products of the World's Largest Exclusive Motor Builder

L. G. S. FREE WHEELING . . . . With Positive Lockout Control

"LIMOUSINE" Convertible Bodies . . "CENTRAL" Standard Bodies

COLUMBIA AXLES—Specialized Products of a Pronounced Leader in this Field

CORD CORPORATION

CHICAGO

Divisions of Cord Corporation:

AUBURN AUTOMOBILE COMPANY . . . . Auburn, Indiana
LYCOMING MANUFACTURING COMPANY, Williamsport, Pa.
CENTRAL MANUFACTURING COMPANY, Connersville, Indiana
L. G. S. DEVICES CORPORATION . . . Indianapolis, Indiana

COLUMBIA AXLE COMPANY . . . . Cleveland, Ohio
DUESENBERG, INC. . . . . Indianapolis, Indiana
LIMOUSINE BODY COMPANY . . . . . Kalamazoo, Michigan
STINSON AIRCRAFT CORPORATION . . Wayne, Michigan

SPENCER HEATER COMPANY . . Williamsport, Pennsylvania
CENTURY AIR LINES, Inc. . . . *Terminals:* Detroit, Toledo, Cleveland, Chicago, South Bend, Bloomington, Springfield, St. L[illegible]
CENTURY PACIFIC AIR LINES, Ltd. *Terminals:* Sacra[illegible], San Francisco, Oakland, San Jose, Fresno, Bakersfield, Los [illegible], San Diego, El Centro, Phoenix, Tucson

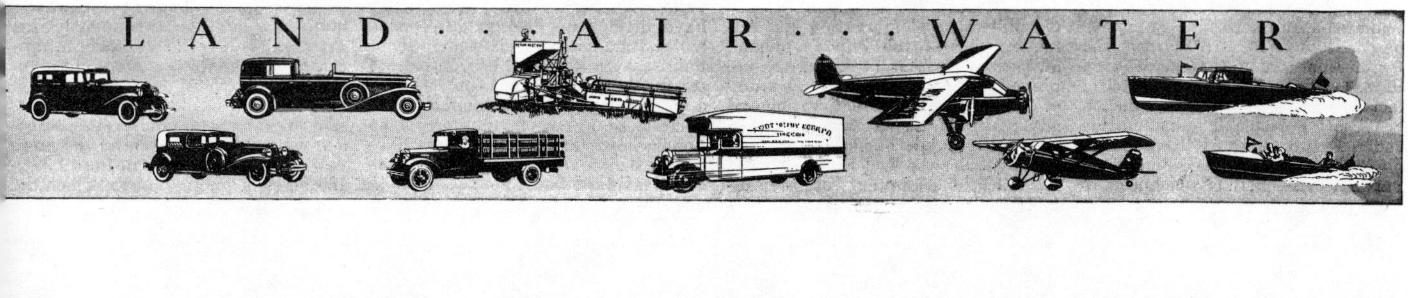

17. Turbulence & Triumph

A company's product **can be no better than its** policy.

Cord had taken payment in 140,000 shares of Aviation stock. What would make the difference was the fact that he immediately began a private program of accumulating more shares—all of this stock he could lay his hands on from various outside sources.

By November, 1932, he had managed to build this nest egg up to around 800,000 shares by buying in the open market. Now Cord held one of the largest blocks of stock in the holding company, and had secured assurance of support from other large holdings.

> "When E. L. Cord sold his Century Air Lines to American Airways last April," observed *Business Week* in the fall of 1932, "most people thought the aggressive builder of Auburn and Cord motor cars, Lycoming motors, and Stinson planes was through with the air transport business. But it seems he isn't through."

It was a classic understatement. Cord seemed almost ready to control the company.

Then came the unexpected. By the proposed issuance of 2,000,000 new shares the president of Aviation Corporation announced a plan to acquire some of the assets of North American Aviation, Inc.

Creating these additional shares would practically halve stockholders' existing shares. Cord, considering the prospects of this 28% ownership of the company reduced to less than 17%—in which his market purchases, for his intentions, would have been in vain—swung into wild and wonderful action.

By his own timetable, perhaps, Cord wasn't quite ready to move, but his hand was forced. He immediately unleashed legal batteries to block the deal and a violent struggle was forecast.

> "It was a nasty fight. Mr. Cord bought big newspaper space to tell stockholders that banking interests (Lehman Brothers, W. A. Harriman) were endeavoring to help themselves at owners' expense. The management bought equally big space," reported *Business Week,* November 23, 1932, "to describe Cord's unsuccessful venture in the air transport business."

Cord's ideas reflected their vitality. He contended that aviation should be brought down to a commonplace mode of travel through the medium of lower rates and more frequent schedules.

Harriman decided to withdraw. Frank A. Vanderlip, another strong figure in Aviation holdings, had always admired aggressive young financiers and was willing to help Cord. The unwieldly board of directors, thirty-five strong, was racked by dissentions. Some directors were jealous of Cord, claiming all he wanted was to compel Aviation to buy his motors and planes.[9]

---

[9]Probably partly true, inasmuch as several years later he would succeed in selling Lycoming Motors and Stinson Aircraft to an Aviation subsidiary.

"The old-fashioned battle for stock control of Aviation had raged through the summer and fall and put the old timers in Wall Street's board rooms in a reminiscent humor," wrote Arthur D. H. Smith. "It ended the first of December, 1932, with young Mr. Cord in the saddle. He had wrested control of the great Aviation Corporation of Delaware from a group of hardy, experienced gentry."

Nobody present could quite understand how this flesh-and-blood Horatio Alger had managed the feat. Subsequently the board of directors was cut from thirty-five to sixteen, eight of each faction. Not long after, one of the old faction retired and the board that remained was in the motor man's favor.

The Aviation Corporation, with its fifty or sixty subsidiaries, thousands of miles of airlines and mechanical adjuncts; Auburn in the popular price field but with unique appeal; Cord for the *avant garde;* Duesenberg for the high and the mighty with an aura all its own; subsidiary suppliers almost like General Motors—this whole structure was erected, first and last, by one young man's wits and daring.

18. A Legendary Life

Most of us will not think through a problem to the end, we are afraid to be different, hesitant to act on our own initiative. It may be the safest plan in the long run, but battles are not won simply through playing it safe. Suppose Grant or Pershing had never permitted their men to do anything but play safe! I think it is the same in civil life. Get the facts, make your plan, then act, regardless of what outsiders or friends may say. The worst you can do is to fail—the experience is worth the effort.

E. L. Cord had progressed from certain obscurity to the helm of vast enterprise by bringing to bear the hair's breadth practicality of his Scotch ancestry against whatever limitations happened to be built-in to each situation along the way. It was the sometimes alarming speed with which he acted on his decisions to make the most of every opportunity that set this man apart from other tycoons of commerce.

"His hurried, boyish manner had capitalized the promise of his start and along the way he had acquired more friends than enemies," continued Arthur D. H. Smith. "He would put over other shrewd deals too.[10] Some of them he wouldn't bring off fully; from others he would make handsome sums."

While Cord's diverse interests in transportation—on land, in the air and, later, at sea—would become legendary, automotive historians were to remember Cord in retrospect even more for another transportation adventure, at this juncture, several years yet to come.

In the Cord L-29 model Mr. Cord had literally put the horse before the cart. The logic of the idea had distinguished the car's promotion, won prominent advocates among the socially elite and, in short, created a new status symbol.

But the average middle class motorist who could have afforded the Cord had turned out to be a traditionalist who enjoyed more the continuity of engineering, gradual improvement and nominal departure from the norm that characterized the products of other manufacturers.

The fact that the new Cord was not "tried and true" on the road had been made much of by sellers of other makes. They had quelled public excitement for the car at every turn with tales of unreliability in anything new, particularly in an engineering approach as radical as front-wheel drive.

The Cord was, indeed a beautiful car, conceded some, so good-looking, they said, that it didn't *have* to be a *good* car too. "Sure it's handsome, maybe so pretty you won't notice its downright dangerous engineering design." They said it was unsafe because the rear end was free to skid.

[10]A couple of years later he would pick up the New York Shipbuilding Company for an outlay of two million dollars. On the boards were Navy contracts worth nearly fifty million dollars.

THE EVENING TRIBUNE

San Diego, Cal., Saturday, Nov. 9

INSURANCE RATES LOW ON NEW CORD

AUBURN, Ind., Nov. 9.—Collision insurance rates on the new Cord front drive car have been set by the Board of Underwriters at the lowest figure of any car in its price class.

These rates were placed following exhaustive tests in the Underwriters' laboratories and were based on the small amount of damage that could be done to the vital parts of the car in head-on collisions and similar accidents.

The exceptional construction of the Cord front drive chassis frame, the ample protection of the large tubular, seamless front axle to the gears and other parts made this low rate possible, N. E. McDarby, director of sales, said in comment.

Fire and theft rates were also placed at a low figure by the board, the distinction of the Cord playing an important part in the low theft rate.

Of special note in Board of Underwriters findings was that the conspicious configuration of the Cord was a plus consideration toward affixing a low theft insurance rate.

This was not a valid objection to the Cord. It was, in truth, well-engineered and rarely broke loose in cornering. (For the record, it cornered more safely than some contemporaries with conventional rear-wheel drive.)

Rumors were also circulated that the front tires couldn't take both the strain of steering and the stress of driving and so frequently blew out with perilous results.

This was not an objective criticism of front-wheel drive. Front tires did give substantial service with traditional safety.

There came to be those who persisted in the feeling that the horse was placed *too far* before the cart. Drive wheels were positioned at the very front of a long wheelbase in which much of the car's body weight was located far to the rear; it was pointed out that when the engine weight transferred to the rear on a severe grade the front drive wheels would lose traction.

There was perhaps a trace of truth in this objection. When uncertain surfaces like loose gravel, or snow and ice, appeared on a very steep hill, occasionally, the wheels were bound to spin. Rear-wheel drive cars had been known to spin wheels under certain adverse conditions too. No owner of record ever disposed of his Cord in dispair.

For all practical purposes a more compact chassis layout would have resolved this problem of wheelspin and laid its critics permanently to rest.

For those comfortably situated individuals who dared to be modern and to be different, for Errett Lobban Cord who wanted a car that would be seen and known, and for little boys everywhere, the Cord front-wheel drive had been a great and exciting adventure from beginning to end . . .

EXCLUSIVE ADVANTAGES

A natural span of time was necessary for so different an automobile to prove itself. Confirmation is not lacking today. It is abundant and conclusive. The experience of more than four thousand owners constitutes an unparalleled record in all motor car history. Today the Cord ranks supreme, the undisputed leader in the fine car field. Doubt has given way to conviction; prejudice to admiration! There is nothing to wait for, no reason to put off enjoying the exclusive advantages obtainable only with front-drive. Especially, now that this car-of-tomorrow is made available today at new prices comparable to ordinary standard cars. We welcome an opportunity to let you drive the Cord and see for yourself why it offers the greatest fine car value on the market.

BROUGHAM $2395 · SEDAN $2395 · CONVERTIBLE CABRIOLET $2495 · CONVERTIBLE PHAETON SEDAN $2595

Prices f.o.b. Auburn, Indiana. ***Equipment other than standard, extra. Prices subject to change without notice.***

AUBURN AUTOMOBILE CO., AUBURN, IND.

CORD

FRONT DRIVE

19. The Fountain of Youth . . . with Four Wheels

We submit it as a simple statement of fact that this car requires no selling to those who can afford it.

The L-29 was not to be the end of the front-wheel drive cars from the Auburn Automobile Company. It would prove only a forceful first act, for the pull-instead-of-push concept was to continue to intrigue Errett Cord in the years immediately to come.

A new opportunity would arise for Cord to exercise his *ultimate prerogative* once again a few seasons later.

Eventually, *Fortune* magazine would call Cord "a mechanical exhibitionist." It would be recognition of sorts for the second series Cord which would appear publically out of the blue in the mid-'thirties to become a worldwide sensation for the inspired sculpture of its body lines. The old hill-climbing bugaboo would be licked. The new Cord would again precurse the styling of the whole automobile industry—this time for all cars, everywhere.

For E. L. Cord, more fortune, more fame, and more fun lay in a new day just ahead. This second Cord, introduced as the model 810, was destined to settle into American history as the sole automobile design ever to be recognized as a *timeless classic.*

Hearts of motor enthusiasts all over the country would skip a beat one fall evening in 1935 when they spread open their favorite magazines to find this announcement.

The man and his first 810, photographed at his Hillcrest Drive estate.

438 524

NEW MODEL REGISTRATIONS BY YEARS
Tabulating United States Sales Only

	1929	1930	1931	1932	TOTAL
Alabama	0	2	5	0	7
Arizona	4	3	1	0	8
Arkansas	0	4	1	0	5
California	91	258	84	25	458
Colorado	4	12	16	3	35
Connecticut	10	26	18	1	55
Delaware	3	4	0	0	7
Florida	9	39	22	4	74
Georgia	10	12	13	1	36
Idaho	2	2	4	1	9
Illinois	121	287	218	28	654
Indiana	35	93	82	21	231
Iowa	11	20	14	3	48
Kansas	0	8	14	3	25
Kentucky	11	13	13	2	39
Louisiana	0	6	12	1	19
Maine	0	4	2	1	7
Maryland	6	9	17	3	35
Massachusetts	29	72	41	5	147
Michigan	31	60	52	6	149
Minnesota	17	16	17	2	52
Mississippi	0	0	1	0	1
Missouri	13	39	51	10	113
Montana	3	12	4	2	21
Nebraska	3	14	8	0	25
Nevada	4	3	4	0	11
New Hampshire	0	3	0	0	3
New Jersey	32	71	63	22	188
New Mexico	0	1	0	0	1
New York	150	350	273	121	894
No. Carolina	2	4	7	0	13
No. Dakota	0	3	1	0	4
Ohio	59	105	106	20	290
Oklahoma	16	20	11	0	47
Oregon	1	6	11	0	18
Pennsylvania	62	115	89	18	284
Rhode Island	12	14	6	0	32
So. Carolina	0	1	4	1	6
Tennessee	1	15	3	0	19
Texas	8	29	29	4	70
Utah	3	13	3	1	20
Vermont	0	10	1	0	11
Virginia	2	15	11	7	35
Washington	18	22	18	6	64
West Virginia	1	11	14	7	33
Wisconsin	10	37	38	2	87
Wyoming	2	2	1	1	6
District of Columbia	3	10	11	3	27
TOTAL	799	1879	1416	335	4429

SERIAL NUMBERS BY YEARS*

1930 Series
Began August 11, 1929

1931 Series
Began January 1, 1931
2928720 to 2930153

1932 Series
Began January 1, 1932
2930154 and up

*Located at front end of frame on right side. Also appears on plate attached to front floorboard, right side.

ENGINE NUMBER located on left side of engine, at rear. Also appears on serial number plate.

BODY NUMBER located near floorboard serial number plate.

A complete reproduction of the Shop Manual begins on the next page.

CORD FRONT DRIVE

Model L-29

Shop Manual *for* Service Mechanics

Auburn Automobile Co., Auburn, Ind.

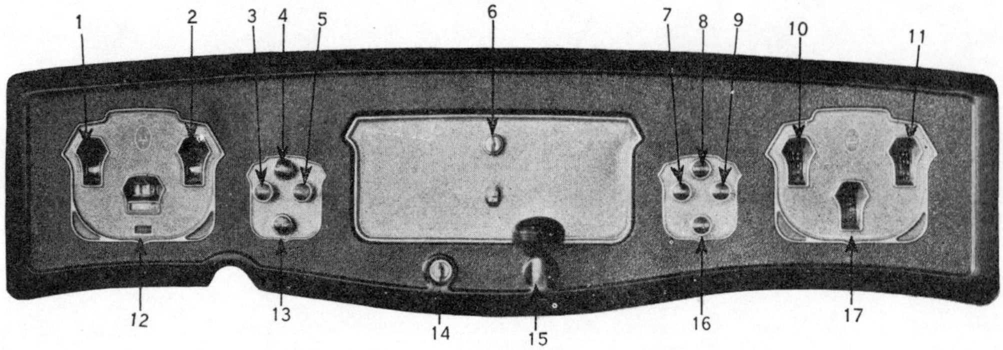

INSTRUMENT PANEL

1. Engine Heat Indicator
2. Oil Pressure Gauge
3. Spark Control
4. Windshield Wiper Control, left
5. Gasoline Throttle
6. Glove Compartment
7. Carburetor Choke
8. Windshield Wiper Control, right
9. Manifold Heat Control
10. Gasoline Gauge
11. Oil Level Gauge
12. Speedometer
13. Instrument Light Switch
14. Ignition Lock
15. Gear Shift Lever
16. Starter Control
17. Ammeter

SERVICE

This Manual, covering Service adjustments on the new Cord Front Drive Model L-29, is designed to assist the service organizations of our distributors and dealers in the upkeep of these cars. It is not an office manual. It has been compiled by the mechanics in our Front Drive Division and is intended to help the mechanics in your Service organization.

This first Cord Model has been developed through years of experimental work in the hands of trained specialists. The mechanical features of the car are all correctly designed, and, with some exceptions, follow standards with which service stations are familiar. By careful observance of instructions covering the unusual features of this Model, service mechanics will find the operations in connection with adjustments very simple and easy to perform.

Lubrication is an important factor. Carry in stock the proper lubricants which will be needed for this Model. Sell the owner on the idea of your systematic and correct inspection and lubrication service. He will appreciate your interest in his car and it will increase your business.

Before disassembling units, note carefully how they are assembled. It will aid you in taking them apart and in reassembling them. Carefully clean and inspect all parts and see that relubricating is properly done, where needed, before restoring them to place. New gaskets and cotter pins should be used in place of the old ones.

Check carefully everything that is removed from an assembly and see that it gets back in its proper place.

In making replacements, use only genuine Cord parts.

Careful attention to details in connection with all operations will increase sales.

OPERATING INSTRUCTIONS

Study the location of all instruments and controls on instrument board and familiarize yourself with their operation.

Starting the Engine:

First see that oil in crankcase is up to proper level, radiator is filled with clean, soft water and that you have a sufficient supply of gasoline in tank.

See that the gear shift lever is in neutral position (shift lever knob pointing straight upward).

Unlock ignition by turning key one quarter turn to the right.

Retard the spark by drawing spark control out part way, and draw gasoline throttle part way out.

In cool weather the carburetor choke knob should be drawn out.

Now draw out the starter control. If starting motor pinion does not engage flywheel gear, release starter control and after a pause, draw it out again.

As soon as engine begins firing, release starter control and push carburetor choke back to original position gradually, or until the engine runs smoothly.

Return the gasoline throttle to original position to avoid racing the engine. Push the spark control in as far as it will go, for correct driving position.

CAUTION: Do not race the engine, when lubricant is cold and car is standing still, as it might cause serious damage.

Do not attempt to start the engine or allow it to run in a closed garage.

Chassis Lubrication:

Immediately after starting the engine and before starting the car, depress the pedal of the Bijur Chassis Lubricator. The pedal is located on floor board above clutch pedal within reach of the drivers left foot. Press the pedal downward as far as possible, then remove the foot.

Starting the Car:

Release hand brake and disengage clutch by pushing forward the clutch pedal. Turn gear shift lever to left and move it forward into first speed or low gear position. Allow clutch to engage gradually and at same time slightly increase the engine speed with the foot accelerator, or the gasoline throttle which beginners may at first find it easier to use.

When the car is under way, disengage clutch and draw shift lever back to neutral, turn it to right and draw outward into second or intermediate speed. Allow clutch to engage slowly, again slightly increasing the engine speed. When a speed of ten to fifteen miles per hour is attained, push the gear shift lever straight forward into third or high speed position, and allow clutch to engage. This is the position used for general driving and the speed may be controlled by the foot accelerator.

In making the shift, pause slightly in neutral. Practice the shifts so they may be made without clashing the gears.

Should road conditions necessitate dropping to a lower speed, disengage clutch, reduce the engine speed, move gear shift lever to desired position, increase engine speed, and allow clutch to engage. The shift should be made quickly in order to retain the momentum of the car.

To reduce speed, when in slow traffic, or to make a short turn, disengage clutch and slightly depress brake pedal.

To Stop the Car:

Slow down; disengage the clutch; move shift lever to neutral. Brake car speed gradually with the right foot pedal, a moderate pressure only being needed to engage the hydraulic four wheel brakes, and bring the car smoothly and quickly to a stop.

To Back the Car:

After car has been brought to a full stop, disengage clutch, turn shift lever to left in neutral position and draw it outward into reverse gear position. Engage clutch and slightly increase speed of engine. Watch the steering carefully, do not back rapidly, and always be ready to operate clutch and brake pedals instantly.

The car is equipped with a back-up light controlled from shifting rod and engaging automatically for the reverse operation at night.

To Stop the Engine:

Lock the ignition by turning key to the left. Set the hand or emergency brake before leaving the car.

"WEARING-IN" A NEW CAR

When a new car is placed in operation, the cylinder walls, pistons, piston pins and rings, as well as all bearing surfaces, are tightly fitted. The first 1,000 miles of operation will impart a glass-like finish to all surfaces, depending however upon correct lubrication and care in operation.

During the first 500 miles the car should not be driven in excess of 25 miles per hour. After this period the rate of speed can gradually be increased to 35 and for short distances to 45 miles per hour. After 1,000 miles the car can gradually be speeded up to the maximum speed desired.

LICENSE DATA AND GENERAL INFORMATION

Car Serial Number	
Engine Serial Number	
(Those numbers are stamped on plate mounted in body near right front door).	
Cylinder Bore	$3\frac{1}{4}''$
Stroke	$4\frac{1}{2}''$
Number of Cylinders	8
S.A.E. Horse Power Rating	33.8
Developed Horse Power	125
Piston Displacement	298.6 Cu.In.
Firing Order	1,6,2,5,8,3,7,4
Capacity of Crankcase	8 Quarts
Capacity of Cooling System	$5\frac{1}{2}$ Gallons
Wheel Base	$137\frac{1}{2}$ inches
Length over all, including bumpers	196 inches
Length, without bumpers	186 inches
Width over all	75 inches
Capacity of Gasoline Supply Tank	20 Gallons

LUBRICATION

Constant and correct lubrication of all wearing parts is vitally important. Careful attention to this feature will result in the maximum amount of wear and satisfactory service. It is just as important to use the proper quality of lubricants as it is to apply them correctly and at proper intervals.

Chassis:

Daily, or during every 100 miles of continuous driving, depress the pedal of Bijur Chassis Lubricator. When first placing the car in service or after a long period of disuse, give the pedal a number of strokes to fill the system with oil.

Engine:

Every 500 miles the crankcase should be drained and refilled with 8 quarts of oil conforming to the required specifications listed on page 11.

Generator:

Every 1,000 miles, add 8 to 10 drops of good grade light engine oil in front and rear hinge cap oilers.

Starting Motor:

Every 1,000 miles, add 8 to 10 drops of good grade light engine oil in the oiler on commutator end bearings.

Distributor:

Keep grease cup filled with good clean, medium cup grease, and give it a complete turn every 1,000 miles. At same time apply a drop of oil to breaker arm pivots and wick beneath rotor, and lubricate cam with vaseline.

Steering Gear:

Keep housing filled with lubricant, using any one of those listed in lubrication schedule under STEERING GEAR.

Front Driving Unit:

The transmission and differential parts of this unit must be kept filled to proper level with Whitmore's Auto Gear Protective Composition No. "0".

Check the lubricant in wheel universals every 5000 miles and relubricate with Alemite grease.

The differential universals should be checked every 10,000 miles and packed with a fibrous graphite or a good heat resisting grease.

Drag Link:
Fill the cups with good clean cup grease every 500 miles.

Front Axle Tie Rod:
Fill the cups with good clean cup grease every 500 miles.

Front Wheel Bearings:
Clean and pack with good clean cup grease every three to six months, depending upon the service. A grease plug located on flange may be removed and cup grease added at intervals, when needed.

Rear Wheel Bearings:
Clean and pack with good clean cup grease every three to six months, depending upon the service.

See the text under headings BIJUR CENTRAL CHASSIS LUBRICATOR; SERVICE BRAKES; WIRE WHEELS, and HOUDAILLE SHOCK ABSORBERS, for directions regarding the lubrication of these units.

In the owner's manual we recommend that their Cord Front Drive, model L-29, be taken to the dealers for lubrication service in order to insure the use of correct lubricants in the various units.

COOLING SYSTEM

The Radiator, of approved cellular type, is connected through pipe and hose lines to water pump mounted on crankcase, affording ample water circulation.

The Fan is driven by the accessory shaft through a V type belt which is adjusted by loosening the bracket nuts and raising bracket until right tension is secured, after which the nuts must be drawn tight. Do not draw the belt too tight but bring it only to a snug tension.

The water pump bearing, fan bearing and fan countershaft bearing receive lubrication through the Bijur central chassis lubricator.

A set of radiator guards, operated by a thermostat and especially designed for this model, is mounted in front of the radiator. The thermostatic action is controlled by the temperature of the water in the system, guards opening at approximately 130 degrees.

The actuating temperature can be regulated by loosening the jam nut on stud located in center of upper tank. However, this is set at the factory for action at the most satisfactory operating temperature and should not be changed.

The guards open inward, therefore, the operation is not affected by wind resistance while driving at high speed.

The capacity of cooling system is 5½ gallons. Use soft water whenever possible. The radiator should be drained and flushed occasionally to remove collected sediment. If car is to be unused for a time, drain out the water, running the engine a minute or two to insure perfect drainage. Do not fail to refill the system before again using the car.

In freezing temperatures, anti-freeze solutions should be kept in the cooling system. Denatured alcohol is a practical anti-freeze solution, but on account of its tendency to evaporate, the strength of the mixture should be frequently tested with a hydrometer and alcohol added when needed to maintain the proper gravity.

The protection afforded by a denatured alcohol solution is shown below:

Denatured Alcohol *(By Volume)*	Water *(By Volume)*	Begins to freeze at *(Degrees Fahr.)*
4½ pints	39½ pints	27°
9 "	35 "	19°
14 "	30 "	10°
17½ "	26½ "	– 2°
22 "	22 "	–18°

On arrival of warm weather, drain out the mixture and refill with clear water. The system can be quickly drained by opening the drain cock in water pump intake manifold at bottom of radiator.

When pouring alcohol in radiator, do not allow it to get on the hood, as it will ruin the lacquer finish. If this should happen it must be wiped off at once to avoid spotting.

Do not pour cold water into an empty or partly empty radiator while the engine is hot, as it might cause serious damage.

ENGINE ADJUSTMENTS

Cylinder Head and Gasket:

To remove cylinder head, drain water; disconnect the upper hose and spark plug wires from cylinder head; loosen distributor set screw. Lift the distributor off cylinder head out of the way. Remove cylinder head and then the gasket. Handle gasket carefully.

Replacement of gasket and head is more important than the removal. If gasket is not in good condition, renew it. See that surfaces of cylinder head, gasket and block are clean. Put gasket in position on the studs and press it down on cylinder face and replace the head.

The cylinder nuts should be tightened gradually and in such a way as to equally distribute the pressure throughout the entire head.

Tighten center nuts first and work both ways toward the ends. This will prevent strains in cylinder head casting.

The driving tongues and slots for distributor are offset so it can be reassembled without disturbing the timing.

Pistons:

Pistons are hand fitted, special aluminum alloy of the Invar-Strut type, which permit closer fitting than possible with cast iron.

To remove them it is not necessary to take off the cylinder head, nor is it necessary to drain the water system unless you intend removing cylinder head. Drain off the oil.

Remove the oil pan from crankcase. Turn crankshaft with starting crank until a connecting rod is pointed straight down. Remove the cotter pins, nuts and connecting rod cap. Turn the crankshaft until the piston slides by the crankshaft. Then assemble, at once, the cap and nuts on connecting rod.

In fitting pistons, use a shim .0015″ thick and ¼″ wide placed along the length of piston directly opposite the slot in skirt. It should pull freely with the fingers. To check the fitting a shim of same width but .0025″ thick should stick in same position so it cannot readily be pulled out with the bare fingers.

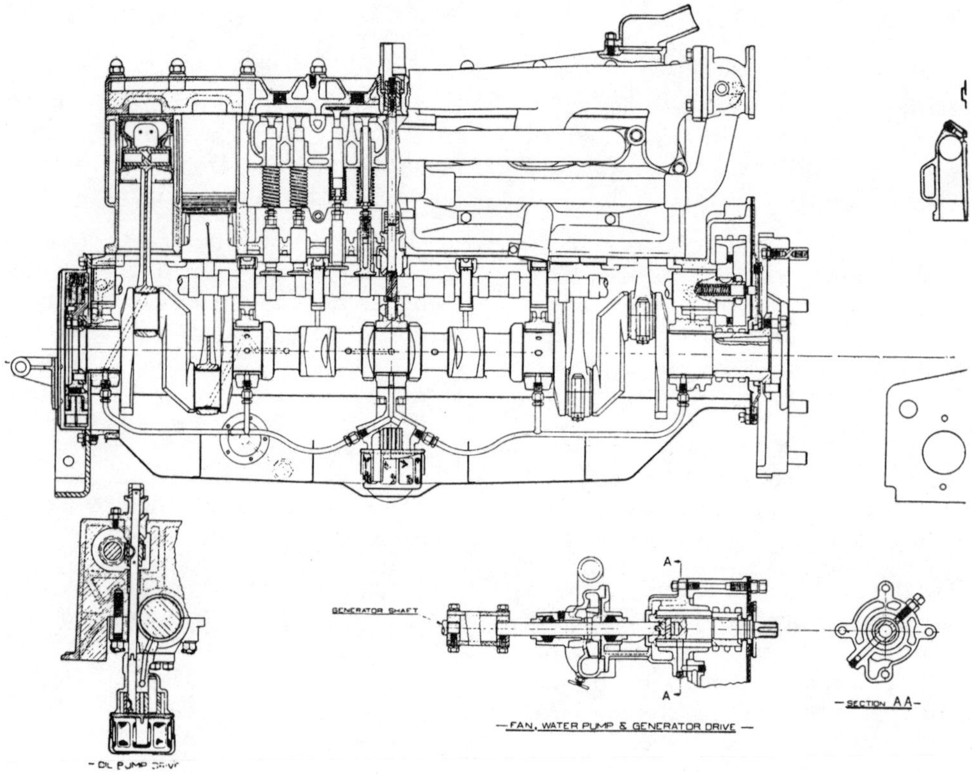

Piston Pins:

When connecting rod is removed, test the pin for looseness in piston bosses. If necessary to fit new pins the bearing surfaces in piston must be reamed smoothly and in perfect alignment. Fit pin tight enough so when the assembly is held by the piston, the free end of rod will, with a slight push, drop of its own weight.

Piston Rings:

Each piston is equipped with four rings, two 1/8" compression and two 3/16" oil regulating rings.

When the rings become worn to any extent they should be replaced at once. New rings should have about .0015" side clearance in grooves and .006" to .012" gap between the ends.

Connecting Rod:

The connecting rod cap must be replaced in exactly the same position it was originally. No. 1 connecting rod and cap, for example, have a "1" stamped on side of rod, also on cap. These numbers must be on same side.

Pistons and rods must be returned to same cylinder from which removed. Cylinders are numbered from front to rear and the rods from rear to front. The large end of rod is offset 1/16". In replacing rods see that they are installed with offset on same side as originally. The short side of rod is assembled nearest to main bearing. When the oil jet holes in large end of rods are on opposite side from camshaft, the assembly is correct.

Rods are hand fitted at factory to a clearance of .0015". This is checked by fitting a piece of paper .0015" thick and 1 1/8" square between the shaft and bearing and drawing up the nuts tightly. The rod should then just support its own weight, but a very little pressure should move it.

Adjust when wear of .004" or more has taken place. It can be done by filing off face of cap but care must be taken to keep the surface straight.

A loose connecting rod bearing is most noticeable on a hard pull. It is possible to locate the loose bearing by listening closely or by removing oil pan and noting any looseness in the cap. Pressing against cap and rocking crankshaft will show which bearing needs adjustment.

Main Bearings:

As no shims are used, adjustment is secured by filing off faces of caps, being careful to keep surfaces straight. The proper clearance between crankshaft and main bearings is .0025" to .003". Adjust after wear of .003" has taken place. Never fit bearings so tight that shaft cannot be turned by hand with a .002" feeler 1/2" wide assembled between bearing and shaft. Bearings are bronze backed, babbitt lined.

Valve Grinding:

When valves become pitted and scored enough to cause loss of compression, they should be reground in their respective seats.

To remove valves drain the water and remove cylinder head. Remove the valve cover plates from side of engine and with a suitable lifter raise the valve springs and take out the conical shaped valve spring supports. (Be careful not to drop them through the oil holes in cylinder base into crankcase). Lift out the valves.

When grinding, place under the head a spring of sufficient tension to hold valve from its seat when not under pressure from the valve tool. Place a little coarse grinding compound on valve and work it into the seat with an oscillating movement of valve, always bearing lightly on valve and making not more than one-half revolution of valve before reversing the direction of motion, otherwise grooves in facing will result. When all pits and black spots have disappeared and valve presents a dull, silvery appearance finish grinding with a fine compound.

The valve face should have a surface free from grooves and pits but need not be polished. It will acquire this in use. Each valve should be ground in its own seat.

To test whether the seat is perfect, mark lines across face of head about 1/8" apart with a soft pencil. Then replace valve and make a quarter rotation backward and forward. All pencil lines should be broken. If not, continue grinding until all lines are broken which indicates that valve is seating all around.

After grinding is completed, wash valves and seats with kerosene to remove all traces of compound and see that none of it gets into cylinder bores.

Valve Adjustment:

To insure proper fitting, the clearance between end of valve and head of adjusting screw on valve tappet must be .006″ intake and .008″ exhaust with warm engine. The clearance is adjusted by removing valve cover plates and adjusting screw on top of tappet with suitable wrenches. Make sure that the lock nut is tight.

Valve Timing:

The firing order is 1-6-2-5-8-3-7-4. Valves are timed as follows:

Intake open upper dead center.

Intake close 45 degrees past lower dead center.

Exhaust open 50 degrees before lower dead center.

Exhaust close 10 degrees after upper dead center.

When checking valve timing the clearance between valve stem and tappet must be exactly .010″. This clearance should then be reset to .006″ to .008″ for quietness. The timing is correctly set at factory. No change is possible or necessary unless front end chain has been removed for some reason.

Ignition Timing:

The ignition is semi-automatic advance, the distributor head rotating in order to advance the ignition manually. To secure correct timing, the flywheel must be set so No. 1 cylinder is 12.8 degrees ahead of top dead center on firing stroke, that is, turn crank clockwise until mark on flywheel lacks four teeth of reaching top center position. In this position set the spark control at full advance. Then set the distributor so contact points are just breaking for No. 1 cylinder. A small amount of variation can be taken up by loosening clamp on advance arm and turning distributor head. Rotating distributor clockwise advances the ignition and anti-clockwise retards it. No. 1 dead center mark on flywheel should be opposite center line of opening in flywheel housing used for timing purposes.

With this spark setting we recommend the use of non-detonating fuel for best all around results.

Ignition should not be advanced beyond the point where a spark knock occurs, except under full load conditions.

Front End Chain:

Any excess slack which may develop in the chain is automatically taken up. The tension on tightener spring is set at the factory and no further adjustment is required. Should it be necessary to remove the chain, proceed as follows: After the front driving unit and clutch are drawn off, remove the flywheel; take off the plates covering water pump drive shaft and crankshaft; remove the 6 cap screws which support oil pan; remove starter; take out 2 studs to your right as you face the assembly; then draw off the outer plate of chain case cover.

Then take the cotter pin out of automatic tightener shaft and draw off the inner cover plate.

Now pull out the inside member of tightener which contains the spring, leaving the revolving sprocket ring in contact with the chain. After the inside member is withdrawn the chain can readily be removed.

To replace the chain, turn crankshaft until cylinders Nos. 1 and 8 are on upper dead center. (There is a hole, closed by a pipe plug, in the head of cylinder No. 8 for small rod to determine when the piston is at exact top position). Then turn camshaft until the first two complete teeth you see, sighting over the top of flange on crankshaft, are those with the prick-punch marks. A square laid across top of crankshaft will assist in determining correct position.

Now wrap the chain over the sprockets and under the tightener stud. When replacing the tightener, push it around into the chain until chain is taut, and wind up the spring one and a half turns, using a tool made from 15/16″ diameter stock with hacksaw slot in end to engage the spring.

Reassemble all parts which were removed, using new gaskets in replacing chain case cover plate and plate over crankshaft.

Compression:

Compression in all cylinders must be equal. Check for uniformity by rocking the engine against the compression of each cylinder with the hand crank, or with a suitable compression pressure gauge.

Camshaft:

End thrust of camshaft is taken by rear face of sprocket against the front bearing boss in crankcase. No end play exists because of a specially designed, automatic spring plunger, which bears against a hardened plug in chain case.

The camshaft bearings should not need replacement during the life of the car. If for any reason new bearings should be required, fit them with a clearance of from .0025″ to .0035″ between shaft and bearings.

Cylinder Block:

It is important when replacing cylinder block to see that the cylinder base stud nuts are drawn up tightly. In attempting to locate an engine knock, first see that all nuts, especially those on extreme front and back ends, are tight. A loose cylinder block will cause a dull heavy knock similar to that caused by a loose main bearing.

Manifolding:

The manifolding is designed to give the least resistance to gas flow and is provided with a variable heat control to reduce the length of warming-up period and prolonged use of choke when starting with a cold engine.

The forward end of exhaust manifold is equipped with a specially designed damper valve controlled from instrument board. This valve is closed by drawing out the dash control which forces the exhaust gases around intake riser and thence through the by-pass tube to muffler pipe.

The valve must be opened as soon as engine reaches a proper operating temperature, to prevent loss of power due to exhaust back pressure while valve is closed.

Use of this valve reduces crankcase dilution and provides best operating conditions at all times.

Crankshaft:

The crankshaft, accurately balanced, statically and dynamically, is drop-forged of high carbon, double heat-treated steel. The counter-weights (which reduce bearing pressures and distortion) are forged integral with the shaft.

A Lanchester torsional vibration dampener is fitted to the end of crankshaft.

Storing the Engine:

When storing the engine, drain crankcase, refill with fresh oil and run the engine a few minutes. Drain the radiator and open drip cock on water pump. Remove spark plugs and pour two or three tablespoonfuls of oil into each cylinder, preferably castor oil. Turn engine over several times to distribute the oil over cylinder walls and valve mechanism. Oil should be injected into cylinders at intervals of three to six months during storage and before putting engine into service. When starting engine for the first time after it has been in storage, run it slowly for a few minutes.

Muffler:

The muffler is equipped with a by-pass valve controlled by a throttle on floor board within the driver's reach. The valve opens when the control is drawn up, permitting the exhaust gases to escape without going through the baffle plates. This reduces back pressure and increases the power at high speeds. Naturally the exhaust noise is louder while this valve is open.

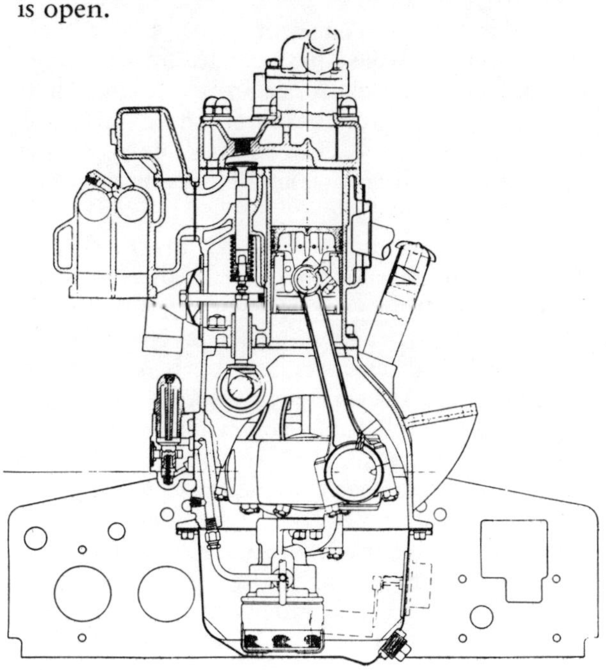

LUBRICATION SYSTEM

The full pressure oiling system is self-contained in upper half of crankcase, permitting removal of oil pan without disturbing any piping.

Oil Pump:

The gear type oil pump is operated by a shaft driven by a spiral gear on camshaft. It is bolted to center main bearing cap about even in height with normal oil level. The oil strainer is secured to bottom of pump and completely submerged in oil. The pump will never lose prime.

The oil pump may be removed for cleaning or inspection by taking off lower half of crankcase and disconnecting the oil manifolds. Whenever the crankcase is removed, the oil strainer should be removed and cleaned.

Oil Circulation:

Oil is drawn from reservoir through strainer and is pumped to main bearings. Main bearings 1, 2, 4 and 5 are supplied by copper tubing manifolds connected to bottom of bearing caps. The center bearing is supplied through a drilled passage in oil pump.

Oil is forced to connecting rod lower bearings through drilled passages leading through crankshaft from main bearings. A small hole is drilled in each connecting rod that indexes with its respective crankshaft hole once per revolution, emitting a jet of oil which lubricates cylinder wall.

Passages conduct oil under pressure from front main bearing to chain tightener stud, around the stud to the accessory drive bearing. Oil holes in the revolving sprocket ring of the automatic tightener register with oil passages in the stud. At every revolution of the tightener ring several shots of oil are supplied to the chain and sprockets. The surplus oil from front end drains back into oil reservoir.

The piston pin bearings, cylinder walls and valve operating mechanism are oiled by spray thrown from connecting rod bearings. Troughs cast on upper side of camshaft bearing supports collect the oil and feed it to camshaft bearings through drilled holes. The valve stems are lubricated by oil spray through large holes in cylinder base.

A branch from the oil manifold leads to the oil regulator on right side of crankcase.

Oil Pressure Regulator:

The piston type regulator automatically controls the maximum oil pressure. The piston valve is held in a closed position by a spring until excessive oil pressure forces it down, when the surplus oil is by-passed to crankcase

The regulator is adjusted in following manner: Disconnect oil line leading from regulator to oil gauge. Remove the cylindrical air chamber which is screwed into top of regulator body. Withdraw the steel plunger, noting that head end points up. Remove the spring with a hooked wire and then insert or remove a small washer under the spring. Adding washers will increase the pressure; the removal will reduce the pressure. Do not change the setting by more than one washer at a time as the adjustment is quite sensitive.

The oil pressure with warm engine and oil should be ten pounds at idling speed, and at speeds of 50 m.p.h. or over the pressure should show a minimum of thirty-five pounds.

If these pressures are not obtained, the regulator should be adjusted.

Oil is poured through filler tube on side of crankcase. Keep filled between the two marks on bayonet gauge which is to be inserted in filler tube. About eight quarts are required to fill to high level. Oil should not be carried above the high mark.

The oil should be drained and renewed at the end of each 500 miles of driving. The drain plug is located in the bottom at left side of oil pan .

The oil pressure gauge indicates the oil circulation only and does not show when the supply in crankcase is running low.

The oil level in crankcase is registered by the oil level gauge on instrument board and this gauge should be examined frequently, when engine is not running, to determine oil supply.

A Purolator oil filter is mounted on dash under hood on right side. The crankcase oil is passed through the filter where all dirt, sludge and abrasive substances are removed and the clear oil is returned to the oil pan.

After approximately 8,000 to 12,000 miles of service the efficiency of the filter is lessened, due to accumulated foreign matter in the cartridge, and the cartridge should be replaced. This cartridge (our part No. N-1-935) is the complete filter less brackets and pipe fittings.

LUBRICATION RECOMMENDATIONS

In selecting the correct grade of engine oil, all factors in connection with design and operation of engine under all conditions have been given consideration.

When freezing temperatures are encountered, an oil of somewhat greater fluidity than oil suitable for summer temperatures should be used.

Our engineers recommend a high quality oil of the body and character of Gargoyle Mobioil BB for summer use, and Gargoyle Mobiloil Arctic for winter use (32° below), as at low temperatures an oil of greater fluidity is essential to insure safe and quick distribution.

These recommendations come within the range of S A E viscosity numbers 40 for summer and 20 for winter.

GENERAL SPECIFICATIONS

Type: Eight cylinders enbloc, four cycle, detachable vertical L head.

Bore	Stroke	Piston Displacement	Rating N.A.C.C. H.P.	H.P. Developed
3¼"	4½"	298.6 Cu.In.	33.8	125@3300

Firing Order: 1-6-2-5-8-3-7-4.
Cooling: Centrifugal water pump.
Ignition: Battery.
Intake: For 1½" Dual Carburetor.

Detail and Dimensional Specifications

Camshaft: Six bearing, .15-.25 carbon steel, cams integral.

Camshaft Diameter: 1⅛".

Camshaft Bearings:

	Diameter	Length
Front	2.038"	2⅛"
1st Inter.	2.007"	1"
2nd Inter.	1.991"	¾"
3rd Inter.	1.975"	¾"
4th Inter.	1.959"	1"
Rear	1.944"	1⅜"

Connecting Rod: "I" Beam section, .30-.40 carbon steel. Length (center to center) 9".

Connecting Rod Bearings: Diameter and length 2⅛" x 1½".

Connecting Rod Bolts: Nickel Steel 7/16"—two per rod.

Crankshaft: Five bearing, counter-weighted, .40-.50 carbon steel, double heat treated.

	Diameter	Length
Front Bearing	2⅜"	2-11/16"
1st Inter. Bearing	2⅜"	1-11/16"
Center Bearing	2⅜"	1-15/16"
2nd Inter. Bearing	2⅜"	1-3/4"
Rear Bearing	2⅜"	1-7/8"

Piston: Invar-Strut—Length 3-15/16".

Piston Rings: Two ⅛" compression, two 3/16" oil regulating.

Piston Pin: Diameter ⅞".

Valves: Effective working diam. (port diameter). Intake 1-7/16"; exhaust 1-5/16".

Valve Lift: 11/32".

Chain: The 1¾" wide silent chain drives camshaft and the fan, water pump and generator drive.

Flywheel: Diameter 14-5/32" out to out; 112 teeth; 3-1/5 degrees per tooth.

FUEL PUMP

The AC Fuel Pump, mounted on right side of engine and actuated by the camshaft, draws gasoline from the twenty gallon supply tank at rear of car and supplies it to the carburetor. It will deliver the correct amount of gasoline at all speeds and loads, under all road conditions and will give continuous service during the life of car.

The pump will not deliver more fuel than the engine can use.

Water and dirt are removed from the gasoline before it reaches the valves. No vapors are emitted as the system is entirely closed.

Fire hazard is reduced to a minimum as the only fuel under the hood is that in the carburetor bowl, fuel filter, and the short pipe between the two.

It is self-priming. Should the tank be entirely emptied only ten to fifteen engine revolutions are required to pump gasoline to carburetor.

It is an integral part of the engine and requires no lubrication.

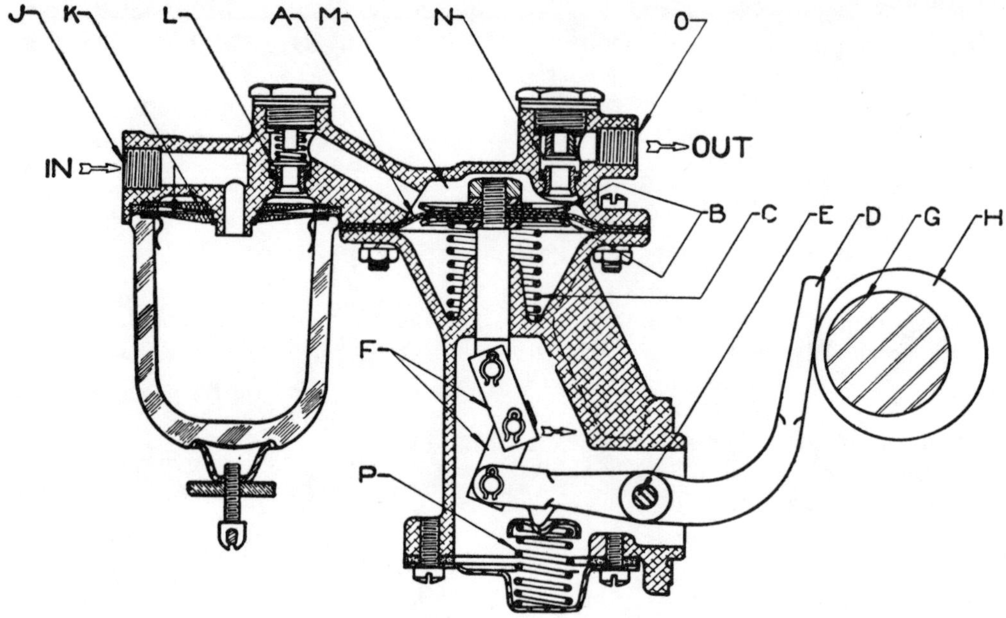

OPERATION OF FUEL PUMP

As camshaft (G) revolves, the eccentric (H) moves rocker arm (D) which is pivoted at (E), pulling linkage (F) together with diaphragm (A) held between metal discs (B) downward against spring pressure (C), creating a vacuum in pump chamber (M).

Fuel from rear tank enters at (J) through strainer (K) and suction valve (L) into pump chamber (M).

On the return stroke, spring pressure (C) pushes diaphragm (A) upward, forcing fuel from chamber (M) through pressure valve (N) and opening (O) into carburetor.

When carburetor bowl is filled, the float in float chamber will shut off the inlet needle valve, creating a pressure in pump chamber (M). This forces diaphragm (A) downward against spring pressure (C) where it will remain in the downward position until the carburetor requires further fuel and needle valve opens. Spring (P) is merely for the purpose of keeping operating lever (D) in constant contact with eccentric (H) to eliminate noise.

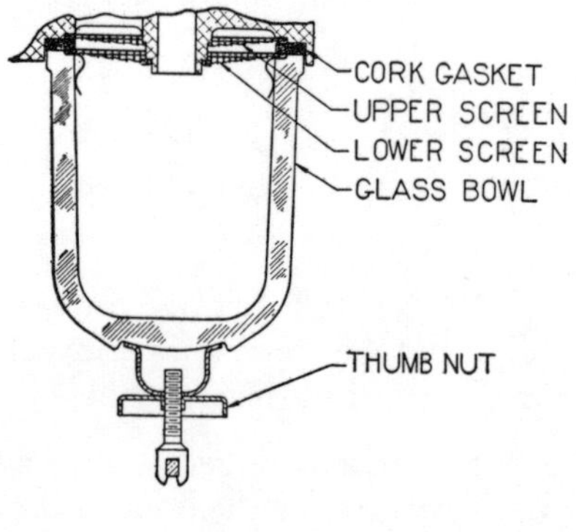

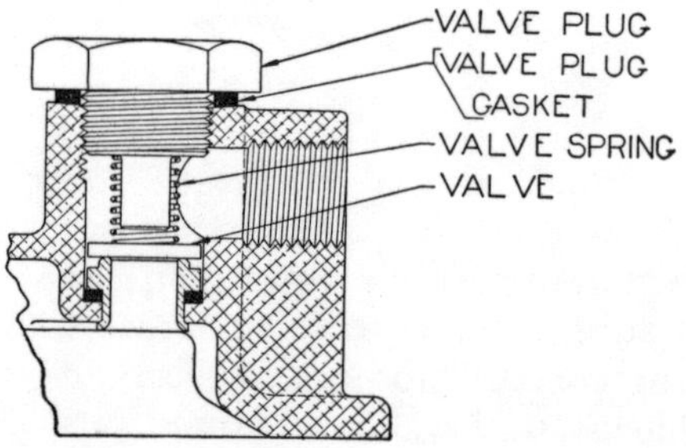

Service on the AC Fuel Pump is available through United Motors Service Branches and authorized AC Service Stations, as they will have parts and fixtures needed for replacement and repairs.

We are listing below a few service operations that are easily performed and will take care of minor troubles which may develop.

In some instances the fuel pump may be blamed for trouble caused by some other condition. Check the trouble carefully before replacing the pump.

The glass bowl should be removed and cleaned occasionally as required, as the accumulated sediment and water in bottom of bowl can be easily seen.

IMPORTANT: Do not attempt to disassemble the pump further than described below, as it is necessary to use a special fixture in reassembling the pump when once taken apart. If these remedies do not correct the condition, replace with a new fuel pump and return the old pump to your nearest United Motors Service Branch, or authorized AC Service Station.

SERVICE SUGGESTIONS

Lack of Fuel at Carburetor

Check as follows:

Cause	*Remedy*
Gasoline tank empty.	Refill.
Leaky tubing or connections.	Replace tubing and tighten all pipe connections at fuel pump and gasoline tank.
Bent or kinked tubing.	Replace tubing.
Glass bowl loose.	Tighten thumb nut, making certain that cork gasket lies flat in its seat and is not broken.
Dirty screen.	Remove glass bowl and clean the screen. Be sure the cork gasket is properly seated when reassembling.
Loose valve plug.	Tighten valve plug securely, replacing valve plug gasket if necessary.
Dirty or warped valves.	Remove valve plugs and valves. Wash valves in gasoline. If damaged or warped, replace them. See that there are no irregularities of valve seat which prevent proper seating of valves. Place valve in valve chamber with polished side downward. Make certain that valve lies flat on its seat and is not left standing on edge. Reassemble valve plug and spring and see that spring is around lower stem of valve plug properly. Use new gasket under valve plug if necessary.

Leakage of Fuel at Diaphragm

Check as follows:

Cause	*Remedy*
Loose cover screws.	Tighten cover screws alternately and securely. CAUTION: Do not disassemble pump body. NOTE: Sometimes there appears to be a leak at the diaphragm, whereas the leak actually exists at one of the pipe fittings and the fuel has run down the pump to the diaphragm flange, appearing to originate there.

CARBURETOR

Schebler Duplex Model "S"

When installing a new carburetor or in making adjustments for best results, the following precautions should be observed:

Be sure that the entire system and fuel lines

are free from sediment or foreign matter. Dirt will clog the lines and stop the flow of gasoline or flood the carburetor. Water will start rust, cause hard starting and freeze in the line in cold weather.

Check the ignition for proper timing and operation. Breaker points must be free from pits and properly spaced, usually .018″ to .024″. See that spark plugs are clean and points have proper gap, usually .025″ to .030".

Try the engine for compression, as proper carburetion cannot be obtained with faulty ignition or bad compression in one or more cylinders. Bad compression may be caused by scored cylinders, bad valve seats, warped valves, poor piston rings, or improper tappet clearances.

When an idle adjustment cannot be obtained, it might be due to some irregularity in the gasoline supply system.

Check the intake manifold gaskets for leaks by pouring a little gasoline over each gasket. Should there be a leak, the engine will immediately speed up and run smoothly for an instant.

Worn intake valve stems and guides will also cause trouble at idle speed.

CONTROL HOOK-UP: One standard hook-up is made as shown in cut. The control tubing is fastened securely in the clamp and screw assembly (M) with tubing projecting about 1/16″ beyond the clamp and the control wire in binding post (O) so there is about 1/16″ play between loose lever (D) and screw (P) when the throttle is closed. After tightening binding post (O) straighten out the control wire so loose lever (D) does not bind the dash control lever (S) and cause it to stick open when moved.

IDLING ADJUSTMENT: The duplex carburetor has two idle adjustments as shown at (A) and (E). The engine should be thoroughly warmed up before adjusting the idle. Both the spark and gasoline throttle must be fully retarded.

Turning (A) to right (clockwise) makes the mixture leaner in the throttle barrel on the side toward (A); to the left counter-clockwise) makes the mixture richer. Turn (E) just as if it were connected to the same shaft as (A) in same directions to richen or lean the mixture in the throttle barrel on the side toward (E).

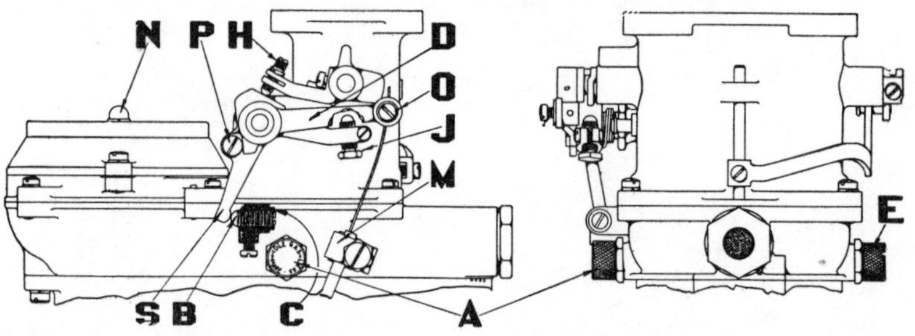

To adjust (A) disconnect and ground the spark plug wires leading to the cylinders fed by (E) and speed up the idle just enough to keep engine running. Adjust (A) rich or lean until engine starts to stop from being too lean when the air valve is held down 1/32″ off its seat.

To adjust (E) do the same as for (A) by

disconnecting spark plug wires to the cylinders fed by (A).

The two cylinders at each end are fed by (A) and the four center cylinders are fed by (E).

Connect all spark plug wires and check the idle with all cylinders firing. If the mixture seems rich or lean turn off or on *both* adjustments the *same* number of clicks.

To change the idle speed, adjust idle stop screw (H).

RANGE ADJUSTMENT: This adjustment is only effective in the driving range at speeds from 20 to 40 miles per hour and does not affect acceleration or hill climbing with wide open throttle.

The adjustment is made by turning the range adjusting screw (B) to the left for a lean mixture and to the right for a rich mixture in the driving range.

This adjustment as shipped from factory will usually be found to be best, unless a lean or richened mixture is necessary at speeds from 20 to 40 miles per hour.

To obtain the factory setting, turn the range adjusting screw in or out so the head is flush with bushing (C). If the range adjustment is changed it is necessary to readjust the idle mixture.

INSTALLATION AND SERVICE FOR NECO ELECTRIC GASOLINE GAUGE

The Neco Electric Gauge is a current balancing instrument being in its accuracy completely independent of changes in battery voltage. In the dash unit illustration you will notice two magnetically opposed coils of equal characteristics. The junction joint of these coils is brought out to a terminal on back of the instrument, and from there connected to battery. The other ends of each coil are brought out to terminals on the back of the instrument for connection with tank unit.

The tank unit consists electrically of a potentiometer, the ends of which are connected through the wiring harness respectively to the coil terminals on dash unit. A rotor in tank unit is connected through gears to the float. This rotor contacting at varying points around the inside periphery of the potentiometer, grounds it at the particular point of contact. This electrical connection creates two parallel circuits from upper terminal of dash unit to the ground in tank unit. These parallel circuits, vary exactly in their resistance with the changing level of gasoline in the tank, thereby causing corresponding changes in current flow.

Through the coils in dash unit travels a magnetizable vane mounted in an aluminum carrier to which the pointer is affixed. As the relative current values of the two coils in the dash unit change, their relative magneto motive forces change correspondingly, hence the vane will assume varying positions dependent upon the relative strength of the two coils.

For example, in the zero position the tank

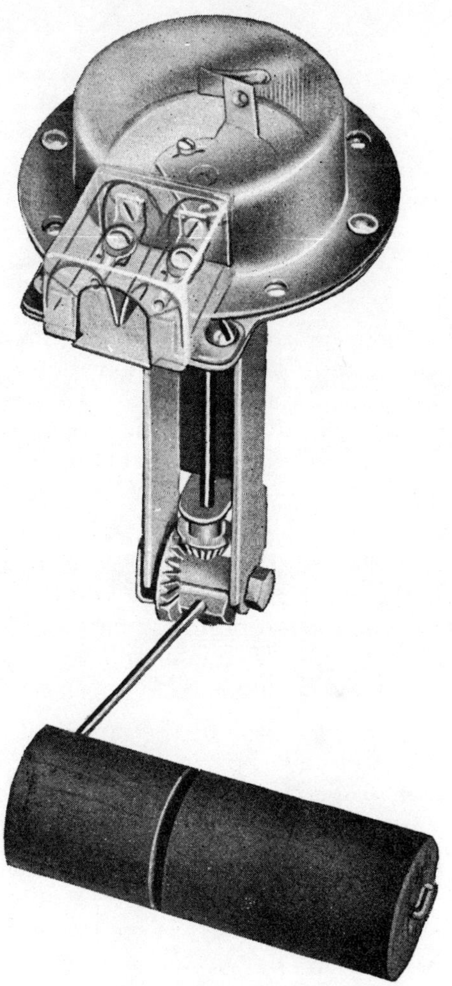

TANK UNIT ASSEMBLY

unit contactor is at one end of the potentiometer in such a position that the entire resistance is admitted to the circuit of the right-hand dash unit coil and completely cut out of the left-hand dash unit coil, giving a predominant magneto motive force in left-hand coil, causing the pointer to assume a zero position. As the gasoline tank is filled, the rotor cuts out resistance from right-hand coil circuit and introduces a corresponding amount to the left-hand circuit until in the half full position, the resistance of both circuits is exactly equal and the magneto motive forces of both coils is therefore equal. This action continues correspondingly until the rotor reaches the extreme full position introducing all the resistance into the left-hand coil circuit and cutting it all out of right-hand circuit, thereby giving a full reading.

Since the one coil is actually balanced against the other and the same voltage is actuating both, a variation in the battery voltage will affect both coils equally and will not disturb the gauge reading.

In the construction of the gauge, all resistances and positions of parts are absolutely fixed, so that if properly installed and under normal service, no attention should be required.

The current consumption of gauge is very low and is negligible in-so-far as car operation is concerned.

The diagram shown above illustrates the wiring circuit of the gasoline gauge. It is important that the circuit of the gauge should be exactly as shown in diagram, and that all connections be securely made. If the instructions are not followed to the letter, the gauge will not operate efficiently and is liable to be damaged electrically.

In cases where connections appear to be correctly made and the gauge operation is faulty, the dash and tank units should be connected with additional wires outside the regular harness, which will indicate whether or not the fault may lie in the harness and will help to show the exact location of the trouble.

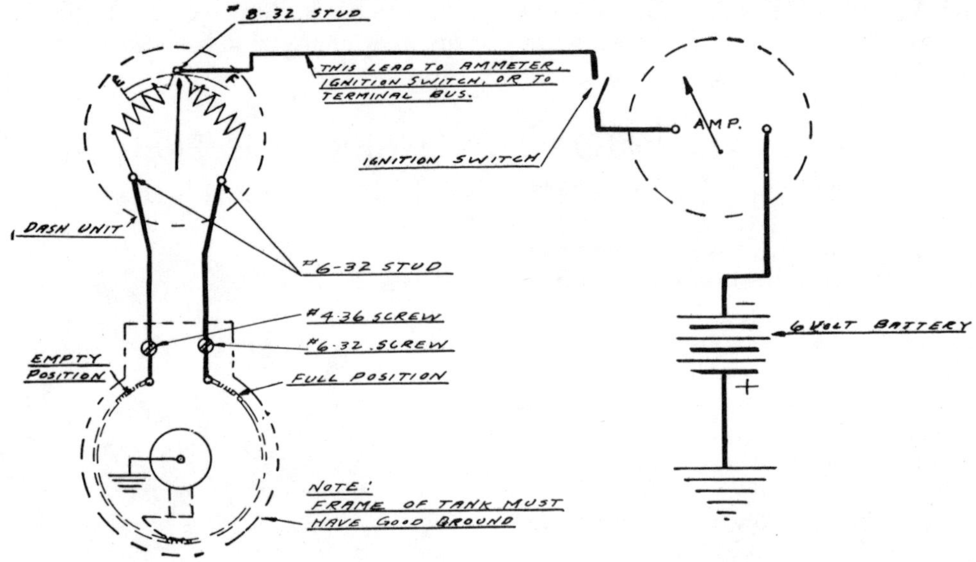

TESTING THE GASOLINE GAUGE

DASH UNIT: When examining the gas gauge for trouble, if the pointer reads at an intermediate point on the dial, such as 1/4, 1/2 or 3/4, one end of a piece of wire should be held on the bottom stud, left hand, and the other end grounded. If the gauge is correct the pointer will read "empty". The end of the

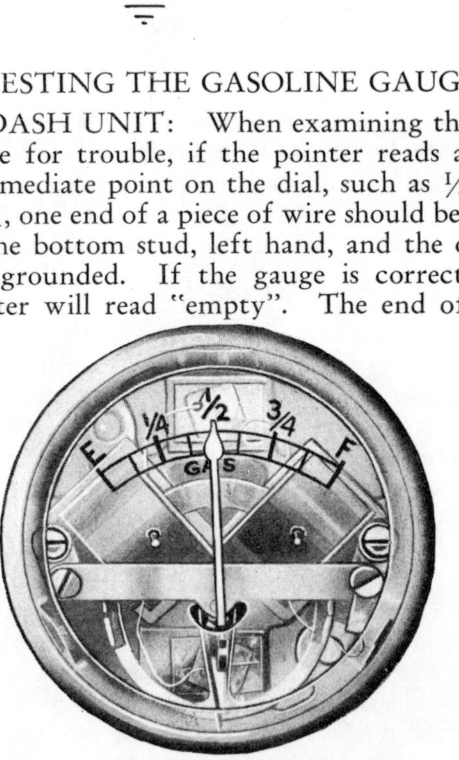

DASH UNIT

wire should then be held on the right hand stud and if the gauge is in good condition, the pointer will read "full".

However, when the pointer reads "empty", if the gauge is in good condition the pointer will read "½" when a piece of wire is held on both of the bottom studs and the other end grounded.

Carefully inspect the two wires between the dash unit and tank unit for short circuits, breaks, or grounds and see that all connections are tight.

TANK UNIT: Should any trouble be located in the tank unit, it should be removed and returned to the factory for inspection. It cannot be adjusted without special tools and for this reason the cover of the tank unit is riveted into place so it cannot be removed.

When necessary to remove the complete tank unit, it should be punch pricked so it can be replaced in exactly the same position.

TROUBLE CHART

Cause	*Gauge Action*
1. Break in battery line, or no ground in tank unit.	Gauge will be inert, assuming any position regardless of gasoline level, depending only on instrument balance.
2. Reversed connections in tank or dash unit.	Gauge will reverse its reading.
3. Ground in zero coil line.	Gauge will read from empty to ½ full only.
4. Ground in full coil line.	Gauge will read ½ when tank is empty and operate to full when tank is full.
5. Break in zero coil line.	Gauge will read full under all conditions.
6. Break in full coil line.	Gauge will read empty under all conditions.
7. Short circuit between two wires leading to tank unit.	Will read ½ at all times if connected with tank unit; no definite reading if disconnected.

Do not attempt to lubricate either dash or tank unit.

Do not use gasoline or oil in cleaning tank unit parts. Use alcohol only.

NOTE: The service data and testing chart applying on the electric gasoline gauge will serve for the electric oil gauge also.

NOTE: In cases where fault is found conclusively to lie within the units themselves, the complete unit should be returned to us for inspection.

ELECTRIC EQUIPMENT

The Delco-Remy electrical equipment supplied for this model consists of the following units:

941-T Generator
724-N Starting Motor
658-W Distributor
528-U Ignition Coil

This equipment is guaranteed by the manufacturers and is serviced through United Motors Service and their authorized stations.

Car Wiring: In order to maintain electrical efficiency all wiring connections must be kept tight and clean. Loose, corroded, or rusty connections are harmful to the equipment and if in the charging circuit they reduce the generator charge into the battery, if in the ignition circuit they will cause irregular firing of engine, and when in the light circuit will cause either a flickering or dim light.

Cables should be examined to make sure they are not rubbing any place and wearing off the insulation. Should a lead be disconnected at any time while making repairs, its terminal must not touch any metal part of the car as this would short circuit the wiring and possibly result in damage to some part of the electric system. It is best to tape the end terminal.

GENERATOR

The generator is a six volt, two pole, round over-hanging frame type. The rotation, viewing the drive end, is counter-clockwise. It is mounted by means of an S. A. E. type base mounting.

The relay is mounted on generator frame. The generator is third brush regulated and thermostatically controlled. The armature rotates on annular ball bearing in either end frame. Both bearings are oiled through hinged cap oilers in end frames. The application of eight to ten drops of light engine oil every 1000 miles provides sufficient lubrication to keep bearings in good condition. The end frames are held in place by means of two through bolts.

The brushes are carried in swivel type holders and are provided with springs that cause the brushes to bear on commutator with a pressure of fourteen to eighteen ounces.

Thermostat: The third brush control is supplemented by a thermostat which is an automatic switch operated by the heat inside the generator. When the internal temperature reaches 165 degrees F., the contact points open and a resistance is placed in the generator field with the result that the generator output is reduced approximately 40%. This type of control permits the use of a higher charging rate on short drives and for a longer period in cold weather which helps to quickly restore the battery current taken by the starting motor and lights.

Third Brush Adjustment: The generator output is adjusted by changing the position of the third brush. To do this, loosen the round head locking screw at one side of the bearing cover on commutator end frame. Remove the cover band and shift third brush in direction of armature rotation to increase the output and in opposite direction to decrease it. When adjustments are completed tighten the round head clamping screw securely and replace cover band. Do not depend on the dash ammeter when adjusting generator output. Connect an accurate reading portable ammeter to the generator relay terminal.

Test Specifications: The generator is set at factory to conform to following specifications:

GENERATOR

Rotation viewing drive end—counter-clockwise.

Brush spring tension—14 to 18 ounces.

Field reading—4.0 to 6.1 amperes at 6.0 volts.

Maximum cold output — (Thermostat closed) 19 to 21 amps. 8.35 to 8.5 volts, 1450 R.P.M.

Maximum hot output—(Thermostat open) 9 to 12 amps. 7.35 to 7.65 volts, 1800 to 2000 R.P.M.

Relay cut in 6.75 to 7.5 amps. discharge.

The above readings are taken at generator relay terminal and will be approximately two amperes higher than dash ammeter will indicate.

Care and Maintenance: The bearings should be lubricated with eight to ten drops of light engine oil every 1000 miles. The cover band around the frame should be removed once a year for inspection of commutator and brush connections. If commutator is dirty clean it with No. 00 sandpaper. Never use emery paper on commutator and never use oil on commutator or brushes.

Examine the brushes to see if they are unduly worn and see if all electrical connections are clean and tight. Never attempt to adjust the thermostat as this can only be done at the factory.

Cutout Relay No. 265-B: The relay automatically connects the generator to battery circuit when the terminal voltage of generator is equal to or greater than the terminal voltage of battery. It automatically opens the generator circuit when the speed of generator is such that the voltage falls below terminal voltage of battery and prevents it discharging back through generator.

The relay is adjusted to close or cut in at 6.75 to 7.5 volts and to open at a maximum discharge of 2.5 amperes. The air gap between core and armature with points closed should be .012″ to .017″. The contact point opening should be between .015″ and .025″.

The generator can be removed from engine by disconnecting the wire leading to ammeter. Remove the four cap screws holding generator to the mounting on engine. Then loosen one of the generator coupling clamps and lift the generator off.

STARTING MOTOR

The starting motor is a 6 volt, four pole, 4 brush series wound unit, mounted to flywheel case by means of a No. 1 S.A.E. flange mounting.

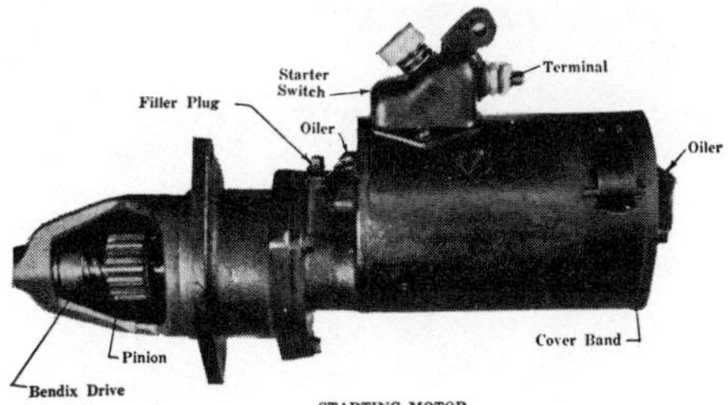

STARTING MOTOR

The motor has a 22 to 14 gear reduction and is fitted with an eleven tooth bendix drive. The brushes are held in swivel type holders and are provided with springs that cause the brushes to bear on the commutator with a pressure of 24 to 28 ounces. This may be checked by attaching a small spring scale to the head of the brush screw and using a direct pull.

The armature rotates in plain cast iron bearings in the end frames. The final drive is through a bendix pinion carried in a stub shaft. The stub shaft rotates in a plain bearing in the drive end frame and a graphite bronze bushing in bendix housing. The bearing in bendix housing is oilless and requires no additional lubrication. Eight to ten drops of light engine oil in hinged cap oilers every 1000 miles will provide the bearings with sufficient lubrication.

Test Data:

Rotation, viewing drive end—clockwise.

Brush spring tension—24 to 28 ounces.

No load—70 amps. 5 volts, 3500 R.P.M. (bendix).

Lock torque—600 amps., 3 volts, 22 ft. lbs. torque.

Eleven tooth outboard bendix drive.

22 to 11 gear reduction.

Care and Maintenance: Add eight to ten drops light engine oil in hinged cap oilers every 1000 miles. The bearing in bendix housing is inaccessible to oiling and requires no additional lubrication. Remove filler plug and repack gear case with graphite grease once a year.

The cover band around the frame should be removed once a year for inspection of the commutator and brush connections. If commutator is dirty, clean with No. 00 sandpaper. Examine the brushes to see if they are unduly worn. See if electrical connections are clean and tight. Never use emery papr on commu-
and tight. Never use emery paper on commutator and use no oil on commutator or brushes. Do not oil the spiral screw shaft on bendix drive. remove the unit from the engine and thoroughly clean the drive.

To remove the starting motor disconnect the starter cable also the control wire, then remove the three cap screws holding it to engine block.

DISTRIBUTOR

The distributor is semi-automatic advance type with condenser. The rotation is counterclockwise, viewing the top. The head and rotor are the single jump spark type. A four lobe cam and double breaker arms are used to fire the cylinders in proper order. The manual advance of 15 degrees is obtained by rotating the distributor in its mounting. The automatic advance of 15 degrees is obtained through two spring-controlled centrifugal

DISTRIBUTOR

weights that require no adjustments. As the speed of engine increases, the weights are gradually thrown outward, which advances the cam in the direction of rotation, causing points to open earlier, thus advancing the spark. The distributor shaft revolves in a grey iron bearing in distributor housing. The shaft is lubricated by a grease cup on side of distributor base. Turn down grease cup one-half turn every 1000 miles.

The spring tension on breaker arms should be 17 to 21 ounces. Check by attaching a small spring scale to the breaker arm at contact point. The two breaker arms must open exactly 45 cam degrees apart. To obtain this adjustment one breaker arm is movable. Set the stationary arm and synchronize the movable arm to it.

Condenser: The cartridge type condenser is mounted on distributor housing. It is placed across the breaker points to reduce arcing and burning and assists the coil to deliver a hot spark.

Test Data:

Rotation, viewing top—counter-clockwise.

Contact point opening—.018″ to .024″.

Spring tension—17 to 18 ounces.

Automatic advance starts—800 R.P.M. engine.

Maximum automatic advance—15 degrees at 3600 R.P.M. engine.

Manual advance 15 degrees engine.

Care and Maintenance: Turn down grease cup every 1000 miles. Apply drop of oil to breaker arm pivots and wick located beneath rotor every 1000 miles. The cam should be lubricated with a small quantity of vaseline every 1000 miles.

Keep contact adjusted and wires pushed firmly into distributor head.

The distributor can be removed from engine by taking off the cap so the wiring will be out of the way, then disconnect the dash control and remove the screw holding it to the base.

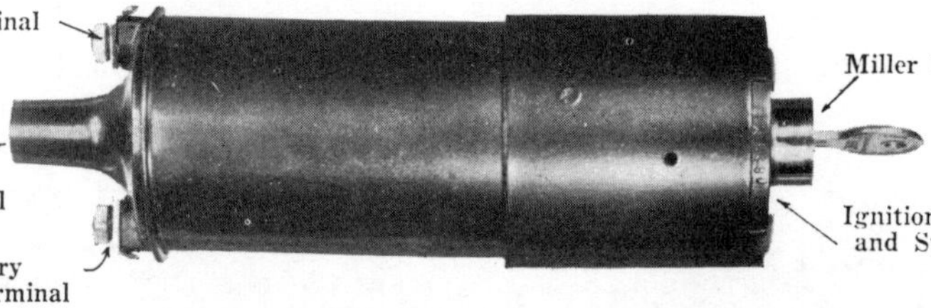

IGNITION LOCK COIL

The contact point openings should be .018″ to .024″. To adjust the point opening put the breaker arm on a lobe of the cam. Loosen the hold-down screw and move the breaker plate with the eccentric adjusting screw. Tighten hold-down screw when adjustments are completed.

IGNITION COIL

The model 528-U coil is a combination ignition and lock coil and is mounted on the dash. The moulded top supports both the primary and high tension terminal. It requires no attention other than to keep all connections clean and tight.

The ignition switch is fitted with a Miller lock and interrupts the primary circuit inside the coil.

TO SYNCHRONIZE BREAKER ARMS ON THE EIGHT CYLINDER DISTRIBUTOR WITH FOUR LOBE CAM

One set of contact points is stationary and the other set is movable. Adjust stationary set first and complete the synchronizing by adjustments to the movable set of points.

To set contact opening of arm (A) turn distributor shaft in its direction of rotation, which is counter-clockwise, (viewed from top) until rubbing block of breaker arm (A) is on lobe of cam. Loosen screw (B) and turn screw (C) to get contact opening, which is .018″ to .024″ and preferably .022″. Tighten screw (B).

Again turn shaft until rubbing block of breaker arm (D) is on lobe of cam. Loosen screw (E), turn screw (F) until points open between .018″ and .024″, preferably .022″. Tighten screw (E).

Put synchronizing tool over cam, locking it with the slide through showing the arrow that points in direction the shaft rotates as viewed from top.

As rotation is counter-clockwise, turn shaft in this direction until breaker arm (A) breaks contact. Note marking on N side of synchronizing tool that is in line with point (X) which is the edge of slot in distributor base rim. Continue turning shaft until the same marking on M side of tool is in line with point (X). Loosen screws (G) and (H) and turn screw (I) until arm (D) breaks contact.

Check by rotating shaft again. Tighten screws (G) and (H). Also check contact opening of breaker arm (D) and if it was set before at .022″, it should still be within the limits. If outside of these limits, reset the point opening and synchronize arms again. Make no adjustments to arm (A) but confine the adjustments to arm (D) to complete the synchronizing.

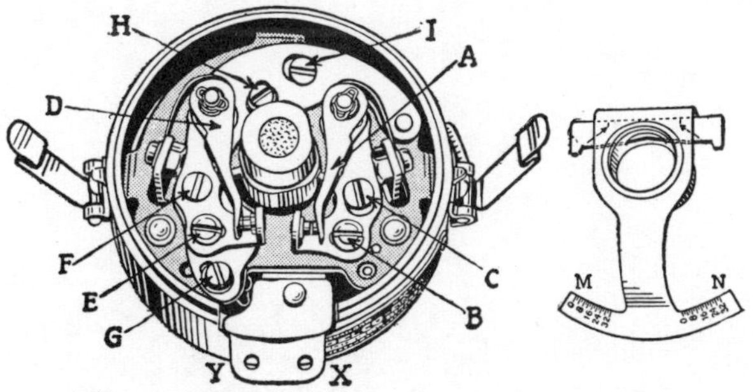

The graduations on the tool represent engine degrees and the breaker arm must not be out of synchronism more than two engine degrees.

The eye cannot detect the moment the points open, so to get an accurate synchronizing adjustment, connect an ammeter in the ignition circuit at distributor terminal. If on the car, make sure ignition switch is "on".

The instant the ammeter needle drops back to zero, the points open.

If points become dirty or rough, dress them with a fine grade hone. Under normal conditions they will acquire a gray finish.

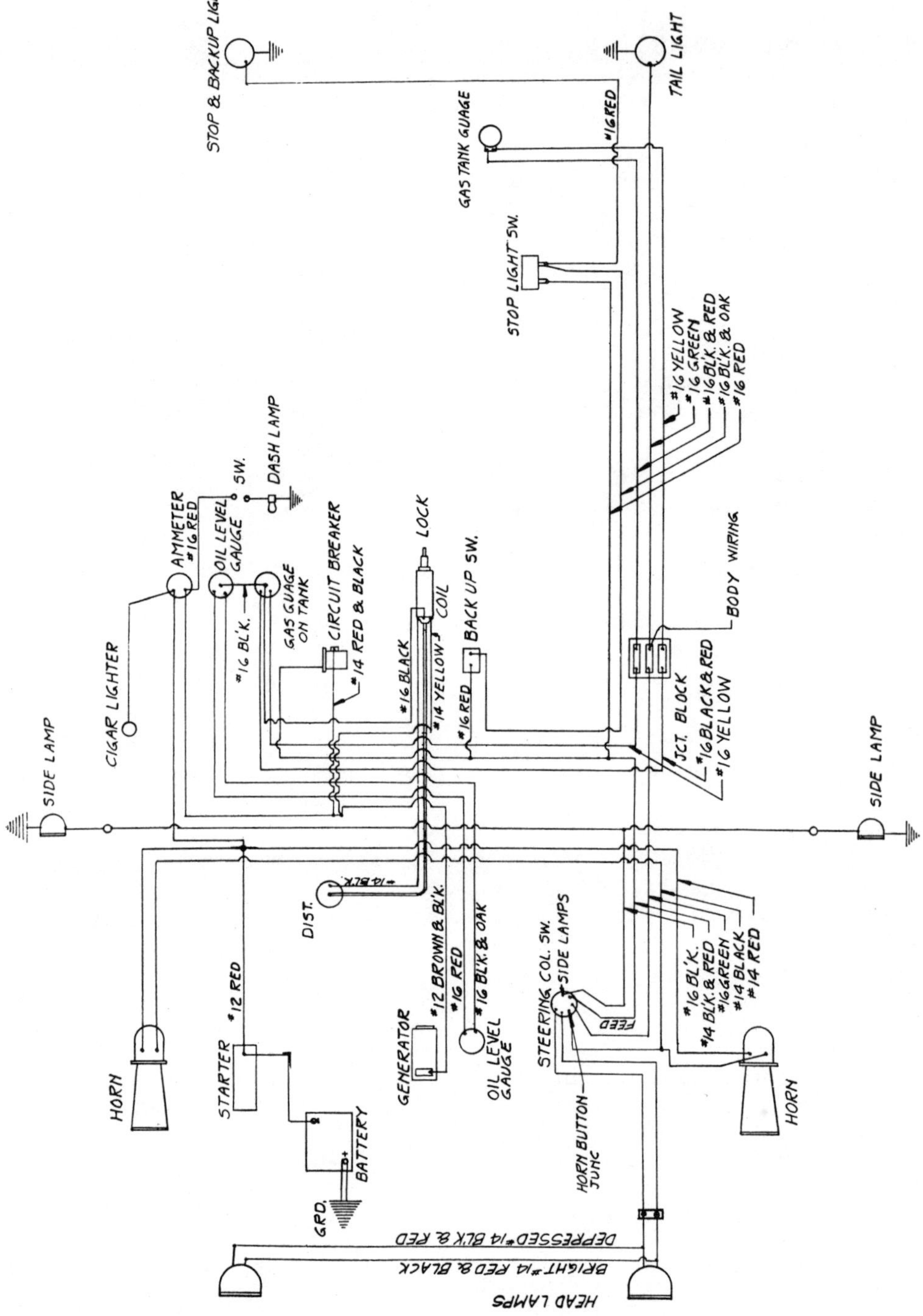

WIRING DIAGRAM

BIJUR CENTRAL CHASSIS LUBRICATOR

The Bijur Central Chassis Lubrication System provides positive and accurate lubrication to the following parts:

Water pump bearing	1 point
Fan bearing	1 point
Fan countershaft bearing	1 point
Clutch release bearing	1 point
Rear spring front hinge bolt	2 points
Rear spring rear shackle bolts	4 points
Clutch and brake pedal cross shaft	1 point

A single push on the Bijur pedal which is conveniently located above the driver's left foot is all that is necessary to completely oil the above bearings. When delivering new cars it is suggested that the Bijur foot pedal be given a number of strokes to completely fill the lines. being released it is an indication that the lubricator tank is empty. It should be filled immediately as under no circumstances should the chassis bearings be permitted to go without oil.

All oil passing from the tank into the oil line is filtered through a dense felt filter disc at the tank outlet. If proper oil is used this filter should never need attention. If oils containing suspended wax, grease, graphite, or other foreign substances are used the filter will become clogged, indicated by an unusually slow return of the lever. It is then necessary to remove and clean the filter.

Never use "Black Oil" or old crankcase oil. Either will clog the tank filter disc, and the

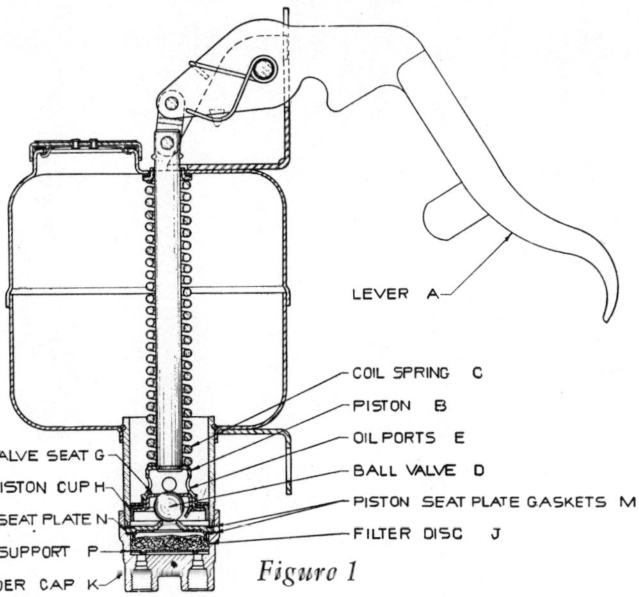

Figure 1

acid, water and kerosene in old crankcase oil will corrode and ruin the system.

After the car goes into use the pedal should be depressed daily before starting the engine, and at least once in every 100 miles of continuous driving.

The pedal should be depressed more often when driving over wet or muddy roads in order to keep water out of the bearings.

The pedal after being depressed and released will return to its original position slowly. At ordinary temperatures (70 degrees F.) with moderately heavy oil it will take about four minutes to return pedal to normal position. In cold weather it will require a much longer time.

Should the pedal spring back instantly on

As chassis bearings are exposed to water, snow, mud, etc., the chassis lubricating oil should be free from suspended matter, have good penetrating and water excluding properties and be thick enough to remain in the bearings for considerable periods.

It should be anti-corrosive, free from any tendency to gum and have lubricating value. For cars in unheated garages it should remain fluid in cold weather.

Dealers may secure from Auburn Automobile Company the correct oil for the Bijur system, put up in convenient containers. It is suggested that they carry in stock a supply sufficient for their trade requirements.

Operation of Bijur System:

Depression of lever (A) by the left foot of driver raises piston (B) against the downward pressure of spring (C). The piston is hollow and contains a valve (D) and is provided with oil ports (E), so that on the upstroke of the piston, oil flows through the hollow piston, past seat (G) of ball valve (D), to the lower end of piston below cup leather (H).

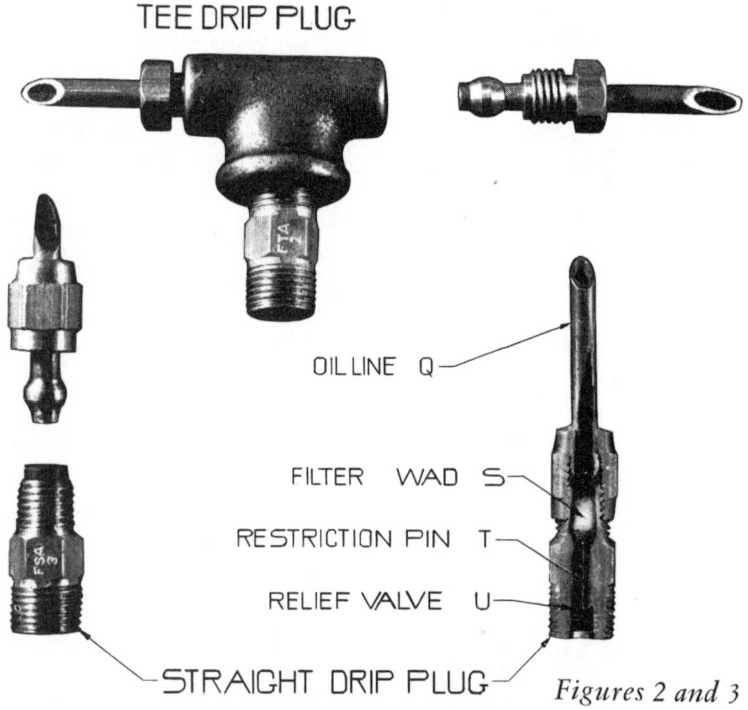

Figures 2 and 3

Upon removal of the foot the backward rush of oil lifts the ball valve against its seat, so that the measured charge of oil trapped below cup leathers is forced by the pressure of spring (C), through filter disc (J) into chassis pipe line. Filter disc (J) prevents any solid matter in improper oil from entering pipe lines.

Drip plugs are either straight to receive the end of an oil line (Q) or have a "T" head to permit the line to be carried on beyond.

Each drip plug contains three elements: A felt filter wad (S), which filters all oil entering the fitting and protects the restriction crevice and relief valve from such foreign matter as may be in pipe line. This filter cannot become clogged, as all fresh oil entering the lines is filtered by the tank filter disc. The restriction crevice which governs the rate of oil flow consists of a very accurate hole in which lies an accurately sized pin (T) so the clearance between pin and hole provides the correct restriction for the flow of oil needed.

All holes are of same size, but pins are of different diameters. All drip plugs are numbered according to flow rate, the numbers ranging from 0 to 5 as the rate increases.

The relief valve shown at (U) opens while the line is under pressure from the tank and allows the oil to escape. Whenever the tank pressure ceases the valve closes and keeps the pipes full of oil for next operation.

Drip Plugs are adjusted when made and cannot be disassembled without destroying their proper operation. Each drip plug, if removed, must be replaced by one of same rate number, and same type as indicated by letters stamped on each.

Cleaning Tank Filter Disc:

Disconnect both pipes from the double outlet by backing off the hexagon headed connections. Cap (K) should now be unscrewed with a wrench applied to flat part of cap. In the cap, note position of ring gaskets (M) and piston seat plate (N) before disassembling, then lift these out, exposing the white felt filter disc. Unless this is covered by a deposit, it is not necessary to clean it. If so coated, it may be removed, washed in benzine, carbona, cleaning fluid, or even gasoline, until clean and white. Leave wire gauze disc (P) in cap with ridges against cap. Replace felt disc with printed side next to gauze. Lay one ring gasket on top of felt so it rests upon metal ledge of outlet cap. Now replace piston seat plate with hollow side facing felt. Lay second ring gasket on outer edge of piston seat plate, and the cap assembly is ready to be replaced on tank and screwed home with a wrench as far as it will go.

Inspect the feed lines occasionally.

HORNS

SPARTON SOS TYPE

Should a horn fail to operate, remove horn motor cover by pulling directly off, giving a sharp rap downward with the hand.

Cover is held in place by spring clips at top and bottom and does not screw or twist off. See that all connections, including those at button, horn and fuse block, are properly tightened.

Adjustment can be made by turning screw S-38 to left or right. If screw is turned too far, the horn will have a tendency to "stutter", therefore great care should be used in making adjustments. Hold adjusting screw S-38 in place with screw driver in slot, while loosening nut S-37.

If a horn develops trouble which you are unable to overcome, consult an official Sparton Service Station, if one is in your vicinity, or report the trouble direct to the factory.

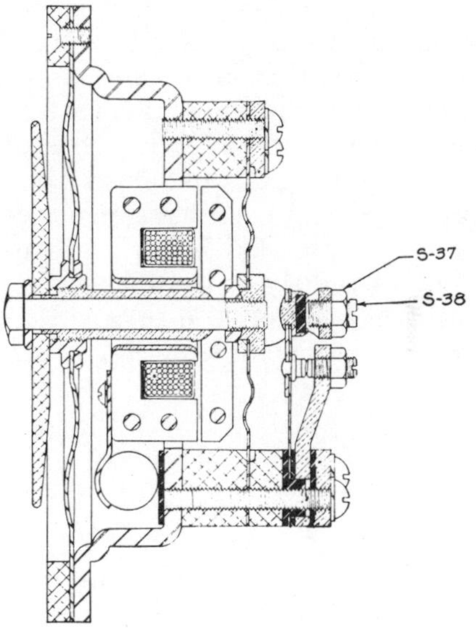

STEERING GEAR

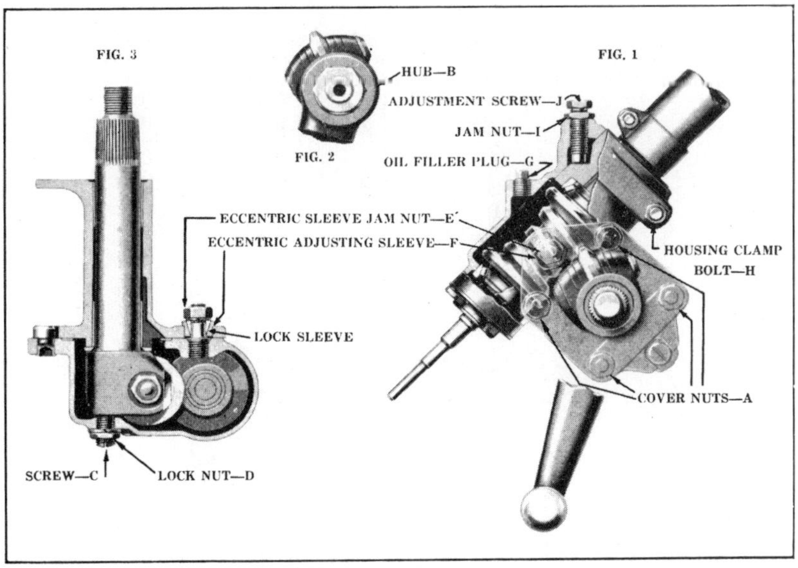

When making Steering Gear adjustments, jack up the front wheels of car and remove the drag link from steering gear arm.

Loosen the frame bracket bolts and turn steering wheel from extreme to extreme to correct any misalignment that may exist between the various supports. Tighten these bolts securely. Loosen instrument board steering gear bracket and column. Column must not be sprung in any direction.

Adjustment of End Play in Cross Shaft:

See that housing cover nuts, A (Fig. 1), are tightened securely. Turn hand wheel to either extreme and back an eighth of a turn. Gripping ball arm at hub B (Fig. 2), shaft should rotate freely without end play. Adjust as required by means of adjusting screw C (Fig. 3) at side of housing next to engine. Be sure to lock securely with lock nut D (Fig. 3) and reinspect end play and freedom of action.

Adjustment for End Play in Column:

To adjust for end play in column or between worm and roller bearing thrusts, turn steering wheel to either end stop and back up ⅛ turn or point where there is lash of ball arm. This leaves column bearings free of side thrust. Loosen housing clamp bolt H (Fig. 1) and jam nut I (Fig. 1) on housing sleeve adjusting screw J (Fig. 1). Turn down adjustment screw as tightly as possible with a 6″ wrench and then back off 1/6 turn. Set jam nut and housing clamp bolt securely. Turn hand wheel from extreme to extreme positions and test for stiffness.

Adjustment for Proper Mesh of Roller in Worm:

Turn hand wheel to mid-position of its complete travel or turning limits. The wheel key-way should now point straight upward toward roof of car. Correct to this condition by shortest movement. Shake ball arm to determine amount of lost motion. Loosen housing cover nuts A (Fig 1) ¼ turn, eccentric sleeve jam nut E (Fig. 1) ½ turn. Turn eccentric adjusting sleeve F (Fig. 1) clockwise gradually, checking at each movement the amount of lost motion still existing at the ball arm.

Adjust only tight enough to eliminate all lash of ball arm and no more, being sure to finish movement of eccentric adjusting sleeve F in clockwise direction.

Turn hand wheel throughout full travel to test for free operation. If too tight, turn eccentric adjusting sleeve F counter-clockwise

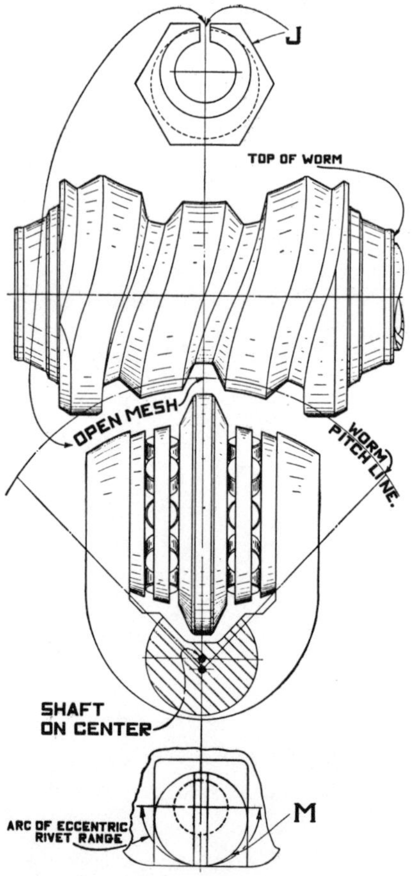

FIG. No. 4

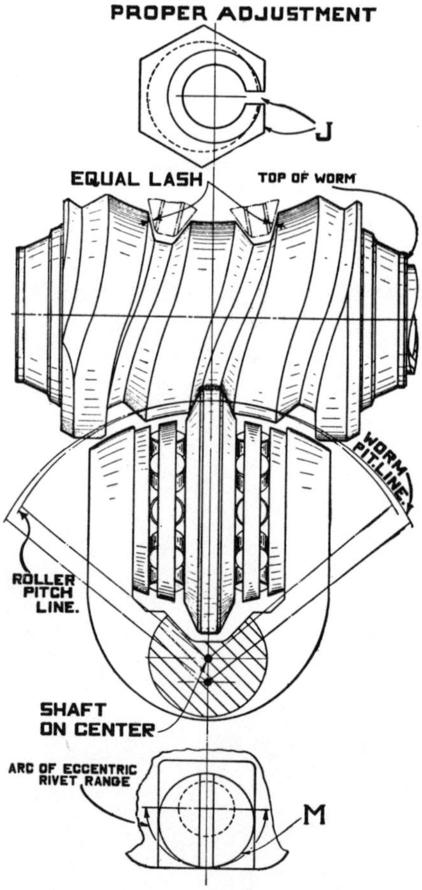

FIG. No. 5

to free, and readjust as above more carefully. Tighten eccentric adjusting sleeve jam nut E securely first, and follow likewise with housing cover nuts A. This is important.

In nearly all instances the foregoing adjustments will suffice. Should there be improper centralization of roller contact, adjustment must be made as follows:

The pitch radius of worm is longer than radius of arc described by roller. See Fig. 5. This provides for closer mesh of these parts at mid-position of the full movement of roller shaft.

The pivotal point of shaft pitch radius must be on same line as is the pivotal point of worm pitch radius and which line is at a right angle to the worm center line. This insures against the possibility of a closer mesh away from mid-position and poor contact of roller face to worm track.

The eccentric rivet M is the means by which conditions due to improper adjustment may be corrected. Turning the eccentric rivet in either direction shifts the roller shaft pivotal point toward or away from true alignment with the pivotal point of the worm pitch radius.

Figures 6 and 7 illustrate extreme conditions brought about by misalignment of the shaft and worm pitch radius pivotal points. Figure 7 shows the shaft pivotal point being too far toward upper end of housing, making for closest mesh at the left hand extreme throw of the steering wheel and for abnormal lash at the right hand extreme throw.

Figure 6 shows same error in opposite direction.

These conditions can be detected by comparing the amount of lash at two positions an equal distance each side of mid-position, the distance being determined by point of least lash farthest from mid-position.

To overcome the condition shown in Figure 7, turn eccentric rivet clockwise (which moves shaft pivotal point toward lower end of

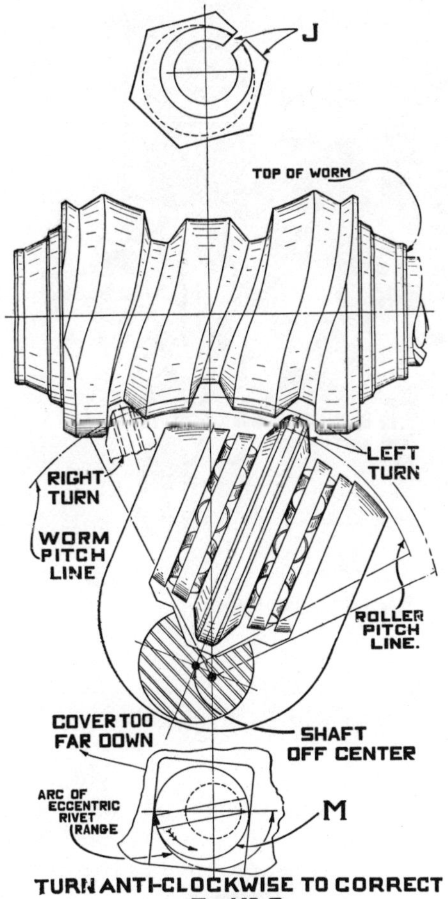

TURN ANTI-CLOCKWISE TO CORRECT
FIG.Nº. 6

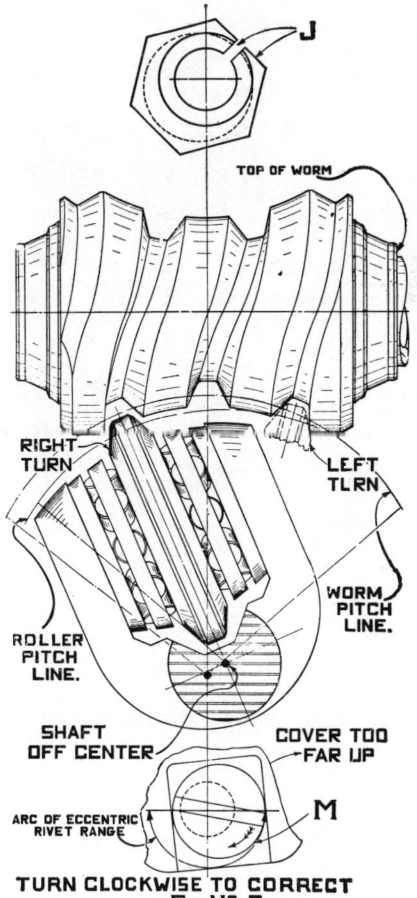

TURN CLOCKWISE TO CORRECT
FIG.Nº. 7

housing) until measured lash at points described above are equal.

Alter mesh adjustment to suit this new shaft pivotal point location.

Movement of eccentric rivet M counterclockwise (which moves shaft pivotal point toward upper end of housing) will remedy the condition shown in Figure 6.

Figures 4 and 5 illustrate proper pivotal point locations, both shaft and worm pitch radius pivotal points being on the line which is at right angles to worm centerline.

Figure 4 shows the open mesh of roller and worm, and Figure 5 the closed mesh at mid-position with equal lash at points equi-distant from mid-position, which is proper alignment and adjustment.

At top of picture the eccentric sleeve for mesh adjustment is shown at positions bringing about open and closed meshes respectively.

If these adjustment instructions are carefully followed, the steering mechanism will function properly.

LUBRICATION

In order to obtain the maximum efficiency of the steering gear, strict attention must be paid to lubrication. It must be done systematically and correctly.

After the steering gear has been mounted in chassis, and every 750 miles thereafter, remove oil filler plug (A) in housing and fill with approved lubricant until it overflows through vent in jacket tube just above adjusting nut.

The following lubricants have been found satisfactory:

Standard Oil Company—No. 20 Steering Gear Lubricant.

Sunoco Special Steering Gear Lubricant.

Whitmore No. O Steering Gear Lubricant.

Gemmer Steering Gear Lubricant.

Avoid use of graphite, white lead or heavy solidified oil.

FRONT DRIVING UNIT

INSTRUCTIONS FOR DISASSEMBLING

Included in this assembly are the Front Axle, Differential, the Transmission and the Differential and Wheel Universals connected by driving shafts, all specially designed for this model. All integral parts of the unit are accurately adjusted at the factory, and aside from thorough and proper lubrication, which is of the utmost importance, they should require no attention.

Should it be found necessary to disassemble the Front Driving Unit, the following operations should be performed in their regular order:

To Remove Radiator: The radiator and head lamps are removed as one complete unit. Disconnect the intake and outlet hose connections; disconnect the headlamp wiring harness on left side of radiator; remove the four

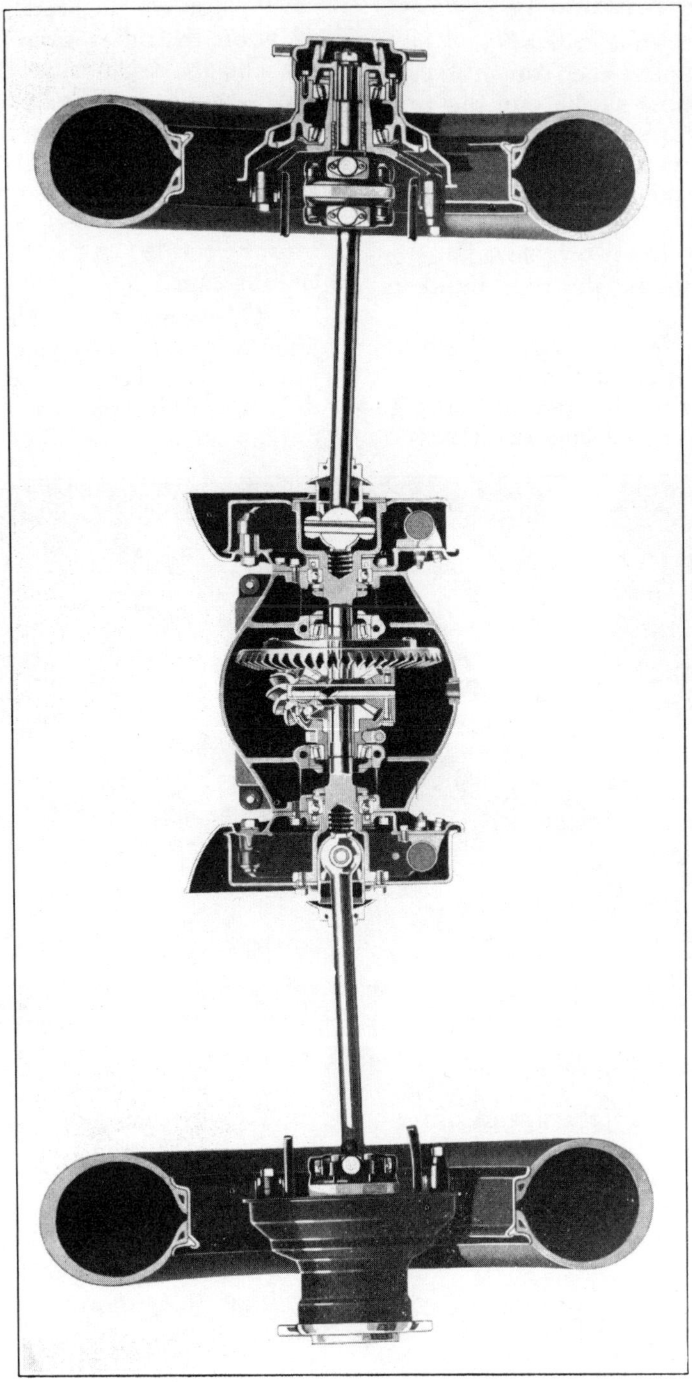

SKELETON VIEW FRONT DRIVING UNIT

bolts holding the radiator braces to radiator, also the two cap screws holding lower extension of shell in place and those holding radiator brackets to frame.

The entire radiator may now be removed.

To Remove Differential Assembly: Jack up the front axle. Remove the front hub caps and draw off the wheels. Take out the four ½″ cap screws holding each spindle. Then take out the four ⅝″ cap screws holding each universal flange on brake drum. Pull out the drive shaft assemblies.

Disconnect brake lines and speedometer shaft. Remove the shock absorber brackets from frame.

Take out the three ⅜″ cap screws holding each front fender to differential housing.

Drain off the oil from differential housing. Take off the differential housing front cover. you stand facing it. Next, remove the two bolts, one on each lower corner, also cap screw in center holding differential and transmission together, then the two top corner bolts.

Push in on the starting crank shaft as you draw off the differential.

The above describes the operations in their order, should you find it necessary to take out the differential for replacement of the assembly or of gears only. To re-install, the operations outlined above must be performed in reverse order, after which the differential must be refilled to the oil level plug with proper lubricant.

Replacement of Ring Gear and Pinion: Should it be necessary to replace ring gear and pinion, we advise replacement of the entire differential instead of ring gear and pinion only.

Showing Method of Gauging Bearing Protrusion

Remove brake drum from right side of differential, after which take out the six cap screws holding the brake shield to differential. Work the brake shield out between fender and axle by holding the fender out so it will not interfere.

Looking inside differential housing you will see a cap screw at upper left as you face it. This is one of the cap screws holding differential to transmission case and should now be removed. Next, remove the transmission cover plate by taking out the six cap screws which hold it on. Then remove the cap screw entering at upper right from transmission case as

To insure accurate relation between Differential and Transmission, we must have the exact amount of transmission bearing protrusion. This must be accurately measured with a depth gauge or a Dial Test Indicator, the correct use of which is illustrated in cut.

This protrusion will be the amount in one-thousandths of an inch gauged from face of transmission housing to inside race of bearing, usually running from .245″ to .255″.

This information is necessary in order to supply the shim or spacer fitting between transmission and differential assembly which will be ground to the exact thickness required.

(See differential pinion shim selection chart).

On top face of differential housing you will find a stamped number (A in drawing). You will note the pinion setting etched on face of pinion as shown at (B) in drawing. To this pinion reading add the gauged bearing protrusion (D). Subtract the total of B and D from the number stamped on differential housing (A), and to the result add the actual thickness of the velumoid gasket after it has been compressed.

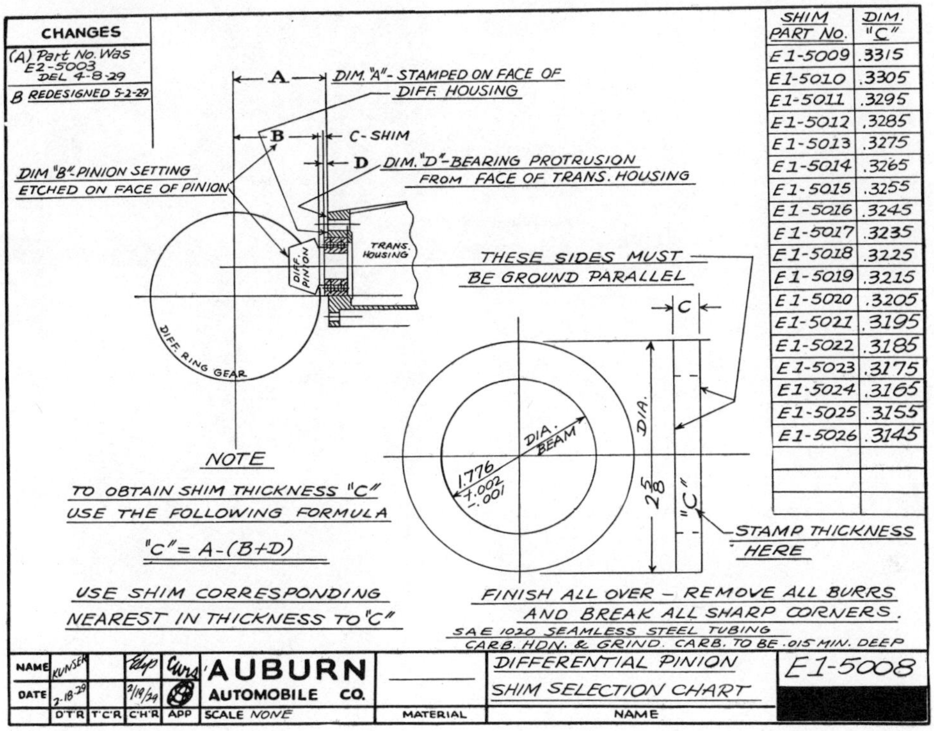

The result obtained by these calculations will represent the thickness of shim (C) which must be used in assembling together the differential and transmission.

For example, assuming the differential housing number (A) to be 6.270, the pinion setting (B) to be 5.718, and the bearing protrusion (D) to be .249". The total of B and D will be 5.967. Subtract this from the differential reading A and the result will be .303. Add the gasket thickness, assumed to be .0125" and you have a total of .3155, the thickness of shim (C), requiring our No. E1-5025.

Upon receipt of the various readings as indicated above, we will be able to supply the correct assembly, including gasket and shim.

However, for the convenience of our Service Stations, the gear ratio and exact shim thickness will be stamped on top of the differential housing and in front of the transmission on right side so they can be read by looking through the radiator shutters. For replacement of differential or parts, these numbers, with the car serial number, must be reported to the factory in corresponding about these parts.

When fitting new differential assembly to transmission, be careful to remove all burrs and any conditions that might prevent a perfect seat.

In changing differential, do not change speedometer drive gear or pinion.

Ring Gear and Differential Bearing Adjustment: These are Hypoid gears and the amount of lash provided is etched on the inside of ring gear. When adjusting back to the proper lash to compensate for wear, check with a dial indicator and see that adjustment is made to the exact lash etched on ring gear,—no more, no less.

This is of the utmost importance.

The adjustment itself is made in the usual manner by backing off on one adjuster and taking up on the other, moving each one notch at a time until the exact lash is obtained.

Removing Transmission: First, take off the radiator and headlamps as described heretofore. Disconnect front fenders from front brake dust shields. Remove the three cap screws holding cap over rubber shackles of upper front spring. Take the lower springs off of frame at spring saddles. Disconnect and remove the front Houdaille shock absorber bracket from frame and arm from axle.

Remove the two 5/8″ cap screws on each side holding transmission to frame. Disconnect the drag link.

Jack up front end of engine back of transmission and put blocking under it. The front wheels, drive shafts and universals are not to be removed if the purpose is to remove the transmission only.

Disconnect the front brake lines and speedometer cable. Take off dust pan under flywheel. Remove battery and battery carrier. Disconnect the Bijur Lubricator System lines leading to fan and clutch throwout bearing. Take out the fan drive accessory shaft and fan to get them out of the way.

Block up under transmission. Place a dolly and blocking under front axle and differential so they can be slid out when disconnected.

Remove front housing cover of differential and top cover plate of transmission. You can then remove the cap screws and bolts holding differential and transmission together and front axle and differential can be moved forward.

Disconnect clutch throwout lever at turnbuckle on left side, also disconnect gear shift lever at front end. Remove the seven cap screws and the two nuts holding transmission to engine.

The transmission can now be removed as a separate unit.

The clutch remains attached to the engine flywheel and is described under a separate heading. See page 33.

The re-assembling of transmission is accomplished by a reversal of these operations.

LUBRICATION

Lubrication constitutes the most important service you can render to the Front Driving Unit. Not only must this service be performed systematically, but the correct lubricants must be used. Dealers should be prepared to supply the proper lubricating service to their owners and should give special attention to this feature on all Cord Front Drive models in their territory, as under proper lubricating conditions the Front Driving Unit should require practically no further attention.

The transmission and differential, insofar as lubrication is concerned, are combined into a single unit.

On account of the Hypoid construction of ring gear and pinion, the lubricant to be used in the unit must be *Whitmore's Auto Gear Protective Composition No. "0". Nothing else will do.*

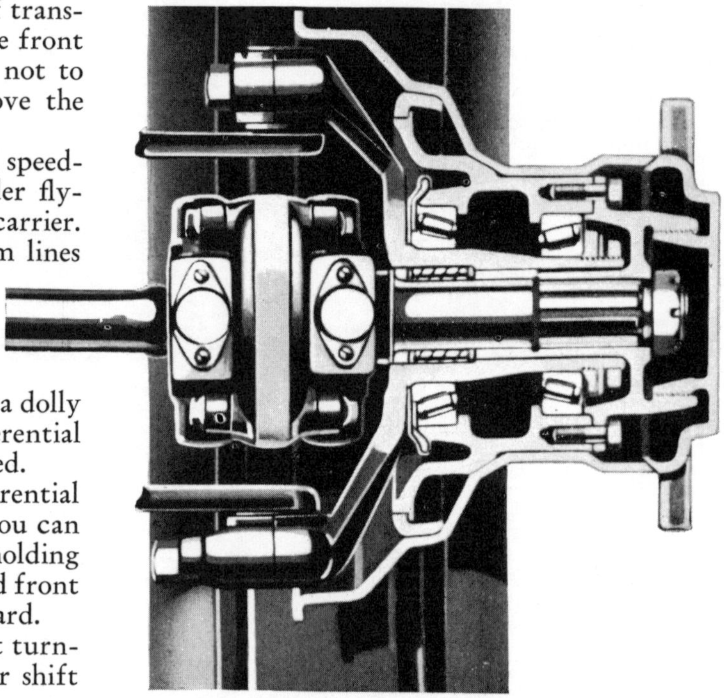

FRONT WHEEL ASSEMBLY

The total oil capacity of this unit is five quarts. The lubricant is supplied to the assembly by removing the 3/4″ pipe plug from oil hole in side of fan bracket on transmission housing. First remove the oil level pipe plug about one-fourth way up from bottom of differential housing. Pour the oil into transmission until it runs out of the differential oil level hole. Then replace the pipe plug in transmission but do not replace differential oil level plug until all drainage has ceased.

The oil circulates back and forth through the assembly. It is carried by the ring gear up into a trough in upper part of differential case from which it passes into transmission housing and from there it flows back through the lower outlet into differential case.

When necessary, replenish the supply of oil but do not draw the oil out of differential. In all cases, replenish with Whitmore's No. "0."

The differential oil level should be checked every 5,000 miles.

The Universal joints require no attention, other than lubrication.

The condition of lubricant in wheel universals should be checked every 5,000 miles. Remove the slotted head oil plug in center ring reservoir, insert the grease gun and force in Alemite grease until all air is expelled and grease begins to come out of crevices in the joint. Replace the slotted head plug.

To lubricate the differential universals, remove the four center bolts from brake drum, back off the flange, and pack the joint with a fibrous graphite or some suitable heat resisting grease, necessary on account of the heat generated at this point. This should be checked at least every 10,000 miles.

NOTE: *The first 1500 cars will have oil filler plug in left side of transmission case., instead of fan bracket.*

The ball sockets of front axle tie rod, and drag link connecting steering gear to front axle, should be lubricated with cup grease every 500 miles. Occasionally wash out the sockets thoroughly with gasoline, and relubricate.

In re-assembling, be absolutely sure that plugs and cotter pins are in correct position and adjustment.

FRONT WHEEL BEARINGS

Cup grease can be forced into front wheel bearings by removing the 1/8" pipe plug in hub. It is necessary to remove the wheel to do this.

However, the bearings should be removed, cleaned, greased and readjusted every six months in ordinary service and oftener if the service is severe. To get at front wheel bearings, jack up the axle so wheel clears the floor and remove hub cap. Then draw off the wheel by hand.

Pull out locking cotter pin and take off the castellated spindle nut. Take off the driving hub by removing the ten cap screws. Then remove the two locking nuts and slip wheel hub off spindle, exposing the bearings.

After thoroughly cleaning and drying the bearings, repack them in good clean cup grease and reassemble.

REAR WHEEL BEARINGS

The rear axle wheel bearings should be removed, cleaned, greased and readjusted every six months in ordinary service and oftener if under continuous service.

To remove bearings, jack the wheel up clear of floor and remove the hub cap. Draw off the wheel. Remove the grease cap. Pull out locking cotter pin and remove the castellated spindle nut. The hub and drum can now be drawn off. This will give access to the bearings. Be careful not to drop the outer bearing on the floor as it might be damaged.

Clean all grease from bearings, spindle, and inside of hub with a stiff brush and gasoline, and after they are thoroughly cleaned and dried, pack the bearings, also the hub between bearing cups, with a good grade of clean cup grease, and reassemble.

It is suggested that at least once a year all front and rear wheel bearings be boiled in washing soda and water.

CAUTION: In reassembling castellated spindle nuts be sure that they are properly locked with cotter pin with ends opened and bent back against the nut.

CLUTCH

The clutch is of dry plate design and will not operate properly if the friction facings are covered with grease or oil.

This condition will cause the clutch to slip under load at high speed and would also be responsible for clutch chatter, or rough, uneven adjustment. A clutch in this condition should be thoroughly cleaned at once. To do this it is not necessary to remove the clutch from the car.

Remove the flywheel inspection plate on right front of engine. Plug the drain hole in bottom of flywheel housing. Pour one-half gallon of naphtha in the clutch through the flywheel inspection opening and start the engine, working the clutch in and out until thoroughly cleaned, then drain off the naphtha and replace flywheel inspection plate. We suggest that this be done every 5000 miles.

The source of oil leakage should be located and eliminated, so there will be no possibility of a recurrence.

To remove the clutch from engine, proceed as follows:

After the Front Driving unit has been disassembled from engine as described heretofore, the clutch will remain attached to the flywheel. Remove the six cap screws attaching it to flywheel and the entire clutch may be drawn off.

It is not necessary to remove the clutch unless some parts of it are in need of replacement. Should the driven member friction facings become so worn that the rivet heads are flush with their surfaces, they should be replaced. Use special care in assembling new facings to the disc. As this member is dished, hand clamps must be used to bring the new facings tightly together before being riveted. If the facings are not rigidly attached to the disc, the unevenness of the facings will cause the clutch to drag. Use only the moulded type facings, such as originally used on the clutch, as the woven type are not suitable and will not give satisfactory service.

The clutch pedal will be the only part requiring adjustment. When clutch is fully engaged, the pedal should have approximately one-half inch clearance or lash so it will not ride against floor board. This adjustment should be checked at 1000 mile intervals.

Occasionally, due to lack of pedal lash, a clutch will slip, causing an intense frictional heat which may develop small local cracks in the facing area zone of the flywheel and pressure plate. These are usually so small that a thorough polishing of the flywheel and clutch pressure plate with emery cloth will make the parts serviceable without replacement.

Many drivers have a tendency to let the left foot rest on the clutch pedal while driving, resulting in a slight up and down movement of pedal while going over rough roads. This practice results in trouble as it is not only harmful to the release bearing, but reduces pressure spring tension, causing slipping, loss of power and rapid wear of clutch parts.

The clutch release bearing is lubricated from the central chassis lubricator and requires no attention.

The clutch fingers are properly set at the factory and should not be distrubed.

SERVICE BRAKES

The Lockheed Internal Hydraulic Four-Wheel brake system brings the brake shoes into instantaneous contact with the drums by means of a column of liquid forced through pipes. This liquid, being incompressible, transmits pressure, applied by the foot pedal, to each brake by means of displacement of pistons in master and wheel cylinders.

Inasmuch as hydraulic pressure is equal on all surfaces, the brakes are self-equalizing and not subject to individual adjustment, except for wear of lining.

The system consists of a Master Cylinder in which hydraulic pressure is originated; a Wheel cylinder operating the brake shoes against each wheel drum, in which wheel cylinder the hydraulic pressure is applied; a supply tank by which the fluid is maintained at a constant volume; and the 'line' consisting of tubing, flexible hose, brackets and unions, interconnecting master cylinder and wheel cylinders.

The master cylinder is fitted with a piston and the wheel cylinders are each fitted with opposed pistons; all provided with cup packings which act as a seal to maintain pressures and prevent loss of fluid.

Operation: Depressing the brake pedal moves the master cylinder piston, thus forcing the brake fluid from master cylinder through the "line" into the wheel cylinders between the opposed pistons, causing them to move outwardly against the shoes, which are pressed against the inner surface of brake drums.

The force exerted is evenly distributed, no braking action taking place until all the shoes are pressed against their drums.

When pressure on foot pedal is released, the return springs on brake shoes retract and return wheel cylinder pistons to "off" position, forcing the brake fluid back through the "line" into the master cylinder.

FIG. 1

The Supply Tank: The supply tank on front side of dash under hood is connected to master cylinder by tubing. It carries the reserve fluid and must be closed at all times except when inspecting, bleeding, or adding fluid, in order to prevent evaporation and the entrance of dirt. By means of a breather in

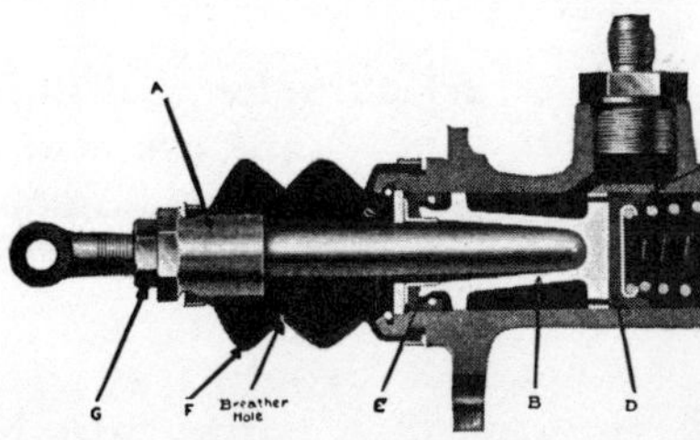

FIG. 2

tank filler cap, air replaces the fluid drawn into Master cylinder. Keep tank three quarters full of fluid.

The Master Cylinder: The compensator type Master Cylinder is connected to brake pedal by a connecting rod which is adjustable at G (Fig. 2). It is designed to automatically maintain a constant volume of fluid in the system, compensating for expansion or contraction of fluid due to temperature changes, or for any loss that might result from gravity seepage.

Rod A (Fig. 2) must be adjusted for clearance where it seats in piston B. There should be ½″ free movement of brake pedal pad before the pressure stroke starts.

Should rod A (Fig. 2) be adjusted tightly against piston B, port hole C will be blocked by cup D, and the compensating action of the Master Cylinder will be destroyed. Cup D must be clear of Port C, when piston B is in its "off" position. This can be determined by as-

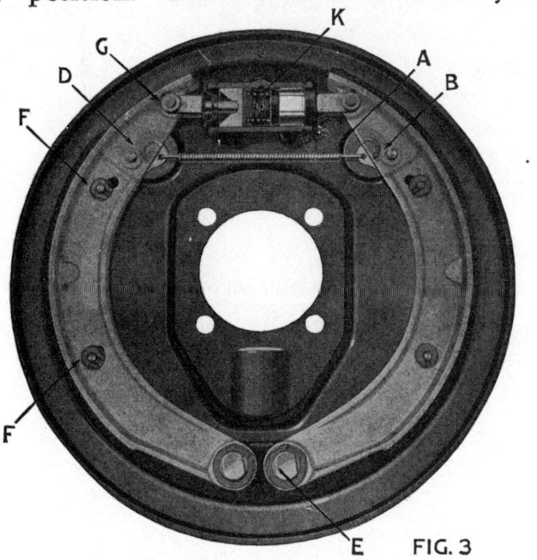

FIG. 3

suring yourself that there is a slight free movement of pedal before the piston starts to move.

Secondary cup E (Fig. 2) prevents fluid from leaking out of Master Cylinder into boot F.

Wheel Cylinder: The stems of opposed pistons in wheel cylinder are connected to brake shoes G. The ends of wheel cylinder are fitted with rubber boots to protect cylinder. At the uppermost position, between the pistons, is a bleeder valve for expelling the air when filling the system. (See L, Fig. 4).

Brake Maintenance: The only adjustment for equalization is such as is necessary to compensate for wear of lining. The frequency of such adjustment will depend upon the service to which the brakes have been subjected.

While the pressure delivered to the brake shoes will always be equal, the brake action may be unequal due to the presence of paint, grease, oil, or other foreign substance on the lining. This condition can be remedied by thoroughly cleaning the lining with gasoline or alcohol and then roughening with a file or wire brush. However, if linings are so saturated with oil or grease that cleansing will not correct the unequal braking effect, the shoes must be relined.

It is imperative that all shoes be relined with lining of the same specifications, otherwise the brakes on individual wheels will not be equally effective in their action. When relining front brakes it is necessary to disconnect the driving shafts at the wheels.

Adjustments: When brake lining becomes extensively worn, manifested by foot pedal going almost to the floor board, and thereby reducing braking effect, necessary adjustments can readily be made to bring shoes into closer relation with the drum. (See Fig. 4).

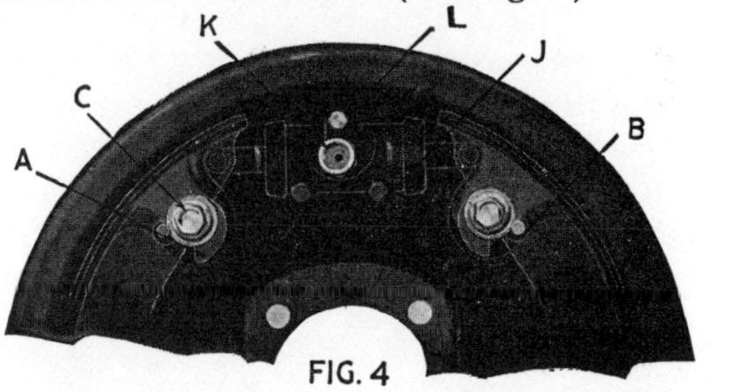

FIG. 4

Jack up wheel to clear ground. Adjust by rotating adjustment cam A against stop pin B on shoe. Rotate adjustment nut C with wrench until shoe comes into contact with drum, then back off adjustment slightly until wheel rotates freely.

Proceed in like manner on the brake shoes of all wheels. To bring shoe into closer relation with drum, adjustment nut must be turned toward rim of wheel when wrench is pointing upwards. The tension of friction spring automatically keeps the cam locked in any position. Correct Clearance for brake shoe is .005″ at heel and .010″ to .012″ at toe.

Brake drums are provided with inspection holes through which shoe clearances may be checked without disassembling.

To Remove Shoes: Remove the washers from anchor pins E and guide pins F. Unhook shoe return spring D. The shoe may then be pulled off. See Fig. 3.

In assembling, these operations are reversed.

To Disassemble Front Brakes: Jack up the car under front axle. Take off the wheel. Remove the four ½″ cap screws holding spindle; remove shock absorber bracket from frame; take out the four ⅜″ cap screws holding grease retaining flange on brake drum. Take out the hub and drive shaft. Take out the two ⅜″ bolts holding brake drum and remove the drum.

The brake shoes may now be taken off in the regular manner.

To remove front brake cylinder, disconnect tubing, take out two 5/16″ cap screws, and the cylinder may now be drawn out.

Bleeding of Line: Whenever any part of the system has been disconnected, it is necessary to "bleed" the system in order to expel all air.

Fill the supply tank with genuine Lockheed Brake Fluid before commencing this operation, and keep tank at least half full of fluid.

The emergency brake must be released. Remove cap screw L (Fig. 4) from end of bleeder connection and screw in bleeder drain provided for this purpose, which is a fitting with rubber tube attached. Allow tube to hang in a clean container, such as a pint mason jar. Unscrew bleeder connection three-quarters of a turn and depress foot pedal slowly by hand, allowing the return spring to bring the pedal back to the "off" position. This gives a pumping action which forces fluid through the tubing and out at wheel cylinders, carrying with it any air that may be present. Approximately ten complete strokes of pedal will be needed to bleed each wheel cylinder.

Watch flow of liquid from hose, the end of which should be kept below surface of fluid, and when all air bubbles cease to appear, or when stream is a solid fluid mass, close bleeder connection. Open connection again to allow drainage of a slight amount of fluid, then tighten bleeder connection securely.

Fluid withdrawn in "bleeding" should not be used again. The bleeding operation should be repeated on each wheel cylinder and fluid should be replenished in supply tank each time.

Should tank be drained during bleeding operation, air will enter the system and re-bleeding will be necessary.

Caution: Do not use a substitute for Lockheed Brake Fluid, as much damage may be done to the system.

Do not allow grease, paint, oil or brake fluid to come in contact with or remain on the lining.

Do not clean rubber parts or inside of cylinders with kerosene or gasoline. Use alcohol.

Do not reline one wheel with a different make of lining than is used on the others, as braking effect will not be equal if this is done.

Do not allow supply tank to be less than half-full of brake fluid.

Brake Fluid: Lockheed Brake Fluid is prepared by the originators of Lockheed Hydraulic Brakes with an exact knowledge of the requirements and the dangers of substitution. To avoid damage to the system, use only genuine Lockheed Fluid. It is put up in convenient containers with instructions for use, and all Auburn Service Stations should carry it in stock.

In addition to our own service facilities on Lockheed Internal Hydraulic Brakes, the Wagner Electric Corporation of St. Louis, Missouri, maintains a nation-wide organization which offers expert assistance in servicing this braking system.

Following is a list of their Service Branches:

Atlanta, Ga.
475 W. Peachtree St. N.E.

Baltimore, Maryland
2018 N. Charles St.

Boston, Mass.
342 Newbury St.

Buffalo, N. Y.
769 Main St.

Chicago, Ills.
1725 S. Michigan Ave.

Cincinnati, Ohio
2125 Reading Road

Cleveland, Ohio
2090 E. 19th St.

Dallas, Texas
2815 Commerce St.

Denver, Colo.
1360 Bannock St.

Detroit, Mich.
2843 East Grand Blvd.

Indianapolis, Indiana
1032 N. Illinois St.

Kansas City, Mo.
1615 Baltimore Ave.

Los Angeles, Calif.
318 W. 15th St.

Memphis, Tenn.
1114-16 Union Ave.

Milwaukee, Wis.
501 Broadway

Minneapolis, Minn.
111 S. 12th St.

Toronto, Canada
217 Dundas St., East

New York, N. Y.
321 W. 54th St.

Omaha, Nebr.
2566 Leavenworth St.

Philadelphia, Pa.
1720-26 Callowhill St.

Pittsburgh, Pa.
5031 Liberty Ave.

Portland, Oregon
327 Flanders St.

San Francisco, Cal.
457 Ninth St.

Seattle, Washington
1918 First Ave., South

St. Louis, Mo.
3029 Locust St.

EMERGENCY BRAKE ADJUSTMENT

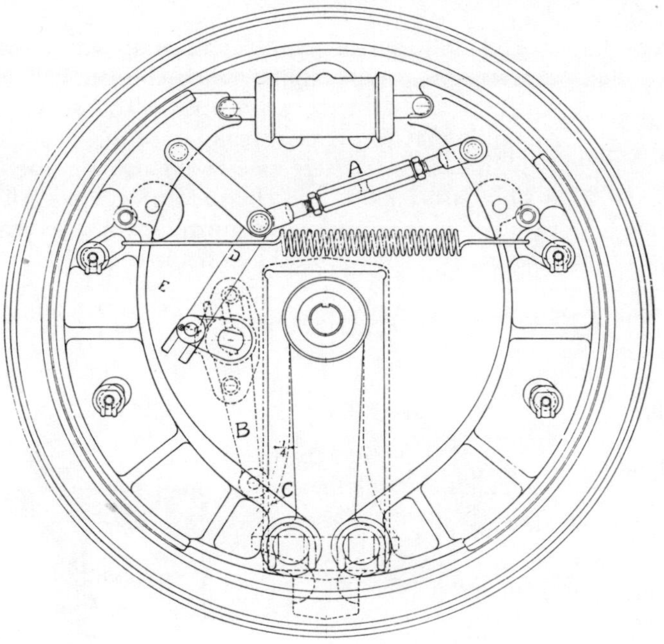

The hand brake is connected to the hydraulic brake shoes on rear axle by correctly designed linkage which provides instantaneous and equal contact of shoes with drums.

When adjustment of hydraulic foot brakes is completed, it will be necessary to readjust the emergency brake by lengthening adjusting link A so yoke D will just touch pin E.

Keep movable parts well oiled. All linkage connections should receive a few drops of lubricating oil at least once a month.

WIRE WHEELS

All hubs and hub caps are plainly stamped RIGHT SIDE or LEFT SIDE. Hubs and caps have right hand threads for right side of car and left hand threads for left side of car.

After inner hubs have been adjusted to axle spindles, be sure to insert cotter keys through castellated nuts and spindles. Wheels are now ready to be mounted.

Clean the taper in hub shell and the other surfaces indicated by arrows on the diagram and apply a light film of grease to these parts. Mount wheel and screw hub cap tight. Arrows stamped on hub cap indicate direction the cap revolves in screwing on. Final tightening of hub cap should be made by several smart blows of a mallet on ears of wing type cap. A wrench is not necessary.

Do not pack hub caps with grease.

After car has been driven about 500 miles, inspect all hub caps for tightness. To do this jack the car up so the inflated tire is clear of the ground.

Loose hub caps result in damage to the wheels. Keep them tight always.

Remove wheels occasionally and clean and grease the tapers and other parts.

Note: Due to the design of these wheels, with thread for hub cap on inside of hub, the hubs are installed on the car just the reverse of other types of wire wheels having thread for hub cap on outside of hub. Such wheels re-

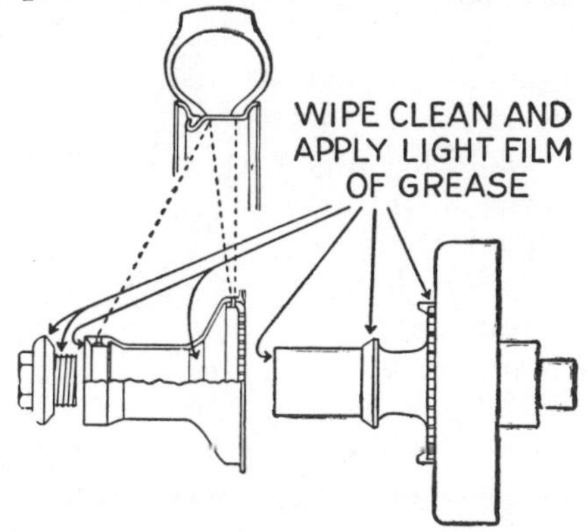

quire hubs and caps with left hand threads for right side of car and hubs and caps with right hand threads for left side of car.

It is necessary to keep in mind this difference in design when installing wire wheels on this model.

When cleaning muddy wire wheels, use a wire wheel brush. To obtain best results, use soft soap and warm water, allowing the soapy water to remain on wheels a few moments to eat off the dirt, then clean with the brush and rinse with clean water.

The wire wheels will sometimes need only one rinsing with spray from hose.

TIRES

Tires should be checked weekly for correct inflation.

Air pressure recommendations are always minimum and must be maintained or reduced mileage and tire troubles are sure to result.

If a valve-inside leaks, replace it with a new one.

After inflation, apply the small valve cap, screwing it down tightly with the fingers. It protects the delicate valve-inside and serves as a double seat to prevent leakage of air.

The standard size tires used on this model is 18″ base x 7.00, and the recommended inflation is forty pounds minimum, front and rear. The air pressure should be checked weekly.

HOUDAILLE SHOCK ABSORBERS

Houdailles are hydraulic shock absorbers and are regulated by turning the needle valve. Adjustment is obtained by varyig the size of valve opening within the instrument which is controlled by the position of the needle valve. A slight movement of the needle valve makes a great difference in the resistance of the instrument. After Houdailles are installed, the needle valves must be adjusted for correct riding position.

To Adjust: In making the adjustment, do not loosen the large hexagon nut. Be sure that shackles and springs are well oiled.

Note position of pointer and turn it clockwise as far as possible. Turn the pointer back, keeping in mind that if turned further back than original position, it will give less resistance. Set the instrument between 2 and 4 for best riding qualities under average driving conditions. Clockwise rotation of pointer increases and anti-clockwise decreases the resistance.

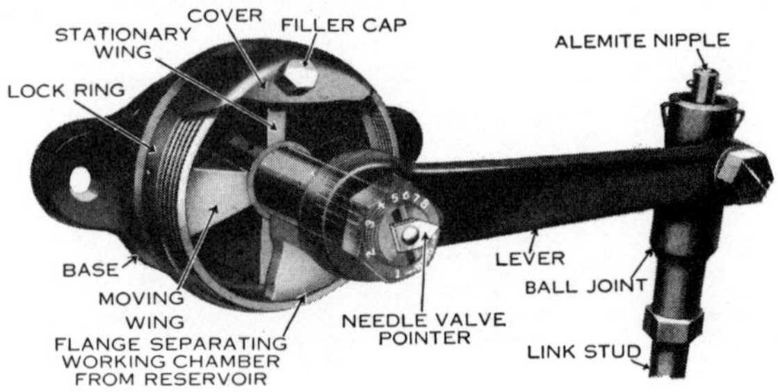

LUBRICATION

Ball points should be lubricated with cup grease on average of 3,000 to 5,000 miles. The fluid to be used in the absorbers is a commercial glycerine solution. Examine its condition on an average of every 10,000 miles and fill to level of the filler cap. Never replenish fluid with oil. It will freeze in the winter or reduce resistance and will not mix with the glycerine in the instrument.

Where the temeprature is below freezing, add 1 to 2 ounces of alcohol to the fluid. Glycerine alone will freeze at 2° above zero.

In warm climate, replenish with commercial or C. P. glycerine.

SPEEDOMETER

The speedometer head (on instrument board) requires no attention and should operate perfectly throughout the life of the car. It is properly lubricated when assembled and under no circumstances, should be taken apart.

If repairs become necessary, before sending the speedometer to the nearest Stwart-Warner Speedometer Service Station, examine the driving equipment very carefully.

Failure to register speed and mileage may be caused by one of the following reasons:

1. Loose connection between the speedometer and the flexible shaft.

2. Loose connection at transmission drive end of flexible shaft.

3. Gears in speedometer drive housing (at transmission) may be stripped.

4. Flexible shaft may be broken.

The flexible shaft consists of a series of links which drive the speedometer by revolving inside of a steel casing. This casing is filled with a special grease when shipped and should be

taken to a Stewart-Warner branch or service station AT LEAST ONCE EVERY 3,000 MILES FOR GREASING.
This is very important for if allowed to run dry, the shaft will break, causing added expense and delay.

If the flexible shaft is replaced at any time, be sure that it is the same length as originally furnished. The shaft should make a sweeping curve from the transmission to the speedometer, avoiding any sharp bends. Be careful that the shaft does not lie against wiring or metal surface as chafing and noise will result.

SHAFT LUBRICATION

Disconnect the upper end tip (at instrument board) and also transmission end; then pull chain out of the casing from the lower end. Cover the links liberally with graphite grease or Stewart lubricant and insert chain in the casing.

DO NOT USE A FLUID OR HARD GREASE, for the oil will work through the casing and the grease will cause excessive friction and will not lubricate properly.

We recommend the use of the SPECIAL STEWART LUBRICANT and it can be procured from any Stewart Distributor or repair station.

A worm gear is fastened to the main drive shaft of the transmission between the rear transmission bearing and the front universal joint. A pinion is mounted in a housing which meshes with the driving worm. The gears receive their lubrication from the transmission.

At the right of the speedometer is a small knob that can be pulled out. By turning the knob you can reset the figures to any tenth of a mile desired or back to zero. Be sure that after resetting the speedometer, you again push the knob to its original position; if you do not, it will fail to record.

EMERGENCY CHART

Caution: Before attempting adjustments, analyze the situation and be sure of the nature of the trouble. Otherwise you may get other parts out of adjustment.

FAILURE OF ENGINE TO START

1. No gasoline.
   If gasoline in tank, see if feed lines are free.
2. Faulty Ignition current, possibly due to failure to unlock switch, or to a broken or disconnected wire.
3. Check for loose battery connection or corrosion between battery post and terminal.
4. Run-down battery indicated by a dimming of lights, with failure to crank.
5. Spark plugs dirty, or points out of adjustment.
6. Contact points in distributor improperly set. Resistance coil may be disconnected or broken.
7. Water on coil, distributor or spark plug terminals.
8. Water in gasoline, or poor grade of gasoline in cold weather.
9. Flooding of carburetor caused by excessive use of choke.

If there is good, clean gasoline in carburetor and a good spark at the plugs, the engine will start under proper handling.

ENGINE STOPS

1. Lack of gasoline. Indicated by a popping noise preceding the final stopping of engine.
2. Disconnected wires.
3. Carburetor flooding.
4. Engine out of oil usually indicated by a knocking in the engine followed by an abrupt stop. If this occurs, let the engine cool off and do not attempt to start it. This may be a serious matter, and the engine should be examined by a good mechanic before attempting to put the car into service again.

This condition may result from a sudden loss of water from the circulating system. If so, do not pour a fresh supply into the radiator until the engine has cooled off.

ENGINE MISSES

1. Broken or disconnected wiring.
2. Spark plug short circuited, dirty, or out of adjustment. Locate the faulty plug, remove and clean it and be sure the porcelain insulation is not cracked. If so, replace it. See that the points are properly spaced—.025 of an inch apart.
3. Loss of compression in one or more cylinders. Valves may be stuck in their guides, or may need regrinding or reseating. A valve spring may be broken, or the adjustment of a

tappet may have become loosened so it is either holding the valve open continually or not raising the valve off its seat at all. An inspection of all tappet celarances will show this.

4. Water in gasoline indicated by engine running and stopping and running again.

5. Improper functioning of gasoline supply system.

6. Overheating.

ENGINE KNOCKS

1. Connecting rod bearing loose. This gives a light knock at high speed or when under a heavy pull.

2. Crankshaft bearing loose. This is distinguished from a loose connecting rod bearing by a heavy pounding under low engine speed or a heavy pull.

3. Gasoline mixture too rich. Adjust carburetor to a 'leaner" setting.

4. Carbon in cylinders, usually due to the use of improper oil. Have carbon cleaned out. Wash out present engine oil in crankcase and begin using an oil of better quality.

5. Worn valve tappet, indicated by a light tapping sound. Tappet adjustments loose.

LOSS OF POWER

Engine will run but will not pull under a heavy load. May be due to:

1. Loss of compression due to leaky valves. Usually caused by too rich a mixture, or too much oil gumming up valve seats. Possibly faulty cylinder head gaskets.

2. Gasoline mixture too rich through some trouble in carburetor, possibly due to grit or foreign matter getting under float valve seat.

3. Carburetor float sticking.

4. Late Ignition.

5. Cold engine. This should prevail only a few minutes after starting out in cold weather, until engine is thoroughly warmed.

6. Lack of oil or water.

7. Dragging brakes.

8. Lack of gasoline usually caused by some foreign matter entering and obstructing the line.

ENGINE OVERHEATS

Stop engine at once and investigate. Some of the causes are as follows:

1. Low supply of water.

2. Lack of proper lubrication.

3. Imperfect gas mixture due to improper setting of carburetor choke.

4. Ignition timed late or driving with retarded spark.

5. Slipping or broken fan belt.

6. Cylinders carbonized.

INSTRUCTIONS FOR ORDERING AND RETURNING PARTS

Read these instructions carefully before ordering parts.

Send a money order, New York or Chicago draft with all parts orders.

Do not use checks drawn on local banks.

This is no reflection on your financial standing but it is necessary in order to avoid a vast amount of bookkeeping and correspondence.

If no remittance is enclosed, we will refuse the order or send C. O. D. at our discretion.

All prices on parts are quoted F. O. B. Auburn, Indiana, and are subject to change without notice.

ORDERING BY MAIL, TELEGRAPH OR TELEPHONE

Give car number. This number will be found upon the name plate inside of body. *This number must always be given with any order.*

If, for any reason, the part cannot be identified, describe the part and its location in the car, enclosing a sketch or return the part for sample if necessary. It is always best to give the part numbers whenever possible.

Never leave anything to be guessed at.

Always consider the right side of the car at the right when *sitting in the car facing forward.*

Some parts are kept in stock painted standard, but most parts requiring painting will have to be painted to order, taking several days' time. *If you want parts painted always state what color and striping.*

We reserve the right to ship parts unpainted if not ordered painted.

State whether we shall ship by Mail, Parcel Post, Express or Freight. Write your name and address carefully and plainly.

If we are not advised we shall use our judgment at the purchaser's risk.

Raybestos

BRAKE SERVICE BULLETIN

PRACTICAL INFORMATION

on the care and adjustment of brakes, prepared by the Engineering Department.
Questions, criticisms and suggestions gladly received. Please file.
F. C. STANLEY, Ph.D., Chief Engineer, E. R. ROSS, Assistant Chief Engineer,
NORMAN LEEDS, Jr., Service Engineer.

THE RAYBESTOS DIVISION, RAYBESTOS-MANHATTAN, INC., BRIDGEPORT, CONN.
Oct.-Nov.-Dec., 1929 CORD FRONT WHEEL DRIVE No. 12A

CORD FRONT WHEEL DRIVE

Figure 1

General

The brakes on the Cord are the conventional internal hydraulic type with two shoes in each drum. The adjustment or relining of the brakes themselves does not present any unusual features. To remove the front brake drums or shoes, however, it is necessary to disassemble the front end, and it is this work which is particularly stressed in this bulletin.

Figure 2

Figure 3

Disassembly of Front End

Jack up the car, using the dead axles for this purpose. Remove the hub caps and take off the wheels, which are held on to the hub with cap screws. Take off the two nuts which hold the shock absorber to the frame and drop the shock absorber down as shown in Figure 1. In order to loosen the shock absorber, it may be necessary to knock the two studs, that hold it, back through the frame.

Figure 4

The next step is to drop the tie-rod assembly which is shown accomplished in Figure 2. This is done by removing the two cap screws, A, which hold this half bracket in place at the bottom half of the kingpin. Note the way in which the bushings and spacers are assembled so that they will be put back correctly.

Removing the live axle is the next step. First remove the four cap screws from the flange at the inner end. Two of these are shown at B, Figure 2. Note that there are six cap screws through this flange but that two of them fit through enlarged holes and hold the drum on. It is not necessary to remove these two cap screws yet. The outer end of the live axle is fastened to the upper part of the kingpin by a bracket, half of which is removable. This half is shown at A, Figure 3. Remove it by taking out the two cap screws and then pull out the axle assembly as the man in the picture is doing. Be sure not to burr the inner end of the axle assembly by hitting it against anything. It will help to have a second man lift the shock absorber up out of the way while the axle is being pulled out. The axle is shown wholly removed in Figure 4.

The next step is to remove the brake drum. Take out the cap screws A, Figure 4, and pull out the drum. The shoes, Figure 5, are then in position to be removed in the regular way.

Raybestos BRAKE SERVICE BULLETIN

Oct.-Nov.-Dec., 1929 | Cord Front Wheel Drive | No. 12D

Figure 5

Adjustment

The adjustments for the brake and instructions for otherwise servicing the hydraulic system are given in our previous bulletin No. 9. Referring to Figure 6, the eccentric anchors, A, A, on the front brakes, may be adjusted from the outside of the car. The adjusting screws are reached underneath the apron.

The mounting of the rear wheels is similar to the front wheel mounting on other cars, and it is not necessary to use a wheel puller. We recommend strongly the use of Raybestos molded lining on both front and rear brakes, catalog No. 138F being for the fronts and No. 103R for the rears.

Figure 6

10M-3-5-30 "B"

Printed in U. S.A.

Index

HARLAN HINEY